INTERNATIONAL LABOR CONVENTIONS

Their Interpretation and Revision

INTERNATIONAL LABOR CONVENTIONS

Their Interpretation and Revision

By CONLEY HALL DILLON

CHAPEL HILL

THE UNIVERSITY OF NORTH CAROLINA PRESS

1942

TO VIRGINIA

FOREWORD

By John G. Winant

Over a period of twenty-one years the International Labor Organization has devoted the major part of its energies to the establishment of international labor standards which would secure for the laboring peoples of the world decent conditions of life and work. These standards, dealing with problems such as social insurance, industrial health and safety, hours of work, child labor and unemployment, have been embodied in formal International Labor Conventions. At the outbreak of the European war in September 1939, 67 conventions had been adopted by the International Labor Conference and 46 of these had, by ratification, come into force as multilateral treaty obligations for member nations. A total of 853 ratifications had been registered by over 50 countries.

The war has delayed but not ended the progress of ratifications —fifteen ratifications have been registered since September 1939— just as it has impeded the progress of national labor legislation. At the same time, however, the war has brought into relief the interrelations of domestic social and economic politics with foreign policy, the interdependence of national prosperity and international stability, and the need for a broader than national basis for social planning. Now beset by the difficulties of organizing our economy in a time of emergency, we are becoming every day more aware of the great problems of reconstruction and adjustment which will face us as soon as war is done. Social values will have to be reviewed, policies, procedures and techniques, revised.

In the past the International Labor Organization has been conscious of the necessity and desirability of keeping legal standards in step with economic realities. In seven instances the Conference has revised labor conventions to meet new conditions. The subject of the revision and interpretation of conventions has become increasingly significant, and in the period of post-war reconstruction will warrant far more attention than it has received in the past.

As yet little has been written on this technical aspect of international labor conventions. Professor Dillon's exhaustive research in this field makes a constructive contribution to the understanding of international labor treaties. Although some phases of the subject are controversial and although there may be differences of opinion concerning some of Professor Dillon's conclusions, his able and scholarly approach to the problem will be of interest and assistance to students of labor legislation, international relations and law. It will be a practical tool for all those concerned with these subjects in planning for reconstruction.

PREFACE

In the field of international law, there is no process of greater importance than that of adjustment. The need of an adequate method of adaptation in the sphere of relations between states is more urgent today than at any time in the past. New methods of international coöperation offer problems of adjustment that are too complex for the rules formerly utilized. This is particularly true of the conventions that grow out of the action of the International Labor Conference. These agreements, in some respects, are quite unlike any in existence prior to the Versailles Treaty. The provisions stipulated in Part XIII of the Treaty and the practice of the organization have given to labor conventions their unusual characteristics. The organization has endeavored to solve the problems of interpretation and revision of labor conventions by utilizing the methods of procedure current in respect to multipartite treaties, and by formulating new methods more in keeping with the special characteristics of labor conventions. It is the purpose of this study to show how these conventions have been interpreted and revised, with the possible effects of these processes on international legal procedure. In endeavoring to accomplish this purpose I have examined the competence of bodies concerned, the efforts to formulate a revisory process, the practice of revision, and the manner in which conventions have been construed. Particular attention has been given to the legal phases of the problem. The conclusion is, in regard to revision, that, while the organization has made a substantial beginning which may affect the technique of treaty making, the merits of the process are yet to be determined. In respect to interpretation the investigation has shown that uniform interpretation is not being achieved.

The world of the future perhaps even to a greater extent than ever before will need scientific procedures to effect satisfactory adjustments in an increasingly complex economic international community. No problems are more vital than those concerned with labor. Men of good will trust that past experience and reason will be universally applied to a just and peaceful solution of these problems. In the present disturbed condition of the relations between states some encouragement may be derived from the recent policy of the United States in the sphere of international collaboration. This return to an active rôle of leadership and responsibility befitting a great industrial nation should assist greatly in the future achievement of a constructive international order.

In preparing this work I have relied on the publications of the International Labor Organization,[1] the Permanent Court of International Justice and the League of Nations, court decisions, general treatises on international law and organization, and periodical publications. A few decisions on labor questions have been reported in official and unofficial compilations of Germany, France, and Great Britain. Generally, the unavailability of published decisions of labor courts has somewhat diminished the value of the study of case law.[2]

I wish to express my appreciation to those who assisted in the preparation of this study. Dr. R. R. Wilson of Duke University who directed the research and preparation of the manuscript as a doctoral dissertation has offered innumerable valuable suggestions and criticism. Dr. Taylor Cole, also of Duke University, has given helpful advice in respect to Chapter VII, "Interpretations in National Courts." Mr. Wilfred Jenks, Legal Adviser of the International Labor Office, made a number of worthwhile suggestions prior to the beginning of the study; later he read the manuscript and gave invaluable criticism. Dr. James T. Shotwell of Columbia University gave constructive assistance in respect to several points. Professor J. Donald Pollitt of Marshall College has materially aided this work by his patient and careful proof reading, although I assume full responsibility for any errors. My wife, Virginia B. Dillon, has rendered invaluable service throughout the entire work. The assistance of the staffs of the Duke University Library, the League of Nations Library, the Library of Congress, and the Geneva and Washington International Labor Offices in procuring materials for research in connection with this study is gratefully acknowledged.

CONLEY HALL DILLON

April, 1941

[1] I wish to call attention to some of the terms used in the body of the study, terms which are peculiar to International Labor Organization materials i.e.: "Adviser," "States Members," "The Netherlands Government," "Labour," etc.

[2] Inquiry of a number of states concerning court decisions interpreting labor conventions has disclosed the fact that such decisions are not available. Accordingly I have been forced to rely in many instances on decisions reported in publications of the International Labor Organization.

CONTENTS

INTERNATIONAL LABOR CONVENTIONS

Their Interpretation and Revision

Chapter I

SUBJECT MATTER AND AGENCIES INVOLVED

ORIGINS

The movement for the establishment of adequate labor standards on a universal scale began many years before there were any definite accomplishments. The first efforts toward this great end were extremely limited and nebulous. Robert Owen (1771-1858) was a pioneer in the realm of social legislation. Yet he cannot be given considerable credit for the beginnings of international labor legislation, as he was essentially an idealist and "had little effect on the subsequent history of labor organizations or on the practical measures of governments." [1] The proposals of Owen were never international conventions.[2]

The economist Jérome Blânqui was probably the first person to propose international labor conventions; writing on economics in 1838-39, he comments as follows:

> "There is only one way of accomplishing it (the reform) while avoiding its disastrous consequences; this would be to get it adopted simultaneously by all industrial nations which compete in the foreign market. Will people be willing to do

[1] Ernest Mahaim, "The Historical and Social Importance of International Legislation," *The Origins of the International Labor Organization,* ed. James T. Shotwell, I, 3. This work is part of a two volume set on the International Labor Organization; Vol. II contains relevant documents. The work will hereafter be cited as *The Origins of the I. L. O.* and all quotations from it are reprinted by permission of the Columbia University Press. I have depended on this work for the historical material with the exception of the places cited. See also in connection with the work of Robert Owen, *The International Labor Organization; The First Decade,* Preface by Albert Thomas, 22; and cf. Paul Perigord, *The International Labor Organization,* 52, for a different point of view. For an excellent detailed analysis of the efforts of individuals and groups concerned in the origins of the Organization, see John W. Follows, Antecedents of the International Labor Organization, MS thesis, Cornell University, 1933.

[2] See comment by E. Mahaim, *Le Droit international ouvrièr,* 183 *et seq.* A valuable account of the economic and political currents that were factors in the international progress toward the betterment of labor standards is given in Lewis L. Lorwin, *Labor and Internationalism,* 1-115. See also Ernest Mahaim, "L'Organisation permanente du travail," *Recueil des cours de l'Academie de Droit International* III (1924), 69-75.

this? can it be done? why not? treaties have been concluded between one country and another by which they have bound themselves to kill men; why should they not be concluded today for the purpose of preserving men's lives and making them happier."[3]

The first attempts to persuade states to put international labor legislation in practice were apparently made by Daniel LeGrand, an Alsatian manufacturer.[4] From 1838 to 1859 he "bombarded" French, British, and Prussian governments with memoranda such as the following, dated in 1847:

> "An international law to protect the working classes against premature and excessive labor, which is the prime and principal cause of their physical deterioration, their moral degradation and their being deprived of the blessings of family life."[5]

These efforts by LeGrand brought no immediate results; yet they marked the beginning of similar attempts by economists, philanthropists, and congresses.

Practical official action was first taken in the direction of international coöperation in the field of labor by the Swiss government.[6] The President of the National Council proposed that the governments of Austria, Belgium, France, Germany, Great Britain, and Italy sign treaties to regulate labor questions in a uniform manner. As a result of this suggestion the Swiss government sent invitations to certain governments asking them to meet in September,

[3] J. Blânqui, *Cours d'économie industrielle* (2ème edition recueillie et annotée par A. Blaise, 1838-39), 119-121. A quotation from the original will possibly best demonstrate the fervor of his appeals. "On a bien fait jusqu'ici des traités de puissance pour s'engaget à tuer des hommes; pourquoi n'en feraiton pas aujourd'hui pour leur conserver la vie et la leur rendre douce? La chose serait au moins neuve, et devrait peutêtre à ce titre un succès; il faut en essayer!"

[4] *The Origins of the I. L. O.*, 3.

[5] *Ibid.*, 5. See also *The International Labor Organization; The First Decade*, 22; Paul Perigord, *op. cit.*, 56-57; *The Annals of the American Academy of Political and Social Science* (hereafter cited *Annals*) in the issue on "The International Labor Organization, "CLXVI (March, 1933), particularly E. Mahaim, "The Principles of International Labor Legislation," 10-11. Cf. Albert Thomas, *Mélanges offerts à M. Charles Andler*, 323-333; and Raymond Weiss, *Daniel le Grand* (1783-1859): *son oeuvre sociale et internationale.*

[6] April 20, 1881.

1889, to consider international action in respect to labor questions.[7] However, the proposed conference was postponed until 1890. Early in that year the German Emperor invited the governments to Berlin for an international conference which was to be a substitute for the proposed Swiss conference.

The Berlin conference was attended by the twelve chief industrial states of Europe.[8] The program of the conference covered the whole field of labor legislation, but the results were only in the form of resolutions.[9] Consequently, the conference was of little value except as a moral aid to future efforts for international labor coöperation.[10]

A private organization proved to be more successful in its attempt to further international labor legislation. This body, the International Association for Labor Legislation, was founded at Paris in 1900. The following year the Association founded an International Labor Office at Basel.[11] The work of the Association was a success, and the high idealism and sacrifice of its personnel have been lauded. The subjects the Office brought to the attention of states were chosen with care and studied thoroughly.[12] The first bilateral treaty originated through the efforts of the Association.[13]

The first international labor agreements were facilitated by the preparatory work of the International Association for Labor Legislation. The Berne Conference met in 1905 and 1906. The meeting in 1905 was at the invitation of the Swiss government, and it was a technical preparatory conference. After this preliminary

---

[7] Belgium, France, Great Britain, and The Netherlands accepted the invitation; Germany did not reply.

[8] Germany, Austria-Hungary, Belgium, Denmark, France, Great Britain, Italy, Luxemburg, The Netherlands, Portugal, Switzerland, and Norway.

[9] These resolutions took the form "It is desirable that. . . ." Naturally, they were quite ineffective.

[10] The lack of preparatory work for the conference was one of the chief causes for its failure. A rather complete description of the various conferences concerning labor questions from 1890-1913 is given in B. E. Lowe, *The International Protection of Labor,* 31-66.

[11] A complete description of this Office and its relations with governments is given in "A Pre-War History of International Labor Legislation," by Sir Malcolm Delevigne, in *The Origins of the I. L. O.,* I, 29-36.

[12] The first subjects considered were night work of women and use of white lead in industry.

[13] A description of the series of reciprocal protective labor treaties that followed this initial agreement is given in B. E. Lowe, *op. cit.,* 137-168. This treaty was between France and Italy, April 15, 1904.

work the diplomats officially representing governments met in 1906[14] and concluded two conventions on the subjects of *Prohibition of Night Work for Women* and the *Prohibition of Use of White Phosphorus in Manufacture of Matches.* An authority on labor legislation says that "the Berne Conventions represented a real innovation in international labor legislation." [15] In 1913 another preliminary conference was held at Berne which was not so fruitful as the former meetings had been.[16] The World War prevented the final conference, which was scheduled to meet in 1914, from being convened.

The Berne Conferences, which were to a large degree the result of the activity of the International Association for Labor Legislation, provided valuable experience for future international action. These conferences demonstrated, by their success along certain lines, the proper methods to adopt; likewise they indicated, in respect to their failure to accomplish certain objectives, the weakness of some phases of their procedure.[17] It is difficult to estimate the value of the work toward international labor legislation prior to the war; however, their worth was considerable in the opinion of one authority, Sir Malcolm Delevigne, who summarizes as follows:

> "Of the four or five leading ideas embodied in the scheme of an International Labor Organization adopted by the Peace Conference in 1919, three, namely: (1) the holding of periodical conferences for the conclusion of international agreements; (2) the creation of a central organ; and (3) supervision over, and enforcement of, the observance of conventions, came from this pre-war experience." [18]

---

[14] All the European governments were represented except Russia, Turkey, Greece, Norway, and the Balkan States.

[15] Statement by Ernest Mahaim in "The Historical and Social Importance of International Labor Legislation," *The Origins of the I. L. O.*, 11. Mr. Mahaim says the term "international labor legislation" is currently used and "is not strictly speaking inaccurate, since any legal system may be called legislation," 12.

[16] See Delevigne, *op. cit.*, 47-54.

[17] Mr. James T. Shotwell expresses a viewpoint in opposition to this position: ". . . the history of the international conferences in the period prior to the World War . . . did not give much to build on. In a very real sense the commission on Labor Legislation of the Peace Conference was called upon to do pioneering work, to draft plans for an organization which had no parallel in the history of politics." *The Origins of the I. L. O.*, I, Introduction, xx.

[18] Delevigne, *op. cit.*, 52.

It is striking, in the light of later events, that an American labor organization was the first body to call attention to the desirability of labor's having a voice in the Peace Treaty. The desire was expressed in part in the form of a resolution made by the American Federation of Labor in September, 1914. "To the end that suggestions may be made and such action taken as shall be helpful in restoring fraternal relations, protecting the interests of the toilers and thereby assisting in laying foundations for a more lasting peace." [19]

While this resolution indicated that American labor realized the importance of giving workers a part in the making of peace, no definite steps were taken by the Federation. It appears that the American Federation did not envisage actual participation by labor in the proceedings of the Peace Conference.[20]

The first notable effort in the direction of active labor participation in the peace conference was expressed by the Inter-Allied Trades Union Conference which met at Leeds, July 5, 1916. It was urged at this conference that an international commission be set up to protect the rights of labor.[21] Although this conference represented only a small minority of organized labor, it received so much publicity that its ideas were influential in labor's share in the Peace Treaty.[22] The majority group of organized workers opposed the Leeds conference and sponsored a counter meeting which convened at Berne in December, 1917. This group proposed a super-legislative body for the formulation of guarantees for labor.[23]

The socialist labor organizations apparently exercised a great influence at the peace conference on the movement to obtain future rights for labor. The Inter-Allied Labour and Socialist Conference met February 24, 1918, and in a memorandum on war

---

[19] *The Origins of the I. L. O.*, II, 3. For full text of the resolution of the American Federation of Labor, see *Report of Proceedings of the 34th Annual Convention of the American Federation of Labor*, Philadelphia, November, 1914, 415.

[20] Carol Riegelman, "Wartime Trade-Union and Socialist Proposals," *The Origins of the I. L. O.*, I, 58. See also Mahaim, "The Historical and Social Importance of International Labor Legislation," *The Origins of the I. L. O.*, 17.

[21] *Ibid.*, 18. For an excellent discussion of the part of organized labor in working out a plan for the protection of their rights see Lewis L. Lorwin, *op. cit.*, 174–196.

[22] Riegelman, *op. cit.*, 64.

[23] These proposals later became the German counter plan for labor organization.

aims[24] favored the unity of the working classes in solving the problem of peace, and proposed that official representatives of labor attend the conference. The members of the conference were also of the opinion that a labor and socialist conference should sit concurrently with the official peace conference. The Inter-Allied representatives of labor met again in September, 1918, and the main principles enunciated by this conference were incorporated in the Peace Treaty.[25]

The activities of these organized bodies of labor prior to the peace conference gave evidence that any satisfactory peace must include a guarantee of the rights of labor.

The participation of labor in the peace conference necessarily required considerable preparatory work. This work was of a delicate and complex nature and required coöperation between organized labor and the Allied governments. The American preparations were not extensive.[26] Dr. John B. Andrews, Secretary of the American Association for Labor Legislation, prepared a memorandum for possible presentation at the peace conference concerning proposals for labor agreements.[27]

The French government began in 1918 to make preparations for the part of labor in the peace conference.[28] The Chamber of Deputies adopted a resolution proposing government support of specific international labor legislation at the peace conference.[29] In addition to internal preparations the French government carried on correspondence with the British government in order that an exchange of points of view might facilitate the conference proceedings.[30] Owing to this preparatory work the French had a

---

[24] See *The Origins of the I. L. O.*, II, Document 9, pp. 52-69.

[25] Reigelman, *op. cit.*, 70. Samuel Gompers represented American labor at this conference.

[26] See Leifur Magnuson, "American Preparations," *The Origins of the I. L. O.*, I, 101. Mr. Magnuson says the experience of Samuel Gompers was the chief "American preparation."

[27] See *The Origins of the I. L. O.*, II, Document 16, pp. 86-88.

[28] See letter from the French Minister for Foreign Affairs to the Minister of Labor concerning labor at the peace conference, November 15, 1918, *ibid.*, Document 18, p. 92.

[29] *Ibid.*, Document 20, pp. 95-96, and Document 21, pp. 97-106. See also discussion of the work of the French government in this connection in *The Origins of the I. L. O.*, I, 88-90.

[30] See Charles Picquenard, "French Preparations," *The Origins of the I. L. O.*, I, 86-87.

general plan to offer the peace conference on the subject of labor legislation.[31]

The preparation of the British for the peace conference was planned more carefully and in greater detail than that of any other government.[32] After some study of the problem the Ministry of Labour favored special machinery for the settlement of labor problems. With this basic idea in mind a definite plan was constructed. The plan provided that the official British delegation to the peace conference should include an independent labor section[33] whose purpose should be to work toward establishing a "Permanent International Labor Organization." [34] At Paris various questions to be solved regarding equality of states, group representation, and the rôle of governments in the labor organization, were given to the labor section of the British delegation.[35] While the peace conference was in session the British labor section communicated with other delegations concerning proposals for a labor organization. Consequently, the complete British scheme formed a skeleton of the final plan for an International Labor Organization.[36]

The Allied statesmen meeting at Paris to draw up the treaty ending the World War were very much aware of the need of considering the demands of labor in their plans. Some of them were constantly in touch with those who were making definite preparations for labor guarantees.[37] In addition to recognizing the need of satisfying specific demands of coherent groups of organized labor the Allied representatives were apprehensive concerning the existing general state of unrest.[38] Accordingly, Mr. Lloyd George

[31] See letter of French Minister of Labor to the Minister of Foreign Affairs, sending proposals for labor legislation at peace conference, listed as Document 21 in *The Origins of the I. L. O.*, 97-106.

[32] See Edward J. Phelan, "British Preparations," *The Origins of the I. L. O.*, I, 110. See explanatory note under Document 25, II, 117.

[33] Phelan, *op. cit.*, 111. [34] *Ibid.*, 112. [35] *Ibid.*, 113-126.

[36] Except the early draft did not contain any provision for a Governing Body. See remarks in *The Origins of the I. L. O.*, I, 118. See also the Memorandum on the Machinery and Procedure Required for the International Regulation of Industrial Conditions, prepared by the British delegation, January 15-20, 1919, in *ibid.*, II, Document 25, pp. 117-125. See also Minutes of the Proceedings of the Commission on International Labor Legislation, No. 2, in which the draft plan submitted by the British delegation is taken as the basis of the discussion, *International Labor Office, Official Bulletin* (hereafter cited as *Official Bulletin*), I (1919-1920), 9.

[37] This was particularly true of the British delegation.

[38] For a brief description of the general state of unrest following the war, see James T. Shotwell, "The International Labor Organization as an Alterna-

proposed a draft resolution which was adopted after a few minor amendments; the final text is as follows:

"That a Commission, composed of two representatives apiece for the five Great Powers, and five representatives to be elected by the Other Powers represented at the Peace Conference, be appointed to enquire into the conditions of employment from the international aspect, and to consider the international means necessary to secure common action on matters affecting conditions of employment, and to recommend the form of a permanent agency to continue such enquiry in coöperation with and under the direction of the League of Nations." [39]

The Commission on International Labor Legislation, proposed in the above resolution, met on February 1, 1919, and held thirty-five sessions, during which the convention establishing the International Labor Organization was formulated.[40] The composition of the American delegation was the cause of some surprise, as it included a representative of labor and a representative of the employers. As the representatives of the other states were government officials, the composition of the American delegation undoubtedly had a decided influence. The selection of Mr. Samuel Gompers, president of the American Federation of Labor, as president of the commission gave labor an added influence.[41] The commission took the British draft as the basis of discussion.[42] This draft was

---

tive to Violent Revolution," *Annals,* CLXVI (March, 1933), 18-19. In this connection Lewis L. Lorwin remarks that, "aroused by the threat of revolutionary movements" the Allied representatives set up the Labor Commission, *op. cit.,* 189.

[39] See *Official Bulletin,* 1-2, for terms of reference and constitution. Also refer to Documents 31, 32, and 33 of *The Origins of the I. L. O.,* II, for the proposals by Powers with special interests. See also D. H. Miller, *My Diary at the Conference at Paris,* XIV, 6-8.

[40] The minutes of the meetings are printed by the International Labor Office in the *Official Bulletin,* I (1919-1920). The French stenographic record has been printed by M. de Lapradelle, in *La Paix de Versailles—La Documentation Internationale;* see note introducing Document 34, Minutes of the Meetings of the Commission on International Labour Legislation, February 1 to March 24, 1919, *Origins of the I. L. O.,* I, 49. An excellent discussion of the work of the Commission is given by Mr. Ernest Mahaim, "L'Organisation permanente du travail," *op. cit.,* 77-83.

[41] Origins of the I. L. O., I, Document 34, p. 150.

[42] *Official Bulletin,* 9, and *The Origins of the I. L. O.,* II, 153; see also E. J. Phelan, "The Commission on International Labor Legislation," *The Origins of*

worked out in complete form prior to the meeting of the Commission and consequently formed an excellent basis for the general discussions. The fact that few changes were made in the British proposals demonstrated that this plan, to a large degree, was acceptable to the Commission. In the discussion of the different parts of the proposed plan the Commission had difficulty in agreeing as to group representation of the Labor Conference. The British scheme called for double representation of government delegates. This method of representation was bitterly opposed by Mr. Gompers and others who favored equal representation of all groups.[43] Most of the proposals were agreed to without a great amount of discussion and debate. There was, however, a wide difference of opinion on the nature of Labor Conventions. The Italian delegation favored the creation of a super-parliament able to make conventions that would have had immediately the force of law. This plan was contrary to the British proposal of conventions which would come into force only after ratification by national legislatures, and it was rejected by the conference.[44] The Commission completed its draft of the Labor Section with optimism concerning the future rôle of the document.[45]

---

the I. L. O., I, 131. This volume also includes the various drafts of the labor section which were considered by the Commission. The draft first considered by the Commission is that of column 2; the drafts are in Part IV, 371-423. "In this section four drafts of the Labor Convention have been printed in parallel columns, in order that each article may be traced from the first complete form of the British text to the final form of the Constitution of the International Labor Organization—Part XIII of the Treaty of Versailles."

[43] Mr. Gompers was supported in this point of view by M. Colliard, French Minister of Labor, and Mr. Bustamente, Latin-American representative; "Minutes of Labor Commission," *The Origins of the I. L. O.*, II, 135-139. For Mr. Gompers' view of the provisions of Part XIII of the treaty, see E. M. House and Charles Seymour, *What Really Happened at Paris*, 319-335. *Cf.* Memorandum by the British delegation on the question of Voting Power at the Conference, *Official Bulletin*, 19-25, and see also remarks by Mr. Gompers, 29.

[44] *Ibid.*, 180. The American delegation made constant reference to the constitutional difficulties in the path of American acceptance of conventions. Other federal states also felt they could not support the British proposal for conventions. Accordingly, Mr. Shotwell, Mr. Frankfurter, and Col. House of the United States collaborated with Mr. Phelan of Great Britain to overcome the difficulty. Mr. Shotwell formulated a "Recommendation" which would be substituted for a convention as regards federal states, see "The Commission on International Labor Legislation," *The Origins of the I. L. O.*, I, 149ff.

[45] See remarks of Mr. Gompers and M. Colliard at the close of the work of the Commission, *ibid.*, 321-322. Also in *Official Bulletin*, 223-224.

Following the completion of the task of the Commission immediate efforts were made to get the approval of its report by the peace conference.[46] This was not an easy task, as there were several obstacles to be overcome. There was some opposition from the British Empire delegation to the "Labor Charter" which had formed no part of the original British plan and which had not been discussed with the Empire delegates.[47] Some delegations desired the amendment of particular sections as a condition of their acceptance. This was particularly true of the Labor Charter, which was drafted and redrafted before it was finally acceptable.[48] With these obstacles, which were not solved without considerable friction, it was difficult to get a session of the conference to consider the report on the work of the Commission.[49] However, after some delay the peace conference accepted the report of the Labor Commission,[50] and the draft clauses on Conditions of Labor were adopted.[51]

The Organizing Committee for the Washington Conference began its preparation prior to the final approval of Part XIII by the peace conference. Through communications with the members of the League the committee was able to gather the necessary information for the initial meeting of the Labor Conference.[52] This

[46] Report of the Commission on International Labor Legislation, Document 48, 366-378; see also *International Labor Office; Report presented to the Peace Conference by the Commission on International Labor Legislation*, Geneva, 1920, 1-26.

[47] This difficulty, which was concerning the quality of status of foreign workers, was solved after a special meeting of the Dominions group, *The Origins of the I. L. O.*, I, 200-207.

[48] *Ibid.*, 212-220.

[49] See *The Origins of the I. L. O.*, II, Document 49, pp. 374-386, and D. H. Miller, *op. cit.*, XVI, 2-10.

[50] *The Origins of the I. L. O.*, II, Document 50, "Proceedings of the Preliminary Peace Conference," Protocol number 4, April 11, 1919, 387-409. See also Proceedings in *Official Bulletin*, 284-308.

[51] Before the final text was adopted Sir Robert Borden made a number of amendments. For a comparison of the original and amended texts see *The Origins of the I. L. O.*, II, Document 52, pp. 412-413. The minutes of the Plenary Peace Conference of April 28, 1919, which adopted the draft articles, are in the same compilation, Document 53, pp. 414-418.

[52] See *ibid.*, Document 61, "Report of the Chairman of the Organizing Committee of the International Labor Conference," October, 1919, 453-468. For a complete discussion of the work of this committee see *ibid.*, I, Part III, "The

committee was responsible for the actual beginning of the work of the International Labor Conference.

This brief survey of the efforts to bring into being an international organization for the protection of labor demonstrates the enormous difficulties that attend such a movement. The forces assisting in building up the organization were of such a diverse nature as to defy complete analysis or description. Idealists, manufacturers, economists, diplomats, labor leaders, politicians, and sovereigns all contributed to the growth of the idea of international labor legislation. The organizations for legislation and for the rights of labor apparently were able through their solidarity to force issues to the attention of statesmen. The conferences resulting from the organized efforts for international labor conventions assisted toward some progress. The insistent need of stabilizing the general conditions of labor growing out of the war was an important factor in forcing a consideration of the betterment of industrial conditions of work. The work of those who were concerned in constructing the Constitution (Part XIII of the Peace Treaty) was a worthy tribute to the practicability of the ideals of their predecessors. The whole process of the formulation of an organization whose purpose is the establishment of universal social justice indicates the slow development of such a movement and the type of difficulty that must be surmounted through international cooperation.

ACTUAL MAKING OF CONVENTIONS

The making of conventions is almost a continuous process. It is difficult to separate the functions relating to preparation in the earliest stages of the procedure from the general activity of the Organization. A purpose of the Constitution is the establishment of "social justice" by an " improvement of the conditions of labor." [53] One of the chief methods of bringing about this purpose is the raising of international legislative standards through conventions.

The Office often conducts research relating to industrial questions without a definite plan for a convention; however, this examination sometimes reveals a need for an international agree-

Washington Conference, the Organizing Committee," by Sir Malcolm Delevingne, 285-304. The documents and a complete record of the work of the conference may be found in *Official Bulletin,* 349-407.

[53] See the Preamble to Part XIII, Treaty of Versailles.

ment.[54] Nevertheless, the preparation of a convention may be the result of special research with that purpose in mind. The suggestion for the study of a topic may be made by the Conference in the form of a resolution.[55] The passage of such a resolution makes research by the Office mandatory. The length of the research period varies considerably. It may continue for a number of years before the subject is ready for conference action.

The work of the Governing Body in the preparatory stages of a convention is extraordinarily important. The agenda of the conference containing the subject matter which may be considered with a view to forming a convention is chosen by the Governing Body.[56] The practice of the Governing Body in this respect is to select a varied number of items of possible current importance at the spring meeting of the Governing Body. The Office prepares law and practice reports on these topics at the request of the Governing Body.[56a] These reports are an evaluation by the Office of the law and practice in the States Members concerned and contain suggestions as to the consultation of governments.[57] In the light of the Gray Reports the Governing Body chooses from one to three items to be placed on the agenda of the conference.[58] In the meantime the governments have received a copy of the Gray reports for their consideration. When the conference meets these reports are used as the basis of discussion.

Following the adoption of the draft conclusions the Office prepares a questionnaire called a Red Report which is sent to the governments.[59] The replies of the governments are given careful

[54] Article 10 provides that the Office shall collect information on labor and industrial conditions.

[55] Article 10 also provides that the Office shall, among other duties, examine "subjects which it is proposed to bring before the Conference with a view to the conclusion of international conventions, and the conduct of such special investigations as may be ordered by the Conference."

[56] See Article 14, which states, "The agenda for all meetings of the Conference will be settled by the Governing Body, who shall consider any suggestion as to the agenda that may be made by the Government of any of the Members or by any representative organization recognized for the purpose of Article 30."

[56a] The Governing Body does not always request that the Office prepare law and practice reports.

[57] The information for these reports is sometime obtained by sending questionnaires to governments. The color of these reports is gray, and they are commonly referred to as Gray Reports to distinguish them from reports concerned with other stages of the process which also have distinctive colors.

[58] This choice is usually made in the October meeting of the Governing Body.

[59] The colors of these various reports emphasize their particular importance.

consideration by the Office, and an attempt is made to make the proposed draft convention or recommendation a reflection of the average point of view expressed.[60] These proposals and the replies of governments are sent to the governments and presented before the Conference in the form of a Blue Report. This report is the basis of the final discussion in the Conference.

In this preparatory procedure, which is directed by the Governing Body and carried out by the Office, there are several decisions of importance to be made. One of these is a determination of the scope of the items to be placed on the agenda. As the determination of the agenda is a function of the Governing Body, it would appear that it alone might have the privilege of defining the items on the agenda.[61] Yet the practice in this regard has not been such as to guarantee control by the Governing Body. In the latest form of procedure, the double-discussion, the Conference has sometimes changed the scope of the agenda against the wishes of the Governing Body.[62] Generally speaking, the care with which an item is defined on the agenda determines whether or not agreement can be reached as to the form of the draft convention or recommendation.

The early work of the Conference demonstrated the fact that the chief obstruction in the path of the framing of conventions was the negotiation among the three groups represented in the Conference. No satisfactory solution of this problem appears to have been found until the adoption of the "double-discussion draft conclusion procedure" in 1929.[63] The adoption of this method was the result of an evolutionary process in which a number of methods were tried.[64] According to the latest double-discussion type of pro-

---

When a preparatory technical conference is held a White Report forms the basis of the discussion. Sometimes reports are made concerning subjects on which no action is to be taken; these are usually called Green Reports.

[60] The greatest care is exercised by the Office in framing the questionnaire sent to the governments.

[61] The power of the Governing Body over the scope of the agenda has varied with the general evolution of the different methods of procedure.

[62] The most outstanding case in this regard occurred in respect to the dockers convention in 1928 and 1929.

[63] See *International Labor Conference* (hereafter cited *I. L. C.*), *Proceedings, Twelfth Session,* I, 1929, 366, 804 f.

[64] In an attempt to facilitate the work a system of "double reading procedure" was adopted in 1924, but under this method the entire convention was opened for discussion at the second reading, so its value was nullified. For text of the standing order providing for this procedure see *I. L. C.*, II, 1925, ap-

cedure, the first discussion is on the draft proposals of the Office and the "law and practice reports." In this discussion no conclusion is reached as to the final form of the convention, but resolutions and conclusions as to the proper items to be considered are adopted.[65] The second discussion of the proposed convention occurs at the next Conference, at which a final decision is reached.[66] It is necessary to emphasize the fact that these methods are changed as the need arises and the whole procedure is in a state of flux.

The actual work in the Conference is done to a large extent by Conference committees. These groups are best suited for the purposes of negotiation and compromise, which are an essential part of any legislation and particularly so in the Labor Conference where the views of three groups must be conciliated. The representation of the three groups on the Conference committee is equally divided.[67] Owing to the preponderance of government representatives in the Conference this would appear to further the success of the process of negotiation. In addition to the standing committees in the Conference there is usually a special committee for each item on the agenda. The Selection Committee plans the day-to-day program of the Conference. The Standing Orders Committee formulates any new rules of procedure.[68]

The basis of the discussion of a special committee is always the

---

pendix 3, *Seventh Session.* In 1926 a "double-discussion" procedure was adopted but this proved to be unsatisfactory as the questionnaire was drafted by the Conference and the delegates did not give the proper attention to drafting; see *I. L. C., Proceedings,* I, 191-200.

[65] The result of this action is published in the Red Report which includes a questionnaire to be answered by governments. This questionnaire is formulated by the Office.

[66] The procedure to be followed by the Governing Body and the Conference is carefully defined by the standing orders of each. In each change of procedure it has been necessary to modify these orders. They may be found in the final record of each Conference and in the *Constitution and Standing Orders of the International Labor Organization.* Hereafter cited *Constitution and Standing Orders,* Published by the Office.

[67] With the exception of the Selection Committee, which has the same ratio as the Conference representation. The representation on committees is in a state of flux at present.

[68] The Credentials Committee and the Committee on Article 408 are two important permanent committees. The former seats the delegates in the Conference, and the latter examines the reports on the application of conventions by States Members.

report of the Office. The members of the committee may suggest amendments to the report, but a new report may not be proposed.[69] The procedure in the committee consists of proposals and debates on these proposals until an agreement is reached among the three equally represented groups. Such an agreement oftentimes cannot be reached without a very delicate compromise.[70]

The conclusions that committees present to the Conference by special Reporters are at first generally discussed. Following the discussion, which may last for only a short period, specific points in the report are examined by the Conference members. Usually the differences of opinion that arise in the Conference are the same as those debated in the committee, and agreement with the committee's report oftentimes follows. In the case of a first discussion of an item, a show of hands and a record vote determine whether the item will be placed on the agenda of the next Conference for final consideration. If the second discussion is taking place the procedure is more complex. Frequently amendments are proposed and voted on and a preliminary record vote on a tentative text is taken. If the required majority is procured, the provisional text of the draft convention is referred to the Drafting Committee. When this committee reports back to the Conference, a vote is taken on the rejection or adoption of the convention.[71]

The procedure involved in the making of conventions demonstrates the complexity of any attempt to conciliate the views of three groups of technical subjects. The long period of time elapsing between the commencement of efforts to prepare a subject for a convention and the adoption of the final conclusion indicates the careful consideration given to conventions. This lengthy consideration is also helpful in arriving at a compromise among the different groups.

GOVERNMENTAL BODIES COMPETENT TO INTERPRET

The Constitution of the International Labor Organization makes a provision for interpretation of conventions. This provi-

[69] The membership of some of these committees is rather large. For example the Committee on the Unemployment of Young Persons in the Nineteenth Session consisted of fifty-two members.

[70] In some instances a minority report is filed which indicates the bitterness of the opposing groups.

[71] The preliminary adoption of a convention is usually a guarantee that the report of the Drafting Committee will be accepted, although the convention on the hours of work in coal mines was defeated in 1930.

sion states that any question pertaining to an agreement concluded under the auspices of the Organization shall be referred to the Permanent Court of International Justice for interpretation.[72] In view of this explicit provision the Permanent Court is evidently the proper body to render an official interpretation. Furthermore, the Court has jurisdiction in respect to any cases arising under a treaty that may be referred to it.[73]

It appears that early in the life of the Organization it was recognized that the procedure of referring the interpretation of clauses of doubtful meaning to the Permanent Court was a method that states hesitated to invoke. In order to remedy this situation it was suggested that the Governing Body render official interpretations.[74] It was believed that such an action taken by the Governing Body would facilitate the interpretation of conventions. Presumably an interpretation by the Governing Body would have followed a direct request and would have been given without any adherence to a complex formal procedure. In spite of the demand for the Governing Body to give opinions it has consistently refused to do so chiefly on the grounds that it has no legal authority on which to base such action.

The constant need of the clarification of articles of conventions has forced the Office to assist in the interpretation of conventions. As the Office receives all inquiries from States Members in respect to the meaning of clauses, it is in a position to consider the matter without delay. In view of its limited competence in this regard its interpretations must necessarily be unofficial.[75] In giving opinions in reply to requests from States Members the Office has been careful to point out that its reading of the meaning of the clauses is not official. The interpretation by the Office is not based on any authority derived from Part XIII or any written rule of the Organization. It is apparently the result of practice by the Office which has received the sanction of the Organization and is now recognized as a useful function.[76]

---

[72] See Articles 423 of the Treaty of Versailles and corresponding sections of other peace treaties.

[73] See *infra,* Chapter VI, "The Permanent Court of International Justice," for a more complete discussion of the jurisdiction of this judicial body.

[74] See *infra,* Chapter VI, pp. 149-150, for a discussion of the position of the Governing Body in this regard.

[75] For a discussion of the position of the Office in respect to interpretations and an analysis of its opinions, see *infra,* Chap. VI, pp. 135-149.

[76] See comment *ibid.*

The bodies competent to deal with questions arising under international labor conventions in the jurisdiction of national states vary considerably according to the organization of the court system and the authority of administrative officials. In Great Britain there are three classes of courts concerned with the labor question. These are the Superior Courts,[77] the Inferior Courts,[78] and certain special inferior courts dealing with matters arising out of labor legislation. These last-named courts are not courts of law in the sense of the regular courts.[79]

In France there are three divisions of courts that have jurisdiction in cases arising under labor laws. The group that contains the greatest variety of courts comprises the Civil or Commercial Courts.[80] The second class is made up of the Administrative Courts, which control the legality of the administrative regulations that apply to labor.[81] Another group of courts which may decide disputes pertaining to labor are the Penal Courts.[82]

The German authorities competent to interpret questions of labor law that may arise under international labor conventions are

[77] The Superior Courts are the House of Lords, the Judicial Committee of the Privy Council, and the Supreme Court. The last-named body is divided into two sections: (1) the Court of Appeal, (2) the High Court of Justice. See *International Survey of Legal Decisions on Labour Law* (hereafter cited *International Survey*), 1932, xxi-xii.

[78] The Inferior Courts consist of the County Courts and Courts of Summary Jurisdiction. *Ibid.*, xxiii.

[79] These special courts are: the Industrial Court, which does not have compulsory jurisdiction and is a conciliation tribunal; the Court of Referees, which deals with disputes arising under certain acts, and the Umpire, to whom an appeal may be made from the Court of Referees. *Ibid.*, xxiii-xxiv.

[80] The lowest ranking of these courts are the Probiviral Courts (Conseil des prud'hommes) and the Justices of the Peace (Juges de paix). The next in rank is the Civil Court (Tribunal civil) which deals with appeals from the lowest group of courts, and the Commercial Courts (Tribunal de commerce), a special tribunal for labor cases. Appeal from these two courts may be made to the Court of Appeal (Cour d'appel) in cases involving 1,500 francs. The highest court of this grouping is the Court of Cassation (Cour de cassation). *Ibid.*, xxv-xxvi.

[81] The lowest court of the administrative group is the Interdepartmental Prefectural (Conseils de prefecture interdepartementaux) and the highest the Council of State (Conseil d'Etat). *Idem.*

[82] These courts are divided into four categories: (1) The Police Court (Tribunal de simple police); (2) the Correctional Court (Tribunal correctionnel); (3) one Chamber of the Court of Appeal, the Chamber of Correctional Appeals (Chambre des appels correctionnels), of the Court of Cassation, *Ibid.*, xxvii.

of a varied character. The State Conciliation Authorities are an important part of the labor relations organization.[83] In addition to these State Conciliatory authorities there are Voluntary Conciliation Agencies. The regular labor courts are the Labor Court of First Instance, the District Labor Courts of Appeal, and the Federal Labor Court of Revision.[84] The administration of labor law in Germany is a complex matter, and the administrative authorities and Administrative Courts interpret laws and regulations to a considerable extent.[85] A special section of the administrative branch which hands down decisions is that of Social Insurance, which pertains particularly to unemployment insurance.[86]

The two chief groups of courts in Italy are the ordinary law courts[87] and special courts for the different departments of law. There is also special judicial and conciliatory machinery for settling collective labor disagreements.[88]

In other Member States of the Organization some variation of the type of court found in the principal states is the general rule. Certain states allow their administrative officials to have wide discretionary power in the interpretation of conventions; others depend to a greater degree on the opinions of regularly constituted courts.

GOVERNMENTAL BODIES COMPETENT TO REVISE

The revision of a convention may mean the changing of some of its provisions to the extent that far-reaching consequences will result. If total revision is accomplished, the subject matter and

[83] These authorities are: (1) the Conciliation Committee; (2) the Conciliator; (3) the Federal Minister of Labor; (4) The Professional Committees of Home Workers. *Ibid.*, xxx-xxxi.

[84] There are also Voluntary Arbitral Courts and Special Labor Courts. *Ibid.*, xxxii.

[85] This interpretation is by Federal Authorities, such as the Federal Minister of Labor, and the Federal Institution for Labor Exchanges and Unemployment Insurance. Likewise, in the individual states, the ministries concerned with labor laws sometimes give opinions. *Ibid.*, xxxiii.

[86] The branches of this administrative authority are the chairman of the Labor Office, the Adjudicating Committee of the Labor Office, and the highest unit called the Upper Insurance Office. *Ibid.*, xxxiv.

[87] These are: the Justices of Peace, Judges of Courts of First Instance, Courts of First Instance and Appeal, Courts of Appeal, and the Court of Cassation. *Ibid.*, xxxv.

[88] These are the Association, the Corporation, and the Labor Judicature. *Ibid.*, xxxvii.

meaning of a convention may be vitally altered. Even the partial revision of an international agreement may essentially change the application of some parts of the convention. The significance of revision is suggested by the fact that before its commencement a serious question concerning the applicability of the treaty must have arisen.

The effect of revision on the instrument being revised would appear to limit the authority of revision to the treaty-making body. It is not conceivable that revision of an agreement by an authority possessing less than the sovereign powers of the representative unit making the treaty could be deemed competent to revise. Thus the revising authority in respect to international labor conventions would reside in the International Labor Conference. This authority is not directly derived from the Constitution, as revision is not mentioned in its provisions; accordingly, it must be indirectly derived from the power of the Conference to make conventions. The Conference is the body with the authority to decide when a convention is acceptable,[89] and likewise it may carry out the revision and adopt the revised convention. As in the case of the making of conventions, the Conference is not competent to carry out revision unassisted. The Governing Body through its prerogative in the preparation of conventions plays an important part in revision. The procedure to be followed in case of revision is defined in the Standing Orders of the Conference.[90] The place of the Governing Body in respect to the agenda of the Conference renders it competent to direct likewise the preparatory revisionary program.[91]

The International Labor Conference in connection with the preparatory work of the Governing Body constitutes the competent revisory organs of the International Labor Organization.

RELATION TO INTERNATIONAL LAW

The subject matter and agencies which are being considered are closely related to international law. One of the express objectives of the International Labor Organization is to set up an interna-

[89] See Article 19, of the Constitution, and *supra,* "Actual Making of Conventions."

[90] Article 6a provides for revision. See *Constitution and Standing Orders* (1934), 27-28.

[91] See Article 14 of the Constitution. For procedure governing revision, see *Constitution and Standing Orders,* 54-55.

tional code of labor legislation. The early efforts of the Organization were to a large extent devoted to the formation of agreements that might be termed a code.[92] Although some contend that the Organization is now attempting to set up labor standards rather than labor laws, its efforts are still in the direction of legal guarantees.[93]

The administrative and judicial agencies involved in the interpretation of conventions are applying international legal principles. In some cases they are reaffirming long-established rules in connection with their decisions. In other instances they are laying down rules that are new, for the subject matter considered may be for the first time directly related to international law. In either case it appears that these agencies are exerting an influence in the realm of international legal practice. The international agencies that interpret should make for uniform application. The national bodies through the assistance rendered by the international agencies may also give interpretations that will be to a degree uniform, although the tendency will apparently be in the direction of some disparity. However, with the assistance of the Permanent Court of International Justice and the Office, general principles may be evolved which will be international.

While these efforts are not so fruitful as they might be, as far as ratifications are concerned, they still look to international standards of labor. The fact that the method of action of the Organization is through a convention, which is an international legal instrument, adds to the Organization's importance in respect to international law. It is, therefore, significant as to its effect on the scope of international legal principles.

The agencies dealing with revision are concerned with a process which requires technical legal rules for a successful completion of the projected changes. To some extent these rules may be derived from past legal procedure. However, much of the revision procedure must be tested by the trial and error method. It may be that from this process principles will evolve which will be of considerable value to international legal procedure. The formulation of a successful revisory procedure would be a distinct contribution to international law.

[92] See the discussion by Ernest Mahaim, "International Labour Law," *International Labour Review,* I (1921), 283.

[93] This point of view is based on the fact that the failure of the Organization to obtain widespread ratifications has caused it to be content with raising standards. See F. G. Wilson, *Labor in the League System,* 163.

CHAPTER II

THE GENERAL PROBLEM OF COLLECTIVE REVISION

IMPORTANCE TO AN INTERNATIONAL LEGAL SYSTEM

"Politics, domestic and international, might be defined as the science or art of the readjustment of institutions to the changing needs of mankind." [1] This statement by a British publicist emphasizes the importance of readjustment to all types of institutions. The perpetuity of any legal system depends to a large degree upon its adaptability to ever-changing conditions. The need for the adaptation of legal rules to meet a variety of new circumstances is especially great in respect to an international legal system which is increasingly coming to be based on multipartite agreements. Treaties to which a number of states are parties must be provided with the proper legal machinery in order satisfactorily to effect the necessary adjustments.[2] As yet there has been no substantial change in the form of the customary treaty, although the modern law-making treaty has a distinctly different function to perform from that of the older bipartite instrument.[3] Owing to the differing characteristics of the bipartite and multipartite treaties there must necessarily be formulated a workable method of revising collective instruments in the light of changing social, political, economic, and technological conditions. The conclusion that there is a need for a process of change which will be more applicable to the modern collective agreement does not exclude

[1] J. F. Williams, *International Change and International Peace*, I (reprinted with permission of Oxford University Press). This volume demonstrates in a masterful fashion the importance of peaceful change.

See Josef L. Kunz, *Die Revision der Pariser Friedens-Vertrage*, for a detailed examination of Article XIX of the Covenant and a rather extensive bibliography.

[2] The following pertinent comment in regard to the need of such machinery and the present lack of it is made by Professor Clyde Eagleton in "International Legislation," *Temple Law Quarterly*, VIII (1933-34), 218-233, at 218: "If a decision of law is made in accordance with an antiquated or unfair law or treaty, it is almost impossible to secure revision in order to provide better justice for subsequent cases."

[3] See an excellent comment on this point by C. Wilfred Jenks, "The Revision of International Labour Conventions," *British Yearbook of International Law*, XIV (1933), 43.

the possible use of *rebus sic stantibus* or other legal rules and principles in changing these instruments.[4] Nevertheless, owing to the complex nature of modern multipartite instruments, an exact parallel cannot be drawn between the application of long-established principles and rules to this type of instrument and their application to bipartite instruments.[5]

The need of a more adequate method of adjusting treaties to conditions is constantly increasing. Prevailing practice concerning clauses providing for modification has failed to provide a method of dealing with the problem in view of the rule of *pacta servanda sunt.*[6] Nevertheless, resort to the doctrine *rebus sic stantibus* will not provide a definite solution to the problem, as a state cannot decide as to the application of this rule itself without violating the basic rule of the sanctity of treaties.[6a] This would appear to lead to the conclusion that the practice of states' revising treaties collectively should be made into a rule which would be applied by a judicial, conciliatory, or legislative body.[7]

It is now becoming generally recognized by states that future conditions and circumstances may make modification of treaties

---

[4] For a discussion of the use of the doctrine of *rebus sic stantibus* see J. F. Williams, "The Permanence of Treaties," *American Journal of International Law* (hereafter cited *A. J. I. L.*), XXII (1928), 89-104. An excellent analysis of the doctrine with the following definition is given by Chesney Hill in *The Doctrine of Rebus Sic Stantibus in International Law* (1934): "A treaty of perpetual or indefinite duration which contains no provision for revision or denunciation lapses, in the sense that stipulations which remain to be performed cease to bind the parties to the treaty, when it is recognized by the parties to the treaty or by a competent international authority that there has been an essential change in those circumstances which existed at the time of the conclusion of the treaty, and whose continuance without essential change formed a condition of the obligatory force of the treaty according to the intention of the parties," 83 (reprinted with the author's permission).

[5] See the discussion of J. W. Garner in which he points out the necessity of the application of the rule of *rebus sic stantibus* until adequate machinery for revision is formulated. "Revision of Treaties and the Doctrine of *Rebus Sic Stantibus,*" *Iowa Law Review,* XIX (1933-34), 314.

[6] See Eagleton, *loc. cit.,* 518.

[6a] An excellent discussion of the limits of this method is given in Charles Fairman, "Implied Resolutive Conditions in Treaties," *A. J. I. L.,* XXIX, no. 2 (April, 1935), 219-236.

[7] See the draft convention and comment on treaties, prepared by the Harvard Research in International Law, in *A. J. I. L.,* XXIX, no. 4 (Oct., 1935), section 2.

desirable and that before such changes can take place it is essential that careful arrangements for this readjustment be made.[8]

ALTERNATIVES TO REVISION

In many instances a procedure permitting reservations may be an alternative to revision as a means of bringing about ratifications.[9] Reservations may be made at the time of signature, when the ratification is deposited, or where an accession is made.[10] A careful examination of the practice concerning reservations indicates that valid reservations must be acceptable to all other parties.[11]

Multilateral treaties vary in their general provisions concerning reservations. Some important agremeents have been hostile to any difference in the obligations of the signatory parties.[12] Other instruments are extremely friendly to the idea of reservations, as is demonstrated by their express provisions concerning the admissibility of such special conditions.[13] In addition to the two

[8] See George Grafton Wilson, "Treaties and Changing Conditions," *A. J. I. L.*, XXIX, no. 2 (April, 1935), 308. A noted British publicist states that "in so far then as treaties are regarded as legislation, it is essential that international law should develop some rule or international society some organ, whereby this process (revision) can be carried out." Arnold McNair, "The Function and Differing Legal Character of Treaties," *British Yearbook of International Law*, XI (1930), 111.

[9] The Draft Convention on the Law of Treaties defines the term "reservation" in Article 13 as follows: "A 'reservation' is a formal declaration by which a State, when signing, ratifying or acceding to a treaty, specifies as a condition of its willingness to become a party to the treaty certain terms which will limit the effect of the treaty in so far as it may apply in the relations of that State with the other State or States which may be parties to the treaty." *A. J. I. L.*, XXIX, no. 4 (1935), secion 11, p. 659. See also comment of Jenks, "Revision of Conventions," *loc. cit.*, 45. A more simple definition is given by Mr. David Hunter Miller, *Reservations to Treaties*, 76.

[10] For a survey of the nature and practice of reservation clauses see H. W. Malkin, "Reservations to Multilateral Conventions," *British Yearbook of International Law*, VII (1926), 142-162.

[11] *Loc. cit.;* see also comment on Draft Convention on Law of Treaties, Article 14, concerning consent; *A. J. I. L.*, XXIX, 874-912, in which the necessity of consent is emphasized in respect to all types of reservations.

[12] See comment on this point by Dr. Ulrich Scheidtmann, *Der Vorbehalt beim Abschluss Völkerrechtlicher Vertrage* (1934), 39ff.

[13] A good example of this type of agreement is the Statute of the Permanent Court of International Justice, article 36, section 2. See comment, Scheidtmann, *op. cit.*, 46ff.

types of treaties mentioned a third group may be regarded as neutral to reservations.[14]

There are several methods which may be followed in formulating reservation clauses. The five stipulations found in the *International Convention Relating to the Simplification of Custom Formalities*[15] cover in an excellent manner the necessary points for valid reservations. These are: (1) the reservations must be accepted by others; (2) further reservations are eliminated; (3) the machinery must provide for dealing with reservations by subsequent signatory powers; (4) assurance of acceptance of reservations which are consistent with the intentions of the original signatory parties; (5) reservations made are placed on record.[16] Some treaties provide for communications with the Secretary General of the League of Nations concerning the reservations they desire to make, and if no objections are received they are to be considered as acceptable to the parties concerned.[17] Other conventions provide that specific communications shall be addressed to the Secretary General, and that he shall call a meeting to determine whether or not the exceptions are acceptable.[18]

In 1927 the Report of the Committee of Experts for the Progressive Codification of International Law made a number of pertinent observations on the admissibility of reservations to general conventions.[19] They declared that no reservations could be valid unless all parties to the agreement consented to them. In the instance of a treaty left open to accession over a period of years, a state becoming a party to the agreement could make no reservations other than those which were agreed to when the treaty was made.[20] The Harvard Research Draft Convention on Treaties has laid down specific rules concerning every step of the reser-

---

[14] Perhaps international labor conventions would come under this classification.

[15] *League of Nations Treaty Series*, XXX, 401-409.

[16] *Ibid.*, Protocol, section 6, p. 409. This provision gives the League Council the right to decide whether reservations shall be made after consultation with a technical body. See also note in *I. L. C., Proceedings* (1928), I, 611.

[17] See *League of Nations Treaty Series*, CXII, *International Convention for the Suppression of Counterfeiting Currency* of April 20, 1929, 384, and also *Treaty Series, Convention Concerning Economic Statistics* (December 14, 1928, CX, 171.

[18] Article 17, of the *Convention on the Abolition of Import and Export Restrictions*, November 8, 1927, *League of Nations Treaty Series*, XCVII, 411.

[19] See *League of Nations, Official Journal* (hereafter cited *Official Journal*), VIII (1927), 881.

[20] *Loc. cit.*

vation procedure.[21] The procedure relating to reservations has been developed over a number of years and now is in workable form.

The insertion of a clause in conventions which will allow amendments to be made is one method of avoiding revision of conventions.[22] Such a procedure allows amendments to be made to provisions concerning points of detail without changing essential articles.[23]

The utilization of denunciation clauses as alternatives to revision is of doubtful value. The purpose of revision is the adaptation of specific conditions to a general situation, for the maintenance of broad obligations already in effect. Denunciation clauses are for the purpose of making individual adjustments without reference to the collective good by absolute termination of obligations. Although unilateral denunciation is not a proper substitute for modification, it is sometimes correctly practiced if the subject of the agreement is technical and the rights and duties of all states are the same.[24] The limitation of the duration of treaties and the allowance of the right of denunciation is becoming a common practice.[25] The use of this type of clause may be a

[21] *A. J. I. L.*, XXIX; see comment on Article 14, "Reservations at Time of Signature"; Article 15, "Reservations at Time of Ratification," 889-906; and "Reservations at Time of Accession," 905-912.

[22] Mr. Jenks states: "There is some authority in international practice for using the term 'revision' to describe procedures involving fresh ratifications by all parties to be bound by the revised convention and 'amendment' to describe procedures which dispense with either ratifications or unanimity." "Revision of Conditions," *loc. cit.*, 46n.

[23] See account of the efforts to establish an amendment procedure by the International Labor Organization, *infra*, Chap. III, pp. 39-43.

[24] See H. J. Tobin, *The Termination of Multipartite Treaties*, 204, wherein it is pointed out that unilateral denunciation is not generally recognized. See also on this point Paul de Auer, "Revision of Treaties," *op. cit.*, 159. The Draft Convention on the Law of Treaties, Article 34, gives the following rule for denunciation; "A treaty may be denounced by a party only when such denunciation is provided for in the treaty or consented to by all other parties. A denunciation must be in accordance with any conditions laid down in the treaty or agreed upon by the parties." *A. J. I. L.*, XXIX, 1173; general comment on the subject of denunciation is given in *ibid.*, 1173-1183.

[25] Mr. Tobin shows that during the period 1815-1825 only one out of twenty treaties contained denunciatory or revisory clauses; but in the period 1919-1932, out of one hundred and fifty multipartite treaties, one hundred contained revision clauses and only eleven had no termination clauses. *Op. cit.*, 269. See also comment by Garner, "Revision of Treaties," *loc. cit.*, 313. Comment on the Draft Convention on the Law of Treaties is made to the effect that of the first

means of a state's obtaining relief from intolerable conditions, but it does not serve the same purpose as revision.[26]

EXISTING METHODS

The necessity for revision is recognized today, as is demonstrated by the general practice of including revisory clauses in conventions.[27] The clauses providing for modification vary considerably as to details, but they contain the following conditions in some form: (1) a set period of years which must elapse prior to their invocation; (2) a provision for a number of states which must agree to set the procedure in motion—many conventions stipulate that one-third of the parties to the convention must be in favor of modification; (3) the naming of the authority responsible for convening a revising conference or to whom communications on the subject shall be addressed; (4) the discretion delegated to the authority following the approval of revision by the required number of states; (5) the number of states required to attend the revisory conference, or to approve the modifications made by the conference or authority empowered to act on the subject.[28]

The stipulations concerning the revision clauses in a few selected treaties will possibly demonstrate the existing practices. It is instructive to note the provisions for amendment found in the sections of the Versailles Treaty which became the constitutions of international organizations.[29] Amendment is provided for in the League Covenant when agreed to by the Council and by a majority

---

seventy-six treaties registered with the League of Nations thirty contained provisions for denunciation, and that an examination of the treaties registered in later years shows approximately the same proportion. *A. J. I. L.,* XXIX, 1177.

[26] See comment on this method by J. L. Brierly, "Some Considerations on the Obsolescence of Treaties," *Transactions of the Grotius Society,* XI, 11-20.

[27] See Tobin, *loc. cit.* Although the general practice is to include revisory clauses, many conventions do not contain them.

[28] See Jenks, "Revision of Conventions," *loc. cit.,* 46. An example of a simple method of proposing revision is given in *Convention for Limiting the Manufacture and Regulating the Distribution of Narcotic Drugs,* which was proposed in September, 1931. This Article (33) provides that a request for the revision of a convention can be made at any time by notice addressed to the Secretary General of the League of Nations, who should inform the other States parties to the treaty, and if the proposal is endorsed by not less than one-third of the members they shall meet to revise the agreement; see the *Official Journal,* no. 12 (1931), 1811.

[29] Mr. Jenks says, "These instruments are on a special footing." "Revision of Conventions," *loc. cit.,* 44, footnote 5.

of the Assembly.[30] The procedure of amendment in the Constitution of the International Labor Organization is somewhat similar to that of the Covenant; it provides for modification by a two-thirds majority vote to take effect following ratification by the Council of the League and three-fourths of its members.[31]

A method of revision for treaties, the value of which has been the source of considerable discussion, is found in Article XIX of the League Covenant.[32] As there has been no application of this Article to changing conditions, no rules of procedure in this regard have developed.[33]

One type of procedure in revision is exemplified by the *Universal Postal Convention* of London, June 28, 1929, which provides for unanimous vote in certain specific instances, a two-thirds vote in other cases, and only a simple majority under certain conditions.[34]

Some revisory articles do not require positive consent to amendments; but if there is no objection on the part of the contracting powers, the amendments come into effect.[35]

---

[30] Article XXVI: "Amendments to this Covenant will take effect when ratified by the Members of the League whose Representatives compose the Council and by a majority of the Members of the League whose Representatives compose the Assembly.

"No such amendment shall bind any member of the League which signifies its dissent therefrom, but in that case it shall cease to be a member of the League." See Treaty of Versailles. In effect the second paragraph of this article necessarily makes unanimous consent a condition of any modification.

[31] Article 36: "Amendments to this part of the present Treaty which are adopted by the Conference by a majority of two-thirds of the votes cast by the Delegates present shall take effect when ratified by the States whose representatives compose the Council of the League of Nations and by three-fourths of its Members." Treaty of Versailles. In practice amendment according to this provision has been very difficult, as is shown by the prolonged attempt to amend Article 37 for the purpose of increasing the size of the Governing Body.

[32] The terms of this Article are as follows: "The Assembly may from time to time advise the reconsideration by members of the League of treaties which have become inapplicable and the consideration of international conditions whose continuance might endanger the peace of the world." Treaty of Versailles. See the following studies of this Article: Aladar Goellner, *L'Article 19 du Pacte de la Société des Nations;* Wolfgang Schneider, *Die Völkerrechtliche Clausula* Rebus Sic Stantibus *und Article 19 der Völkerbundsatzung;* Albert Wignoille, *La Société des Nations et la révision des traités.*

[33] See especially Paul de Auer, *op. cit.*, 168, and for an excellent discussion of the relation of this clause to the doctrine of *rebus sic stantibus,* see J. F. Williams, "The Permanence of Treaties," *loc. cit.*, 89-104.

[34] See *League of Nations Treaty Series,* CII, Article 20, p. 265.

[35] See especially, Article 86, section 9, of the Regulations annexed to the

The modification of the annexes to some treaties is accomplished by special regulatory bodies that possess the power of amending these sections. The International Commission for Air Navigation possesses such authority. This body may receive or make proposals for modification,[36] subject to approval by three-fourths of the total votes of the parties to the agreement.[37] Nevertheless, before any actual proposal can be made it must be examined by the Commission and approved by two-thirds of the States parties to the treaty.[38] Following modifications, such changes must be adopted by all the contracting states before they become effective.[39]

Since 1919 there has been a growing tendency for the inclusion in multilateral treaties of clauses providing for the use of international agencies, such as the Council of the League of Nations, in bringing about modifications.[40] In a few instances the international authority may act on its own initiative, but in most cases action is taken following the request of more than one party to the instrument.[41] Generally the rules of such revisory conferences are fixed by the conferences.[42]

International Telegraph Convention of St. Petersburg (July 22, 1875), as revised October 29, 1925, *ibid.*, LVII, 375.

[36] This authority is given in the following passage: "The duties of the Commission shall be: (a) To receive proposals from or to make proposals to any of the contracting states for the modification or amendment of the provisions of the present convention, and to notify changes adopted"; *ibid.*, XI, 196.

[37] "Any modification of the provisions of any one of the annexes may be made by the International Commission of Air Navigation when such modification shall have been approved by three-fourths of the total possible votes which could be cast if all the states were represented, and shall become effective from the time when it shall have been notified by the International Commission for Air Navigation to call the contracting States." *Loc. cit.*

[38] "Any proposed modification of the Articles of the present convention shall be examined by the International Commission for Air Navigation, whether it originates with one of the contracting States or with the commission itself. No such modification shall be proposed by the contracting States, unless it shall have been approved by at least two-thirds of the total possible votes." *Loc. cit.*

[39] "All such modifications of the Articles of the Convention (but not the provisions of the Annexes) must be formally adopted by all the contracting States before they become effective." *Loc. cit.*

[40] See the survey of sixty instruments in R. R. Wilson, "Revision Clauses in Treaties since the World War," *American Political Science Review,* XXVIII, no. 5 (1934), 907, in which one-third of the group studied have stipulations providing for the action of international agencies.

[41] *Loc. cit.*

[42] *Loc. cit.*

The practice of international unions in respect to revision has been indicative of the general tendency of the development of the collective modification of technical regulations.[43] Briefly, the following generalization may be made concerning the procedure of these international bodies: (1) the permanent organization of the union keeps an account of the needs of the parties and their desire for changes and prepares a plan for revision along the lines suggested; (2) the conventions provide for periodic conferences with the power of revision; (3) where the equality of representatives would work an injustice, weighted voting is substituted for equal voice; (4) where the revision of a convention between conferences is deemed necessary, a fraction of the states may call a revisory conference; (5) protection for dissenting states is provided by requiring the ratification of new conventions and allowing the states not wishing to ratify to maintain the old convention.[44]

The practice of revision as demonstrated by the provisions in treaty clauses appears to reveal that there is no uniform method of modification and that there is no existing tendency in that direction.[45] One reason for this lack of uniformity seems to be the emphasis since 1919 on the necessity of changing "detailed technical regulations." [46] The practice in this regard has special significance in the field of international labor regulations.

SPECIAL SIGNIFICANCE IN THE FIELD OF LABOR

The complexity of the structure of social relationships, within which questions relating to labor arise, necessitates frequent readjustments. Social legislation is not static; it is dynamic. The significant developments of labor legislation since the inception of the International Labor Organization demonstrates the ever-increasing importance of new labor regulations.[47] The existence of an international "legislature," by which new labor laws of universal applicability may be regularly created, gives a special complexity to questions in this field. This new international regulatory authority necessitates the formulation of untried methods of procedure in respect to problems of labor.[48]

---

[43] See Tobin, *op. cit.*, 277. [44] *Idem.*

[45] R. R. Wilson, "Revision Clauses," *loc. cit.*, 907. [46] *Idem.*

[47] See *Legislative Series* (Annual), published by the office, for a complete list of the legislation passed since 1919.

[48] See general comment on "International Legislation" by Arnold McNair, *Iowa Law Review*, XIX (1933-34), 177-189.

The development of procedural methods in the field of international labor regulation is further complicated by the innumerable changes in the world economic and industrial system. Technological inventions may make certain provisions, which were formerly valuable, utterly obsolete. Changes in the political, and particularly the economic, structure of states may make necessary a special consideration of the existing obligation of the state in the light of the new conditions.[49] These economic and political changes may alter the function of the national governmental machinery to the extent that drastic adaptations in respect to international regulations are necessary. The cycle of economic depressions often creates unprecedented economic and social conditions which must be provided for if the international legal system is to serve the current needs.[50]

There is every evidence that the problem of readaptation in the field of labor is one of paramount importance. The multiplicity of factors which may be instrumental in creating new conditions make the need for flexible international labor rules a real one. The fact that the International Labor Conference constitutes an "international legislature" means that there is a definite possibility of relief from a crystallization of existing rules.[51] Nevertheless, the Conference will not be adequate for a solution of the problems unless a workable procedure for modification is formulated in the light of the peculiar characteristics of international labor conventions. These characteristics are due to the fact that these agreements are not independent instruments, but must always be considered in connection with the Constitution of the Labor Organization.[52] This unusual feature of labor conventions has made unsuccessful numerous efforts to provide the proper method of adjustment.

One suggestion that has been made is that conventions be formulated so as to embody only general principles. This would allow the states which were parties to the agreements to decide as to details in the manner they deem most suitable for their respective

[49] The totalitarian states that have come into existence since the World War offer a variety of problems in this respect. The question of the proper obligations of Soviet Russia, in respect to the tripartite participation in the International Labor Organization, is an example.

[50] See comment of Jenks, "Revision of Conventions," *loc. cit.*, 43.

[51] See statement by J. F. Williams to the effect that law is an expression of changes, *International Change and International Peace.*

[52] See description of the organization and its functioning in Chap. I, *supra.*

countries. Such flexibility would make the revision of conventions unnecessary.[53] When this method of making conventions was considered by the Office the view was advanced that such a plan would be in opposition to the wishes of the framers of the Constitution, for they desired international legislation to proceed along more specific lines. The Office thought this fact was evidenced by the two stages of legislation provided for (1) recommendations and (2) draft conventions.[54]

Had the proposal for the adoption of general labor conventions been in accordance with the spirit of the Constitution, such agreement probably would have helped in the adjustment of technicalities, one of the major difficulties. Technical considerations constitute an unusually large percentage of the clauses necessitating modifications.[55] In these cases the matter to be adjusted concerns only some detailed regulation and does not to any degree affect the purpose of the convention. Yet such a stipulation may be of grave importance in the application of a convention. Should the Labor Conference discard in entirety the original convention and formulate a new one? Such an action would be a serious waste of time, a great expense, and would probably reopen questions that had formerly been successfully solved with considerable difficulty. Consequently, it is highly desirable that the method of modification resorted to in respect to labor conventions be capable of making the necessary changes without disturbing satisfactory arrangements.

The opinion has been expressed that conventions should preferably be short and renewable by providing the proper means of revision and denunciation.[56] Owing to the circumstances surrounding certain conventions the average period of denunciation has been considerably reduced in the hope that this stipulation will facilitate the ratification and application of the agreements.[57]

[53] See proposals of Czechoslovakian, Finnish, Japanese, and Swiss governments in this regard, *Report on the Institution of a Procedure for Amendment of Conventions* (1924), 66. This report will hereafter be cited *Report on Amendment*.

[54] *Ibid.*, 67.

[55] See survey in Chap. III, *infra*, of "Technical Questions." See also the purpose of the *Report on Amendment* (1923).

[56] An instructive discussion on this point is given in *I. L. C., Seventeenth Session*, 1933, Report V.

[57] The usual denunciation period is ten years from the date of coming into force. In the case of the coal mines convention, this period has been reduced to five years; *idem.*

The common practice of making reservations to treaties has already been considered. Ratification of agreements, and universal application of the broad principles, can be furthered to a large degree by allowing reservations by contracting states. Notwithstanding the valid use of this method in respect to treaties generally, its use is forbidden in regard to international labor conventions.[58] The reason for the failure to sanction the use of reservations in respect to labor conventions is due to the "peculiar legal character" of such agreements.[59] It has been pointed out above that the consent of the contracting parties to a convention must be obtained before reservations become valid. In the case of labor conventions, the consent of States parties to a convention would not be sufficient. For these instruments are not drawn up by the states alone, but by non-governmental representatives as well; hence States Members would not be authorized to accept reservations.[60] Furthermore, acceptance of reservations by the International Labor Conference would not be effective; for, if the reservation were interpretative in nature, such action by the Conference would not be valid; according to the Constitution only the Permanent Court may give official interpretations.[61] Or, if the reservation were a modification of the text of the original convention, its adoption by the Conference would be equal to the formation of a new convention and the nullification of previous ratifications, as decisions of the Conference are not binding on States Members of the Organization.[62] In addition to these objections it has been stated that the purpose of labor conventions is to protect workers from the dangers arising from international competition, which purpose can be achieved only by a uniform application of conventions.[63]

[58] See the memorandum submitted by the Director of the International Labor Office to the League Council, *Official Journal,* III (1927), 880-881.

[59] *Loc. cit.* See also sections on the making of conventions.

[60] *Loc. cit.* A point of view in opposition to this opinion is expressed by Dr. Scheidtmann to the effect that, up to the conclusion of a convention, states are basically free to act as they please, so the participation of states with reservations is not impossible, *op. cit.,* 53.

[61] See Chap. I, pp. 15-16, *supra.*

[62] The memorandum of the Director of International Labor Organization previously referred to states: "Legal arguments force us to deny the admissibility of reservations on the occasion of the ratification of international labour conventions." *Official Journal.*

[63] The Director pointed to practice in this regard which indicated that the unacceptability of reservations has not raised serious objections in the Labor Conference, *loc. cit.*

Conditional ratification, a form of ratification with reservations, has been considered as a practical means of facilitating the ratification of labor treaties that are not acceptable to certain states under existing circumstances.[64] The state ratifying according to this method does so with the stipulation that its accession to the convention becomes effective following the ratification by certain other parties. This suspension of legal ratification for an indefinite period may facilitate ratification, or, on the contrary, it may hinder the progress of such action by encouraging a conditional accession where in the absence of such a method of procedure actual ratification would be forthcoming.[65] By and large, it appears that this method of reserving full obligations under an agreement would not be a valid substitute for revision, as it would be helpful at best only in respect to bringing about a ratification by other states without changing any provision of a treaty which might be an obstacle to ratification or application.[66]

A consideration of the various alternatives to revision demonstrates their inadequacy as substitutes for the revision of international labor conventions. The unusual characteristics of these collective instruments demonstrate the need of a careful process of revision which will meet the constitutional requirements of the Constitution and make the needed modifications with the least possible inconvenience to the parties involved. The general practice of collective revision, as demonstrated in various multipartite instruments, affords some valuable precedents in this regard. The procedure usually followed in the case of treaties providing for modifications by some stipulated international authority serves to point out the general pathway revisory efforts must take.

[64] See a discussion of this type of ratification as applied by States Members of the International Labor Organization, Chap. IV, "Conditional Ratifications," *infra.*

[65] A discussion of this possibility is given in section cited; see also various proposals for conditional ratification in *Report on Amendment* (1924), 70-76.

[66] See discussion of conditional ratifications in *International Labor Review,* XVI (1927), 755, 770; and in *A. J. I. L.,* XXIX, 863.

CHAPTER III

THE DEVELOPMENT AND PRACTICE OF REVISION

The problem of the revision of international labor conventions may be dealt with by two methods; first, in respect to the procedure of revision and its administration, and, secondly, in regard to the legal consequences of revision. It will be the purpose of this section to take the first method of approach; the legal phase will be considered in a later chapter. The scope of the subject will be further limited here in that technical matters, which are frequently the subjects of revision, will not be considered as to their substantive value in their relation to the provisions to be revised; rather they will be commented on solely to illustrate their relative importance.

THE BERNE CONVENTIONS

At the close of the World War two international labor conventions were in force. They were the Berne Conventions agreed to in 1906 at Berne, Switzerland, on the subjects of the use of *White Phosphorus in the Manufacture of Matches*,[1] and the *Prohibition of Night Work for Women in Industrial Employment.*[2] During the period in which plans were made for the organization of the First International Labor Conference in pursuance of Article XIII of the Versailles Treaty, considerable attention was given to these two conventions in order that they might be integrated in the new system. A special report on the current status of the Berne Conventions, with proposals as to their future place in the constructive program of the Organization, was made by the Organizing Committee for the International Labor Conference to be held at Washington, 1919.[3] As a consequence of this report the following resolution was proposed and adopted by the first Conference; "That this Conference recommends to all members of the I. L. O. which have not yet done so that they should adhere to the Inter-

[1] See *British and Foreign State Papers,* XCIX, 986-989.

[2] *Ibid.,* C, 794-799. For an excellent discussion of the status and the importance of these conventions see *The Origins of the I. L. O.,* I, 36-47.

[3] *League of Nations Report on the Employment of Women and Children and the Berne Conventions of 1906.* Report III (prepared by the Organizing Committee for the International Labor Conference, Washington, 1919), hereafter cited *League of Nations,* Report III, 1-161.

national Convention adopted at Bern in 1906, on the prohibition of the use of White Phosphorus in the Manufacture of Matches."[4]

This recommendation was made in respect to the convention concerning the use of white phosphorus without any discussion of the applicability of the convention by States Members of the International Labor Organization. This convention was recommended in its original form, as conditions concerning its application had evidently not changed since it was formulated.

When the Organizing Committee examined the convention concerning night work for women in industry, they found that for various reasons the details of the original convention were not in complete harmony with the developing policies of the new organization.[5] This decision was reached after the Committee had communicated with and received replies from most of the member states who had adhered to the convention,[6] and also from those which had not yet done so.[7] Accordingly, the Organizing Committee suggested that the convention would require some changes in drafting to make it correspond with certain draft conventions which were being submitted to the Conference.[8] These proposals of the Committee were incorporated in a tentative convention.[9] The work of the Organizing Committee was continued by a special commission constituted for the purpose of making a detailed study of the convention in order to report definitely to the Conference concerning the advisable amendments to be adopted.[10] The chairman of the Committee[11] in reporting to the Conference emphasized the

[4] Resolution proposed by Sir Malcolm Delevingne (Great Britain), *I. L. C., First Session, Proceedings,* Washington, 1919, 171. See also text of recommendation in Appendix, 264.

[5] *League of Nations,* Report III.

[6] Adhering states: Austria, Belgium, British Empire, France, Germany, Italy, The Netherlands, Portugal, Spain, Sweden, and Switzerland. *Ibid.,* 20.

[7] Most of these states indicated that they were preparing to adhere. For details see *ibid.,* 21ff.

[8] These draft conventions concerned the forty-eight-hour week, the age of the admission of children to industry, and others presented at Washington Conference, 1919. See *ibid.,* 52.

[9] *Ibid.,* 53. See also Conclusions of the Organizing Committee on Adhesion to Berne Convention in 1906, *International Labor Conference, First Session, Proceedings, Appendix,* 246-247.

[10] Report of the Commission of Women at Night and the Extension and Application of the Berne Convention of 1906 on the Prohibition of the Night Work of Women Employed in Industry. *Ibid.,* 245-246.

[11] See remarks of Miss Constance Smith (Great Britain), chairman and reporter.

unanimous endorsement of all the principles of the convention.[12] The reporter stated, however, that:

> "In examining the convention it became at once clear that the change in the situation created by the establishment of the League of Nations would necessitate certain changes in the form of the convention, and it also became clear that there was a strong feeling in favor of introducing into the convention certain changes or to speak more correctly, of drafting a new convention." [13]

The changes suggested in the report to be incorporated in the new convention pertained generally to clarifying the provisions of the convention[14] and raising the standards to meet the improved conditions that have come about since the drafting of the Berne Convention.[15] The Committee also recommended that the period granted in the convention of Berne for the passage of legislation by the adhering state should be made shorter.[16] In addition to these changes in the original convention the Committee proposed that a new article be added which would facilitate ratification in certain countries hampered by climatic conditions and backward industrial organization.[17]

The Conference discussion which followed the report of the chairman of the commission indicated that most of the delegates were in favor of the adoption of the proposed new convention without further changes.[18] However, there was considerable dis-

[12] See Report before Conference, *I. L. C., First Session, Proceedings,* 102.

[13] *Loc. cit.* These changes were not suggested by the Organizing Committee. This statement of the Committee, especially the reference to the League of Nations, is not so explicit as it might be. Presumably, the reference is to the system of the League of Nations in general, with particular reference to the International Labor Organization.

[14] In this connection Article I, paragraph 3, which defined "industrial undertakings" was amended so as to be in harmony with the definition embodied in other draft conventions. *Loc. cit.* See also remarks of Mr. Mahaim (Belgian Government Delegate), *I. L. C., Twelfth Session,* 1929, I, 353.

[15] Article I, paragraph 2, stated: "The present convention applies to undertakings in which more than ten men or women are employed." This section was deleted by the Committee, as they did not regard such exceptions justifiable under present conditions. *I. L. C., First Session, Proceedings,* 102.

[16] It was suggested that the wording of Article VIII, paragraph 8, be changed in this regard from "two years" to "one year," *idem.*

[17] This new article was added to the convention particularly to enable India to adhere, *idem.*

[18] See *ibid.,* 103-106.

cussion of the minority report, and two amendments to the majority's recommendations were made from the floor of the conference, but both were defeated.[19] The vote on the adoption of the majority report of the commission was unanimous,[20] and the proposals for the new convention were given to the regular drafting committee.[21]

The action of the Conference commission in making changes in the substance of the convention, which were adopted by the Conference, was contrary to the proposal of the Organizing Committee on the Berne Conventions. This commission favored the acceptance by the Conference of a recommendation providing for the adoption of the Berne Conventions.[22] The report of the Conference commission stated:

> "Careful examination of the terms of the Berne Convention has, however, convinced us that it requires some revision to make it an efficient international instrument at the present time, apart from and in addition to what redrafting of the formal articles providing for ratification, notification, and method of denunciation so evidently called for in the new situation created by the covenant of the League of Nations.
>
> "The commission's proposed changes are few in number and leave the main provisions of the existing convention untouched. It is, however, clear that it would be impracticable to attempt to modify a convention actually in force. The commission therefore recommends that a new convention concerning the employment of women at night be put forth by the conference to supersede the Berne Convention of 1906." [53]

The acceptance of this recommendation meant that a new convention was accepted by the Conference.[24] The Conference did not dis-

[19] Both of these amendments concerned technical changes concerning hours. One was made by Mr. Baldesi (Italian Workers' Delegate) and the other by Mr. Guerin (French) representing the Employers Group; for texts of motions see *ibid.*, Appendix, 269. The minority report of the committee on night work for women on modifications of the Berne Convention of 1906, which is the basis of the amendments is given *ibid.*, Appendix, 246.

[20] *Ibid.*, 107.

[21] For text of the new convention see *ibid.*, Appendix, 260.

[22] See *League of Nations*, Report III, particularly conclusions of the Organizing Committee on adhesion to Berne Convention of 1906, p. 246.

[23] *I. L. C., First Session*, Appendix, 245.

[24] The preamble to the convention adopted does not refer to the Berne Convention. The pertinent passages are as follows:

"Having decided upon the adoption of certain proposals with regard to

cuss the effect of this new convention on the Berne agreement.[25] It would seem, however, that although at the time of adopting the new convention it was not regarded as a revision of the Berne treaty, in reality it became such.[26] It has been previously noted that the object of the two conventions is the same and that they differ only in certain provisions. Also the same states are, or have been, parties to each of the conventions. In fact, the circumstances are similar to those pertaining to a convention that has been revised.

In spite of the similarity of the convention on the employment of women at night to a revised convention, its adoption did not contribute anything of value to revisory procedure. Since the action on this subject was not regarded as a *bona fide* revision, it has not served as a precedent in assisting the Organization in modifying agreements. Possibly the only value that may be attributed to the adoption of this convention in 1919 as far as revision is concerned came from the observance of the effect of two conventions on the same subject existing side by side.[27]

'women's employment during the night,' which is part of the third item in the agenda for the Washington meeting of the Conference, and

"Having determined that these proposals shall take the form of a draft international convention. . . . ." *Ibid.*, 260.

[25] It is instructive to note the actual effect of the new convention upon the old. Mr. Ernest Mahaim gives an excellent account of the situation:

"The Washington Convention was first ratified by Greece (19 November, 1920) and Rumania (13 June, 1921), two States that had not adhered to the Berne Convention. The Washington Convention thus came into force on 13 June, 1921. Then the following ratifications were registered successively: in 1921, those of Great Britain, India, Czechoslovakia, and the Union of South Africa; in 1922, Bulgaria, the Netherlands, Switzerland, and Estonia; in 1923, Italy; in 1924, Austria and Belgium; in 1925, France and the Irish Free State; in 1927, Yugoslavia; in 1928, Luxemburg, Hungary, and Cuba. Altogether, the convention has nineteen ratifications. But it is interesting to note that some States which have ratified the Berne Convention, such as Germany, have not ratified the Washington Convention, and that many of those which have ratified the Washington Convention had ratified the Berne Convention and have not denounced it. The latter include Great Britain, the Netherlands, Switzerland, Italy, Austria, Belgium, France, Luxemburg, and Hungary. In theory, they are therefore bound by both conventions." "Some Legal Questions Relating to International Labour Conventions," *International Labour Review*, XX, no. 6 (1929), 794.

[26] See comment *ibid.*, 793.

[27] See Chap. IV, *infra.*, on "Status of Original and Revised Conventions."

EFFORTS TO ESTABLISH AN AMENDMENT PROCEDURE

In the early stages of its development the International Labor Office became aware of the difficulties in the path of the ratification of an agreement of such rigidity as a draft convention.[28] While the practice of making reservations to treaties is a common one in international law,[29] the procedure of the International Labor Organization does not permit such reservations to its agreements. Consequently, there is not sufficient flexibility in all conventions to allow for the varied conditions which exist in the respective states. In an attempt to remedy this situation the draft committee to the Third Session of the International Labor Conference prepared an article to allow amendments to be made to provisions concerning points of detail without changing the essential articles.[30] This article contained a tentative proposal which the Conference failed to adopt for embodiment in the conventions concluded in 1921,[31] but rather decided to give the matter further careful consideration before making a final decisions.[32] The result of this further examination was the appointment of a special

[28] See the *I. L. C., Report of the Director to the Third Session*, 1921, Geneva, 119; and *I. L. C., Third Session*, 1921, I, 241.

[29] See Chap. II, 23-25, *supra.*

[30] This article was drawn up, to some extent, at the desire of the British Government delegates for modification of certain conventions, yet they opposed the suggested procedure. See remarks of Sir Montague Barlow, *I. L. C., Third Session*, 1921, I, First and Second parts, 300.

The position of the Office on the matter was stated as follows: "In the first place, it seemed necessary where there was some doubt as to the measure of elasticity which might be allowed by the terms of a given article of a convention, that some method should be found whereby the Members of the International Labor Organization should adopt a uniform practice as regards the application to be given the article in question. The second class of case is the case in which some amendment of secondary importance would appear to be required in the terms of the convention itself in order to remove an obstacle to ratification which may have presented itself in more than one country." *I. L. C., Fourth Session*, II, *Report of the Director*, 827.

[31] This proposal advocated that the Conference adopt amendments of technical articles by a two-thirds vote of the delegates present if this vote included that of the Government delegates and one member of the non-Government delegates of the States having ratified. *Third Session*, 1921, I, 299-306; see also *Institution of a Procedure for Amendment of Conventions* (Report submitted to Governments for their observations), Geneva, 1924, 1-2.

[32] The question of amendment was referred to the Governing Body, which recommended reference to the Fourth Session of the Conference.

committee by the Fourth Session of the Conference.[33] This committee found a number of constitutional difficulties in the application of the proposal in question, chiefly concerning the problem of amendment without the consent of the legislatures of states that had ratified the convention.[34] The committee also questioned whether the procedure was in conformity with the treaty of peace.[35] However, these doubts were dispelled by a consultation with the legal experts of the major states concerned.[36] The text of the amending article presented by the commission was:

> "At the request of a member of the Organization after the expiration of a period of two years from the close of the Session during which the present Convention was adopted, Amendments modifying the application of Articles 3, 4, 5, and 6, may be adopted by the conference by a majority of two-thirds of the votes cast by the Delegates present provided that such a majority includes the votes of all the Government Delegates, duly authorized to that effect, and the votes of at least one of the non-Government delegates of each member which has ratified this Convention and which is represented at the session at which the Amendment is adopted. Any Amendment thus adopted shall be registered by the Secretary General of the League of Nations six months after the close of the Session during which it was adopted and shall thereupon be considered as incorporated in the present convention.
>
> "Nevertheless, if one of the members which has ratified the present Convention should consider that the Amendment adopted by the Conference is one requiring the approval of its legislative authorities, it shall within the above period of six months, inform the Secretary-general of the League of Nations, through the International Labor Organization of this fact. In such a case, the Amendment will not be registered

[33] *I. L. C., Fourth Session,* 1922, I, 35; the importance of the question of amendment was indicated by the remarks of Mr. Adatci (Japan), chairman of the Committee of Selection, who stated that the amendment of a convention was "a question which requires very great care because it is one of great practical and legal complexity, and it is necessary to safeguard the sovereignty of each state, a thing of which all states are very proud," 27.

[34] *Report on Amendment* (1924), 20.

[35] *Ibid.,* 3.

[36] The views of the legal representatives of Great Britain, France, Germany, Italy, Belgium, Denmark, Roumania, and Switzerland were that a proper amendment method presented no constitutional difficulties, as consent to a convention containing an amendment would be "proceeding to a delegation of powers," a common practice of public law in most states, *idem.*

and put into force unless and until it has been ratified by the said Members.

"A Member shall give at least six months notice of such request to the International Labor Office, which shall forthwith inform other members of the Organization." [37]

The 1922 Conference gave no decision on this article, and so the committee decided that before any procedure was adopted member states should be given an opportunity to consider the question and make individual observations.[38] The very great caution exercised in approaching this problem indicated its inherent difficulties and its unusual importance. That the new procedure could not apply to conventions already in force, or even those adopted by the Conference but not yet ratified, was evidenced in the memorandum of the Office to the Governments.[39]

The memorandum presented a number of alternatives to the amendment of conventions. These were: (1) conventions embodying general principles only; (2) double-reading procedure; (3) ratification with reservations; (4) the interpretation of conventions by bodies other than the Permanent Court of International Justice.[40] Nevertheless, as these alternatives were received unfavorably by the governments they did not obtain further consideration.

In respect to amendment procedure, the Office emphasized that such action in regard to conventions was limited to the general clause embodied in each agreement.[41] It also felt that the adoption of a definite amendment procedure would guarantee against imaginary difficulties being put forward by states as a pretext for non-ratification.[42] This procedure, the Office considered, must be

[37] *Ibid.*, 6.

[38] The following resolution was adopted by the committee: "The committee is of the opinion that the problem submitted to it is a very difficult and delicate one, and can be decided only after all the information capable of contributing to its solution has been collected and that consequently the conference is not in a position to take a decision on the question of Amendments to Conventions. While emphasizing the importance of the question, the Commission proposes to the conference that it instruct the International Labor Office to undertake a thorough study of the problem, and to prepare a report to be submitted to Governments for their observations at least four months before the next conference," *ibid.*, 6.

[39] *Ibid.*, 14.

[40] *Ibid.*, 7-14.

[41] See standard revisory clause included in conventions adopted at the Washington Conference.

[42] *Report on Amendment* (1924), 15.

instituted in the conventions themselves to insure proper application.[43]

With the receipt of the replies to the communications of the Office to member states, a more comprehensive basis for arriving at an acceptable solution on the proposed amendment clause was possible.[44] The observations of the governments represented a wide difference of opinion on the topic.[45] Of the seventeen states responding to the request of the Office for an opinion on the matter, only six positively favored the adoption of the proposed modification procedure.[46] Ten states opposed the suggested procedure,[47] while one expressed no opinion on the subject.[48] In general, the chief objections to the method of amendment outlined by the Office were: (1) an amendment clause would cause an element of uncertainty to be injected into the general atmosphere of international labor legislation and, consequently, ratification would more likely be retarded than facilitated;[49] (2) the contemplated procedure was too complicated;[50] (3) if incomplete delegations were sent to the Conference by states which have ratified the convention, or if these delegates vote against the amendment, it could not come into force;[51] (4) a draft convention adopted in accordance with Article 19 of the Constitution should not be amended except in accordance with that article;[52] (5) amendments might be used by some states to obtain "specially favorable conditions," thus weakening the force of the conventions.[53] The Office defended its sponsorship of the proposal,[54] and concluded that the objec-

[43] See views expressed *ibid.,* 20.

[44] *Report on Amendment* (1924), pp. 1-93. Following the dispatch of the memorandum to the Governments a further proposal to enable more widespread ratification was proposed by Mr. de Michelis, Italian Government Representative, in a letter to the chairman of the Governing Body dated November 24, 1923. This proposal was to allow "conditional" ratification by States, to be sanctioned by the Conference if justified, 29.

[45] The replies of the Governments of Argentina, Austria, Belgium, Canada, Czechoslovakia, Denmark, Estonia, Finland, France, Great Britain, Hungary, India, Japan, Netherlands, Norway, Sweden, and Switzerland, are given *ibid.,* 31-64.

[46] Belgium, Denmark, Esthonia, France, Hungary, and India.

[47] Argentina, Austria, Czechoslovakia, Finland, Great Britain, Japan, Netherlands, Norway, Sweden, and Switzerland.

[48] Canada.

[49] *Report on Amendment* (1924), 84.

[50] *Idem.*

[51] *Ibid.,* 85.

[52] *Idem.*

[53] *Ibid.,* 87.

[54] For details of replies to the governments' objections, see *ibid.,* 84-89.

tions were concerned primarily with the application of procedure rather than the principle. The chief fear of the states seemed to be that the procedure would become too complicated. The general attitude of opposition of the majority of the governments expressing opinions forced the Organization to decide to wait until 1929 to make a final decision on the matter of the procedure of amendment. At that date the conventions adopted by the First and Second Conferences would be open for consideration of revision.[55]

This prolonged effort on the part of the International Labor Organization to formulate some special procedure for the amendment of conventions in respect to matters of detail failed to provide any tangible results. The failure may have resulted partly from the narrow scope of the objective aimed at, which was the amendment of minor details, perhaps of importance only temporarily, for the purpose of making ratification easier for the individual states. This consideration failed to take into account the more comprehensive question of the permanent introduction of revisory machinery to cope with the entire problem of adjustment.[56] If an amending process such as was suggested had been adopted, it would have possibly further complicated the formulation of a workable revision clause suitable for the whole or partial adaptation of conventions to changing economic conditions.[57]

THE DEVELOPMENT OF REVISORY PROCEDURE

The Constitution of the International Labor Organization contains no provision for the revision of conventions.[58] This lack

[55] This consideration for revision would take place in virtue of the following general article which has been included in all conventions since the first Conference: "At least once in ten years the Governing Body of the International Labor Office shall present to the general Conference a report on the working of this convention, and shall consider the desirability of placing on the Agenda of the conference the question of its revision or modification," *ibid.*, 92.

See decision to postpone consideration of amendment procedure, *I. L. C., Sixth Session*, 1924, I, 544.

[56] A similar point of view is expressed by one writer: "As the discussion progressed amendment became less important and the issue of the general revision of conventions came more to the front." F. G. Wilson, *op. cit.*, 257.

[57] In 1928 and 1929 it was suggested to the Conference that conventions should include a clause for their amendment similar to those in certain League of Nations Treaties. For a discussion of this proposal see "Alternatives to Revision," chapter II, p. 25, *supra*. F. G. Wilson, *op. cit.*, p. 231, states that the abandonment of the effort to set up an amending process was "the burial of an adventure in the speculative fields of international administration."

[58] The instrument provides in Article 36 for its amendment.

of reference to revision may have been due to oversight, or to the belief that the Organization could through experience devise a more appropriate method of modification. At the First Session of the Conference an effort was made to provide for this necessary function by suggesting inclusion of the following article in the conventions adopted by the Conference:

> "The General Conference of the Labor Organization may at any time after five years from the date on which this convention shall first come into force, propose the revision or modification of this convention; and in any case, at least every ten years after the date on which this convention shall first come into force, the Governing Body of the International Labor Office shall consider the desirability of placing on the agenda of the conference the question of the revision or modification of this convention." [58a]

However, this original draft was altered before a report was made by the drafting committee to the Conference; and the article which was included in the conventions adopted by the Conference read:

> "At least once in ten years the Governing Body of the International Labor Office shall present to the General Conference a report on the working of this Convention, and shall consider the desirability of placing on the agenda of the Conference the question of its revision or modification." [59]

In commenting on this article Mr. Manley O. Hudson (legal adviser of the Conference) said that it would be observed that "This article in no way encourages unnecessary action which might disturb settlements already arrived at but it simply contemplates the study of the working of the draft conventions in order that their revision may be considered in case their provisions may appear to have become obsolete." [60]

The limitations of this article are very obvious. It fails to provide for any means of revision prior to the completion of the ten-year period; it makes no mention of the legal implications of revision, nor does it define the competence of organs concerned in the process. Nevertheless, this clause remained the standard revisory formula for the first eleven sessions of the Conference.

[58a] *I. L. C., First Session,* Appendix, 222.

[59] See Article 21 of the *Hours of Work (Industry) Convention* (1919) and corresponding articles of other conventions, *Ibid.,* 256-264.

[60] *Ibid.,* 179.

The failure of conventions to obtain widespread ratification caused an early recognition by the Organization of the need for a modifying process to adopt accepted agreements to the needs of States Members. The attempt, already considered, to formulate a method of amending details was unsuccessful.[61] This effort, as was pointed out above, was too narrow to have solved the problem of revision, had it been successful. The question of revision was first definitely raised at the Thirty-seventh Session of the Governing Body (October, 1927) by Mr. Lambert-Ribot (French Employers' Representative).[62] He proposed that a committee should be appointed to consider the revision of the draft convention limiting the hours of work in industrial undertakings which was adopted at Washington in 1919. This suggestion was referred to the following session of the Governing Body, at which a formal proposal for the revision of this convention was made by the British Government delegate. While no action was taken on this proposal the Governing Body instructed the Standing Orders Committee to proceed to draw up a plan for the general revision of conventions.[63] In addition to this specific demand for revision, the Organization realized that the termination of the ten-year period for the consideration of the conventions of 1919 was drawing near and that the need for formulating a procedure to meet possible revision of these agreements was urgent. Accordingly, detailed discussions looking to a suitable method took place at the Thirty-eighth, Thirty-ninth,[64] Forty-third, Forty-fourth, and Forty-fifth Sessions of the Governing Body, and at the Eleventh[65] and Twelfth[66] Conferences. At the Eleventh Session of the Conference no decision was made on the question, owing to circumstances described by Mr. Mahaim (Belgian Government Delegate), chairman and reporter of the Committee on Standing Orders:

[61] See *supra*, pp. 39-43.

[62] *I. L. C., Eleventh Session*, 1928, II, *Report of the Director*, 22. As early as 1922 the British Government had asked the Governing Body to consider the revision of the hours convention so ratifications could be facilitated. See *Minutes of the Eleventh Session of the Governing Body*, 1922, 126.

[63] *Report of the Director.*

[64] In this session of the Governing Body there was a violent debate on revision. The workers' group opposed the adoption of proposals which might tend to open all provisions of conventions to revision. The employers' group held that revision was preliminary and complementary to modification. *Minutes of the Thirty-ninth Session of the Governing Body*, 1928, 245.

[65] *I. L. C., Eleventh Session, Proceedings*, I, 297-310, 591-612.

[66] *I. L. C., Twelfth Session, Proceedings*, 1929, I, 340-360, 717-803, 807-811.

"We had submitted to us a proposal concerning revision of Conventions which appeared to us to raise so many important problems that we could not take them into consideration. From this point of view the Committee proposes to refer the study of the question to the Governing Body." [67]

The attitude of Mr. Mahaim toward the problem of revision was extremely cautious and doubtful as to the advisability of any obligatory process.[68] This point of view may have been one of the reasons no action was taken on the matter in the Eleventh Session of the Conference.

The seriousness and complexity of the problem was further emphasized by the Director in his report to the Twelfth Session. Commenting on the progress of the Organization, he said:

> Moreover, it is still clear that the machinery of the Organization is far from complete. The first Conventions provided for a consideration of their working and the desirability of revision or modification once in ten years. In the case of these first Conventions this period will soon have elapsed, yet no detailed procedure has been arranged for carrying out these operations. If they are not properly thought out and prepared, these operations might bring down like a house of cards the new and still fragile system of labour legislation which has been built up with such care and effort.[69]

---

[67] *I. L. C., Eleventh Session,* I, 301. The Conference adopted the following resolution to express its wishes in this regard: "The Committee on Standing Orders proposes that the questions relating to the denunciation, revision, modification, and amendment of Conventions shall be referred to the Governing Body for consideration and report."

[68] In speaking of the existing standard revisory article Mr. Mahaim remarked: "In examining this Article seriously, I asked whether it was of value; I wondered whether it would not be better to suppress it. . . . Is it necessary to fix in advance a period of ten years when the question of revision must be taken up? I cannot help from feeling that the obligation imposed on the Governing Body to examine the question of revision is likely to shake the whole basis of international labor legislation. . . . If the period of denunciation is sufficient, I would be ready to suppress the clause providing for the revision of conventions." *Ibid.,* 310.

This expression indicates the fear that any revision at specified periods will destroy the stability and continuity of the work of the International Labor Conference. See also Mr. Mahaim's comment on the many legal difficulties concerning revision, *Minutes Forty-fourth Session of the Governing Body,* 1929, 51.

[69] *I. L. C., Twelfth Session,* 1929, *Report of the Director,* II, First Part, 290.

When the question was further considered by the Standing Orders Committee, it found that there were numerous problems connected with revision that were difficult of solution. The discussion in the Committee on Procedure centered on three questions raised by Mr. Jean Morellet, Legal Adviser of the International Labor Office.[70] The first question concerned the desirability of applying double-discussion procedure to the revision of conventions. Some members favored the use of this method, maintaining that it was the only way a careful study of the problem could take place. They also defended the procedure because it allowed overseas countries ample time to give consideration to the questions proposed.[71] The members taking the opposite view pointed out that the purpose of the first discussion was to define the scope of the question and that the Governing Body had already done that; and, furthermore, if the period of uncertainty over the question of revision was extended over a two-year period the "edifice of international labor legislation would be endangered." [72] Most of the committee inclined toward the last-named view, and so the double-discussion procedure was not adopted.[73] The second question related to the omission of the reference to the possibility of transforming a proposed draft convention which has not obtained the necessary two-thirds majority into a recommendation as applying to conventions revising other conventions.[74] The Legal Adviser was of the opinion that this section should be deleted, as revision could not be effected by a recommendation; the vote of the committee upheld this contention.[75] The last question was, "Should a clause be inserted in the Standing Orders of the Conference stating by way of reminder that the Conference can only amend a Convention in respect of those points which are mentioned in the

---

[70] *I. L. C., Twelfth Session*, 1929, I, Third Part, Appendix I, Note of Legal Adviser, 728-753.

[71] *Ibid.*, Appendix III, Extract from Report submitted by Mr. Mahaim on behalf of Standing Committee, 720. See remarks of Mr. Mertens (Workers' Delegate, Belgium) for a criticism of use of double-discussion procedure in drafting conventions, *ibid.*, First and Second Parts, 364.

[72] Appendix III, *loc. cit.*

[73] *Idem.* The vote was 5-0 against the procedure. The employers abstained from voting in the committee in order not to obligate their group in the Conference, as they desired further consideration by that body.

[74] See Article 6, paragraph 16, of the Standing Orders of the Conference, in *Constitution and Standing Orders*, 1936, 29. (Conference edition.)

[75] Twelfth Session, vol. I, *loc. cit.*

Agenda?" Mr. Morellet favored the insertion of this clause; the employers' group opposed it, asserting it gave the Governing Body power beyond its competence. Nevertheless, it was adopted by the majority of the committee, as the workers' representatives voted for it.[76]

At the meeting of the twelfth session, the chairman of the Committee on Standing Orders[77] gave a report on the revision of conventions and the articles in the Standing Orders of the Conference which would require amendment in order to cover the contemplated procedure. The committee proposed that an entirely new article,[78] entitled "Procedure in case of revision of a convention," be inserted following Article 6 of the present standing orders, and that it should be worded as follows:

> "1. The International Labor Office shall submit to the Conference draft Amendments drawn up in accordance with the conclusions of the report of the Governing Body recommending the revision in whole or in part of the Convention previously adopted and corresponding to the question or questions in respect of which a proposal for revision has been placed on the Agenda. In accordance with Article 400 of the Treaty of Versailles and subject to the provision of Article 402, paragraph 3, of the said treaty, the Conference shall not revise in whole or in part a Convention which is adopted previously save in respect of the questions placed by the Governing Body on the agenda of the session." [79]

---

[76] *Idem.* See also p. 723. An excellent discussion of the position of the various groups on this question is given in F. G. Wilson, *op. cit.*, 254-256.

[77] *I. L. C., Twelfth Session,* 1929, I, 341; see Report of Mr. Mahaim (Government Delegate, Belgium) in which he states the employers' delegates particularly oppose the section of the proposed article giving the Governing Body authority to limit the agenda. See also text of Report of Committee on Standing Orders, 718.

[78] The preface to this article states: "When the revision in whole or in part of a Convention which has been previously adopted by the Conference is included in the Agenda, the provisions of paragraphs 4 to 13 inclusive and 16 of Article 6 shall not apply and the Conference shall proceed in accordance with the following provisions." The provisions referred to "paragraphs 4 to 13 inclusive" pertaining to procedure utilized in drafting a convention which is not appropriate for formulating a revising Convention; instead of these provisions those stipulated in Article 6(a) are followed. For an original text see *Constitution and Standing Orders,* 29.

[79] *I. L. C., Twelfth Session, Proceedings,* 1929; see also *Constitution and Standing Orders, loc. cit.*

In reporting this change Mr. Mahaim pointed out that this modification was the result of a corresponding alteration by the Governing Body of its own standing orders.[80] He also remarked that in both the Governing Body and committee meetings there was considerable discussion in respect to the competence of the Governing Body to limit the subject matter to be placed on the agenda. The debate following this presentation indicated that some of the Conference delegates believed that the use of this power by the Governing Body was a usurpation of the power properly belonging to the Conference.[81] They believed that this proposed change in the Conference rules joined with paragraph 5 of Article 7(a) of the Governing Body's Standing Orders constituted too great a

[80] This new procedure was incorporated in Article 7(a) of the Standing Orders of the Governing Body on April 27-28, 1928, as follows:

Procedure for Placing the Question of Revising or Modifying a Convention on the Agenda of the Conference.

1. When the Governing Body, in accordance with the provisions of a Convention, has to present to the Conference a report on the working of the said Convention, and has to decide if it is desirable to place the question of its revision or modification on the agenda of the Conference, the Office shall submit to the Governing Body all the information which it possesses, particularly on the legislation and practice relating to the said Convention in those countries which have ratified it and on the legislation relating to the subject of the Convention and its application in those which have not ratified it.

2. The Governing Body shall fix the terms of the report on the working of the Convention.

3. It shall consider the question of placing the revision or modification of the Convention on the Agenda of the Conference. This consideration shall not take place until after two months from the date of circulation of the Office report (referred to in paragraph 1) to the members of the Governing Body.

4. If the Governing Body takes the view that it is not desirable to place the revision or modification of the Convention on the agenda, the Office shall communicate the above mentioned report to the Conference.

5. If the Governing Body takes the view that it is desirable that the question of placing the revision or modification of the convention on the agenda of the Conference should be further pursued, the Office shall send the report to the Governments of the Members and shall ask them for their observations, drawing attention to the points which the Governing Body has considered specially worthy of attention.

6. The Governing Body shall, on the expiry of four months from the date of the dispatch of the report to the Governments, taking into account the replies of the Governments, adopt the final report and define exactly the question or questions which it places on the agenda of the Conference. *Ibid.*, 41-42.

[81] See remarks of Mr. Molin (Government Delegate, Sweden), 343, and Mr. Oersted (Employers' Delegate, Denmark), *I. L. C., Twelfth Session, Proceedings*, 1929, 344.

restriction.[82] Article 7(a), one delegate pointed out, allowed the Governing Body to restrict proposals of modification, adopt a final report from replies, and define the question or questions for the agenda; in addition, Article 6(a) of the Conference rules further restricts by providing that the Conference cannot revise, totally or in part, a convention it has previously adopted, save as to questions already present on the agenda of the session.[83] However, this contention does not appear to be entirely a valid one, as it is the proper function of the Governing Body to prepare the agenda, according to the Constitution,[84] and possibly a greater danger lies in proposing topics for the agenda at the Conference when it is too late for a study of the new items. Another objection to Conference initiation of subjects of revision is that, owing to the lack of preparatory work, the question may be so devised that it may make agreement on the final text impossible.[85] As The Netherlands Government Delegate asserted, if the Governing Body does not pay attention to the wishes of the member states they may so inform the Conference.[86] In replying to the criticism of the opposition, the committee chairman, Mr. Mahaim, admitted that the purpose of the proposed changes was to limit the possibility of revision; for, he declared: "We are drawing up international legislation the object of which is to give the greatest possible stability." [87] He further said it was necessary for the Conference to trust the Governing Body and that the belief voiced by some that a convention was a single thing was mistaken, that technical items

---

[82] *Idem.*

[83] See remarks of Mr. Molin, *idem.* One minor change in the Conference rules was the wording "revision or modification" to "the revision in whole or in part." The Standing Orders Committee believed that this made the meaning less ambiguous.

[84] Article 14. In Article 16, paragraphs 1 and 2, provision is made for objections to the items of the agenda. Paragraph 3 states that the Conference by two-thirds vote may propose a subject for the agenda of the following meeting.

[85] A view in opposition to this was expressed by Mr. Molin as follows: "It seems to me doubtful whether in practice the deliberations of the Conference can remain within the limits fixed. A Convention should be considered as forming a whole, all parts of it being connected with each other, and modifications in one article involve inconsequential modifications in others. The fact that the Conference may place on the agenda of the next session items not thought out by the Governing Body is not of great practical importance." *I. L. C., Twelfth Session,* 343. The remarks of Mr. Oersted (Employers' Delegate, Denmark) concurred with those of Mr. Molin, 344.

[86] Mgr. Nolens, *ibid.,* 347.

[87] *Ibid.,* 349.

might be changed satisfactorily without in any wise affecting the whole.[88] When the vote was taken on the changes proposed by the committee, the decisive vote cast in favor of the report indicated that a large majority of the delegates favored the amendments.[89]

Further changes in Article 6 concerning the incorporation of revised portions in the revising convention were proposed:

> The amendments together with consequential amendments of the unamended provisions of the convention under revision as adopted by the Conference shall be referred to the Drafting Committee, which shall combine with them the unamended provisions of the Convention under revision so as to establish the final text of the Draft Convention in the revised form. This text shall be circulated to the Delegates.[90]

As this procedural proposal did not contain any controversial questions, it was adopted without discussion. Following this, a final vote was taken on the whole of Article 6(a) which resulted in its adoption as a part of the Standing Orders of the Conference.[91]

---

[88] As an example of this Mr. Mahaim gave the convention on the minimum age of admission to agriculture, which, he pointed out, could be changed by substituting one word. In doing this, the Governing Body would place on the agenda the term age limit and not the exact age. *Idem.*

[89] *Idem.* The ballot was 75-15 in favor of the proposed changes.

[90] *Ibid.*, 350; this provision was paragraph 6 of Article 6(a).

[91] It was adopted by a vote of 75 in favor and 11 against. The provisions of this article with the exception of those parts already quoted are as follows:

"2. The Conference shall decide whether it will take as the basis of discussion the draft amendments prepared by the International Labour Office, and shall decide whether they shall be considered in full Conference or referred to a committee for report. These decisions may be preceded by a debate in full Conference on the general principles of the proposed revision in whole or in part within the limits permitted by the agenda.

"3. If the draft amendments are considered in full Conference, each of them shall be placed successively before the Conference for adoption. During the debate, and until all the draft amendments have been disposed of, no motion other than a motion to amend the text of one of them or a motion as to procedure shall be considered by the Conference.

"4. If the draft amendments be referred to a Committee, the Conference shall, after receiving the report of the Committee, proceed to discuss the text of each draft amendment in succession, in accordance with the rules laid down in the last preceding paragraph. The discussion shall not take place before the day following that on which copies of the report have been circulated to the Delegates.

"5. During the discussion of the draft amendments the Conference may refer one or more of them to a Committee."

The changes not given detailed consideration were in regard to the consultation of governments before proposals of revision are placed on the agenda. The legal effect and force of two conventions existing side by side was also acted on at this time, and a clause on this point was to be placed in all new conventions.[92]

The measures sanctioned by the Conference, summarized above, represented a notable step in the development of a procedure which would enable the Organization to adapt its efforts to the needs of its members and to retain the gains registered in raising labor standards. It is instructive to note that the procedural changes which made the formulation of a revisory process possible resulted from the adaptation of the standing orders or rules of the two units of the Organization to the needs of the occasion. This solution within the framework of the existing structure gave promise of the success of modification efforts. Nevertheless, it would be difficult to agree with the statement of the Director to the 1930 Conference, holding in effect that articles adopted at the Twelfth Session had solved the problem of revision.[93]

When the Governing Body was considering the draft convention on social insurance to be submitted to the Seventeenth Session of the Conference, it decided the section of the provision concerning the legal consequences of revision needed some modification.[94] The object of the modification effort was to leave to that session of the Conference at which revision might be discussed the choice of deciding whether or not a new revising convention should *ipso jure* involve denunciation of the old convention. In the existing standard article no choice was left to the Conference in regard to this matter. Following the report of the Committee on Standing Orders, the Conference adopted the proposed clause with the understanding that the modified article should be inserted in the conventions drawn up at the Seventeenth Session, but that the article should be referred to the Governing Body for further study before it was permanently adopted.[95] In pursuance of this request, the Governing Body at its Sixty-fifth Session, January, 1934, reconsidered the question and decided to recommend to the Conference

[92] This clause is considered in detail in a subsequent chapter on "Legal Questions in Revision," *infra.*

[93] *I. L. C., Fourteenth Session,* 1930, *Report of the Director,* First Part, 135.

[94] *I. L. C., Seventeenth Session,* 1933, Appendix, III: Report of the Committee on Standing Orders, 501.

[95] *Ibid.,* I, 311-313.

the retention of the amended article in future conventions.[96]

In conformity with this recommendation the following article was adopted by the Conference:

> "1. Should the Conference adopt a new Convention revising this Convention in whole or in part, then, unless the new Convention otherwise provides,
>
> (a) the ratification by a member of the new revising Convention shall *ipso jure* involve the immediate denunciation of this Convention, notwithstanding the provisions of Article X above, if and when the new revision Convention shall have come into force;
>
> (b) as from the date when the new revising Convention comes into force, this Convention shall cease to be open to ratification by the members.
>
> "2. This Convention shall in any case remain in force in its actual form and content for those members which have ratified it but have not ratified the revising Convention." [97]

The adoption of this article made the amending process more flexible and will doubtless provide a workable method of making the necessary changes under ordinary conditions. It was perhaps desirable to give the Conference the right to decide the status of a particular Convention when revised. However, the chief implications of this change were legal, and they will be considered in another chapter.

The experience of the Organization in attempting to adapt conventions to the practical needs of member states demonstrated the need for a revisory procedure which would provide for the revision of conventions at a time other than that provided for in the standard articles. In order to provide for an emergency revision, the Standing Orders Committee in 1934 decided unanimously to propose the following addition to the Standing Orders:

> "6. If at any other than a time at which the Governing Body in accordance with the provisions of a Convention, has to present to the Conference a report on the working of the said Convention, the Governing Body should decide it to be desirable to consider placing upon the Agenda of the Conference the revision in whole or in part of any convention, the

---

[96] *I. L. C., Eighteenth Session,* Appendix, III, Standing Orders of the Conference, 528.

[97] This article was adopted without debate or opposition, *I. L. C., Seventeenth Session, Proceedings,* I, 17.

Office shall notify this decision to the Governments of the Members and shall ask them for their observations, drawing attention to the points which the Governing Body has considered worthy of attention.

"7. The Governing Body shall, on the expiry of four months from the date of the dispatch of this notification to the Governments, taking into account the replies of the Governments, define exactly the question or questions which it places on the Agenda of the Conference." [98]

The addition of this clause to the rules of the Governing Body should be of value in meeting emergency demands for revision. Its adoption was also an indication that some of the early fears concerning the effect of revision on the newly built structure of international labor legislation were subsiding.

Recently, certain special techniques have been devised for revising the provisions of certain conventions.

One of these provides that the conference may, if the item is on its agenda, adopt amendments by a two-thirds majority to certain articles of the convention which have to do with Members States of backward industrial development.[99] Such an amendment must list the name of the Member State to which it applies and this state is obligated to submit this amendment to the proper authorities within a period of one year, or eighteen months in exceptional circumstances, for appropriate action. After this action the formal ratification is communicated and the amendment takes effect. This simple procedure necessitates no action by other states in any part of the revisory process. Another recent innovation is found in the *Safety Provisions (Building) Conventions,* 1937 which links this convention with the Recommendation of the same date on the same subject.[100] According to this provision the "appropriate authority" of each member has the authority to make regulations similar to those recommended in the Recommendation or adopted by the

[98] This proposal was adopted by the Governing Body without opposition, *Minutes of the Sixty-fifth Session of the Governing Body, January,* 1934, 64-66.

[99] See *Minimum Age (Industry) Convention* (Revised), 1937, Article 9 and *Minimum Non-Industrial Employment Convention* (Revised), 1937, secs. 5, 6, 7, 8 of Article 9. *Official Bulletin,* XXII, No. 3.

[100] See a summary of these recent developments by C. W. Jenks in "The Contribution of the International Labor Organization to the Development of Procedures of Peaceful Change," *The New Commonwealth Quarterly,* IV, no. 4 (March, 1939), 54.

conference. This gives each Member State an opportunity to make progressive adjustments in line with conference recommendations without a formal revision.

An unusual approach to the problem of the modification of the provisions of a convention to meet new conditions is found in another 1937 adoption.[101] This provides that if a subsequent convention is adopted containing modifications to meet conditions in certain backward countries,[102] that this new convention shall be deemed joined with the original to form one convention. Thus no special revisory action would be necessary for changing certain provisions.

In 1938 a convention was adopted which contained a special arrangement for modifying certain of its provisions.[103] Under this special procedure the Governing Body may communicate to Members "proposals for improving and amplifying the statistics compiled in pursuance of this convention or promoting their comparability." Subsequently, each ratifying member is obligated to submit such proposals to the competent authorities; they are also to indicate in their annual report the extent to which these proposals are given effect. This new procedure would appear to give the Governing Body authority to make important changes in this convention at any time.

The experience of the Organization in attempting to develop a satisfactory method of amending conventions illustrates the enormous difficulties that are inherent in the problem of revision. The fact that the adoption of a satisfactory method of amendment was such a slow and uncertain process was probably due to a number of factors. One of these was the lack of any precedent, another the differences of opinion on the general subject of revision held by the three groups represented. An additional factor which added to the length of the period of discussion was the importance of the revision of conventions to the whole structure of international labor standards. The complexity of the problem, combined with the need for caution in formulating an untried procedure possibly accounted for the slowness of this development, which

[101] See *Reduction of Hours of Work (Textiles) Convention*, 1937, Article 15, *Official Bulletin, ibid.*, 106.

[102] Listed in Article 19, paragraph 3 of the Constitution.

[103] *Convention Concerning Statistics of Wages and Hours of Work*, Article 24, *Official Bulletin*, XXIII, No. 3, 82.

made for an efficient amendatory process. Recent developments indicate that new techniques will be constantly devised to meet conditions as they arise.

MODIFICATIONS ACCOMPLISHED

The first attempt to put in practice the rules formulated by the Labor Organization for the purpose of revising conventions resulted from the decision of the Governing Body at its June session in 1930.[104] This decision was made by the Governing Body following its consideration of the regular reports made at the end of the ten-year period on the working of the eight conventions adopted by the Conference in 1919 (Washington) and 1920 (Genoa).[105] As these conventions came into force in 1921, it was obligatory that the Governing Body arrive at a decision as to whether they were in need of revision.[106] It was decided that seven of the conventions considered by the Governing Body were not in need of revision.[107] However, the Governing Body decided the eighth convention on the subject of employment of women at night (*Night Work [Women] Convention*, 1919) should be examined in order to bring about certain changes.

After having made this decision the Governing Body, through the services of the Office, compiled a report which contained the existing status of the convention, the observations of governments on the subject, and a brief analysis of the discussions which took place in the meetings of the Governing Body.[108] On the basis of

[104] See *Report of the Governing Body of the International Labor Organization upon the Working of the Convention Concerning Employment of Women during the Night, International Labor Conference, Fifteenth Session,* Geneva, 1931.

[105] This report was made under Article 14 of the Convention and Article 6(a) of the Standing Orders of the Conference. It contains actual facts concerning the working of the convention and an account of the action of the Governing Body culminating in a decision to place the question of partial revision on the agenda.

[106] See the general article adopted in 1919, section 3, "The Development of Revisory Procedure."

[107] These conventions were: (1) *Hours of Work in Industrial Undertakings* (1919); (2) *Unemployment* (1919); (3) *Employment of Women Before and After Childbirth* (1919); (4) *Minimum Age for Admission of Children to Industrial Employment* (1919); (5) *Night Work of Young Persons Employed in Industry* (1919); (6) *Minimum Age of Admission of Children to Employment at Sea* (1920); (7) *Employment for Seamen* (1920).

[108] *I. L. C., Fifteenth Session,* 1931, Report III, *Partial Revision of the Convention Concerning Employment of Women During the Night.* See also *Final*

this investigation the convention was placed on the agenda for revision.

The attempt to revise this convention failed before the revision was completed.[109] Failure was the result, to some extent, of several unforeseen difficulties which indicated the intricate nature of the revisory process. In the first place, the most recent clause concerning denunciation and revision adopted in 1929 was not included on the agenda. The failure to place specifically this item on the agenda meant it could not be discussed at this session, although it should have been an important part of the revising convention. This was an extremely unfortunate occurrence in the first attempt to revise a convention.[110] The second difficulty arose when the Conference had before it at one time two proposals concerning the convention on the employment of women during the night.[111] One proposal was that of the British Government Delegate to exclude from the scope of the convention women occupying posts of supervision and management, the other was a Belgian proposal to insert a provision allowing member states to substitute 11 P.M. to 6 A.M. for 10 P.M. to 5 A.M. as the period during which night work for women would be absolutely prohibited. When the Conference voted on these separate proposals they were approved by a small majority,[112] but when both were incorporated in the text by the Drafting Committee, according to the Standing Orders,[113] the necessary two-thirds majority for the adoption of a convention could not be obtained.[114] One of the chief reasons for the adverse vote on the final adoption of this revised convention was the group division on the question. This difference of opinion was evident in the committee, where a large number opposed a favorable report

Record, I, 322-336, 341-359, 474-479, 718-734. For an excellent comment on the difficulties encountered in this effort to revise, see Jenks, "The Revision of Conventions," *loc. cit.,* 54.

[109] *I. L. C., Fifteenth Sesson,* I, 478.

[110] This convention was based on the old Berne Convention. See Chap. II, pp. 34-38, *supra.*

[111] See remarks of Mrs. Letellier (Government Adviser, France), Reporter of the Committee on Employment of Women at Night, *I. L. C., Fifteenth Session, Proceedings,* 322-324.

[112] The vote was 54-43. *Ibid.,* 348.

[113] This proposal was adopted by a vote of 56-38. *Ibid.,* 358.

[114] The final vote on the revised draft convention was 74-40 favoring revision; but, as a two-thirds majority was necessary for the adoption of a new convention, revision was rejected by two votes. *Ibid.,* 477. See the text of the draft convention submitted by the Drafting Committee, I, Appendix, Third part, 730-734.

to the Conference on the proposed revision.[115] The workers were opposed to revision in the committee and at the Conference, as they averred that it was unnecessary and that only a small number of people would be affected. They feared that its real purpose was to extend the working hours of women.[116] Other objections given by the workers' group were that revision should represent progress and that in this case it represented a reverting to lower standards. They also thought that revision under the existing circumstances would cause legal difficulties.[117] The employers' delegates were solidly in favor of revision of the convention, while the representatives of the government delegates were divided on the question.[118] Accordingly, the linking together of the two articles made the attempt partially to revise the convention a failure. Another vote on the text minus the provisions to which only a small majority would agree was not possible because of the procedure stipulated in the Standing Orders.[119] Thus the revision of this convention was delayed until another session of the Conference.[120]

This first attempt at revision demonstrated the difficulties in the path of such adjustments. The method of procedure followed had to function without confusing the issues to be considered. The fear of the workers' delegates that the consequence of revision would be a lessening of the guarantees of labor had to be assuaged before the revision could be completed. Any questions as to the

---

[115] The vote was 38-28 in favor of revision; see the committee report, *ibid.*, 324.

[116] See remarks of Mrs. Hanna (Workers' Adviser, Germany), Mr. Serrarens (Workers' Delegate, Netherlands), and Mr. Kawamura (Workers' Delegate, Japan). *Ibid.*, 325-329.

[117] *Idem.* For a statement of legal questions involved see the note by Mr. Morrellet in the *I. L. C., Fifteenth Session,* I, Appendix, Third part, 719-730.

[118] See remarks of Mr. Ohno (Government Delegate, Japan); Mr. Oersted (Employers' Delegate, Denmark); and others. *Ibid.*, 325-342.

[119] The text of this procedure may be found in Article 6(a) of the Standing Orders of the Conference and Article 405 of Part XIII of the Treaty of Versailles. Mr. Jenks gives a proposal for remedying this situation, which is as follows: "It might be overcome by an amendment to the Standing Orders providing that, in the event of a revising convention not securing the required majority at a final vote, the Conference may decide, perhaps by a two-thirds majority, to discard some of the proposals which are before it and take a further final vote on a text revised in fewer respects." "The Revision of Conventions," *loc. cit.*, 55.

[120] See discussion of the revision in this connection in the 1934 Conference, in this chapter, *infra.*

legal propriety of the steps in revision had to be made as clear as possible. All the efforts toward revision must necessarily be made in a spirit of compromise and negotiation between groups.

The next trial of revision procedure occurred under unusual circumstances. The convention on the *Protection against Accidents* (*Dockers*, 1929) was placed on the agenda by the Governing Body for partial revision,[121] although it had not yet come into force and was not subject to the regular decennial procedure.[122] This was done by the Governing Body on its own initiative in respect to powers conferred on it by Article 14 of the Constitution dealing with the settlement of the agenda.[123] The decision to revise the convention was reached only after detailed discussion. The Director of the International Labor Office was not in favor of revising the convention. He believed that the difficulties were only of a minor technical nature, and that they could be solved by a broad interpretation by governments.[124] Although other members of the Governing Body held a similar view, the majority favored revision of the convention, since the important maritime countries of Germany and Great Britain would not ratify the existing agreement.[125]

As revision prior to the regular ten-year period was not contemplated in the Standing Orders, the Governing Body had to consider a possible method to be followed. It decided to adhere in so far as possible to the regular procedure of Article 7(a) of the Standing Orders relating to revision.[126] One provision of this

[121] See *Minutes of the Fifty-sixth Session of the Governing Body*, January, 1932; also *Fifty-first Session*, Appendix, 132-145, and *Fifty-second Session*, Appendix, 157. See also *I. L. C., Sixteenth Session*, 1932, Report IV, *Partial Revision of the Convention Concerning the Protection Against Accidents of Workers Employed in Loading and Unloading Ships* (hereafter cited *I. L. C., Sixteenth Session*, Report IV), 1-97.

[122] This convention was adopted at the *Twelfth Session*, 1929.

[123] The Governing Body decided to revise the convention by a vote of eleven in favor and six opposed. *Minutes of the Fifty-fifth Session of the Governing Body*, October, 1931, 635.

[124] The Director feared the revision of this convention would create an unfortunate precedent. *Ibid.*, 624.

[125] Mr. Mertens (Workers' Delegate, Belgium) opposed revision for three reasons: (1) it would prevent certain governments now preparing to ratify the existing convention from doing so; (2) other proposals concerning revision of the convention would probably be offered; (3) no one knew the proper procedure to adopt. Mr. Legett (Great Britain), Mr. Weigert (Germany), and Mr. Oersted (Denmark) spoke in favor of revision as necessary for ratification. *Ibid.*, 624-620. See also *I. L. C., Sixteenth Session*, Report IV, 6.

[126] This corresponds to Article 6(a) of the Conference Rules and Procedures.

article states that when the Governing Body has decided to revise after examination of the report on the application of the convention, this report and related materials shall be sent by the Office to the various governments for their observations. Then a final report is made on the basis of the information received, and the question of revision is placed on the agenda. This procedure was followed, but a legal difficulty was encountered in the fact that the final decision of the Governing Body was made only three months before the Conference met, and Article 15 of the Constitution says States Members must be notified concerning the items on the agenda four months prior to the Conference.[127] The Office considered this legal objection fully but decided that, since the governments had been informed in two letters[128] four months prior to the convening of the Conference of the possibility of revision, the requirement of Article 15 had been practically fulfilled.[129]

When the discussion of the committee's Report on Revision of the Convention came before the Conference, the Reporter stated the topic had been placed on the agenda at the request of the British and German governments, who found in considering ratification of the convention and the act of putting it into effect "that there were certain points on which it was not clear in its meaning, or on which certain practical difficulties arose." [130] The Reporter further stated that this was the most detailed convention the Conference had adopted, and that most of the points in

Minutes of the Fifty-fifth Session of the Governing Body, 634. See *Minutes of the Fifty-sixth Session*, 76. See also paragraph 5, Article 7(a), *Constitution and Rules* of the *I. L. O.*, 46.

[127] The Office sent a letter November 11, 1931, to the governments informing them of the decision taken at the Fifty-fifth Session of the Governing Body and communicating to them the text of the revision proposal. The governments were requested to report their observations as soon as possible and not later than January 1, 1932. By the time of the Fifty-sixth Session of the Governing Body, January 13, 1932, sixteen replies had reached the Office, the majority of which were in favor of immediate revision along the lines proposed. *I. L. C., Sixteenth Session*, Report IV, 7-9. See also the *Minutes of the Fifty-sixth Session of the Governing Body*, 30-33.

[128] November 11 and November 14.

[129] For a discussion of the legal implications involved in the procedure, see subsequent chapter (IV) on "Legal Questions in Revision."

[130] See remarks of Mr. Bruyns (Government Adviser, Netherlands), Reporter of the Committee on the Partial Revision of the Convention Concerning the Protection against Accidents of Workers Employed in Loading or Unloading Ships; *I. L. C., Proceedings, Sixteenth Session*, 1932, 300.

need of change were technical; yet the committee had dealt with these questions in a practical way and almost unanimous agreement had shown the justification for revision.[131] The committee Report stressed the importance of reciprocity in connection with this convention. It pointed out that when the convention was adopted (1929) a recommendation was also adopted on the subject of establishing reciprocity. However, owing to the difficulties in connection with ratification, nothing had been done in this regard. The committee expressed the belief that successful revision would pave the way for reciprocity between the maritime states in respect to the subject matter of the convention.[132]

With such a favorable committee report, it would seem that revision could have proceeded smoothly. Nevertheless, the second speaker in the discussion of the report called attention to the fact that Article 15 had not been observed.[133] He pointed out that, in view of the fact that notification in regard to partial revision of the convention had not been given until the expiration of the specified time, his government (Japan) had not had time to choose the necessary experts for the conference, or to make other advisable preparations.[134] He also stated that in the two letters sent out the original proposals (British and German) were listed, but no mention was made of the later proposals of other governments.[135] The speaker concluded his remarks by declaring he would make no formal protest concerning the matter as both employers and workers desired revision.[136]

The answers to these objections of the Japanese Government Delegate showed that the members of the Conference were willing to defend the past revision proceedings but that some of them were apprehensive respecting the legality of the procedure.[137] To make

[131] *Idem.* [132] *Idem.*

[133] *Ibid.* See See remarks of Mr. Yoshisaka (Government Delegate, Japan). The Japanese Government had made a reservation as to the proposed procedure (304), in her reply to the Office questions, *I. L. C., Sixteenth Session*, Report IV, 8.

[134] *Idem.*

[135] Proposals of Belgium, Italy, Finland, and The Netherlands; see *ibid.*

[136] *Idem.*

[137] Mr. Oersted (Employers' Delegate, Denmark) remarked that the change in procedure was a matter of convenience and that there was no infraction of the Peace Treaty; yet he feared that Mr. Yoshisaka would bring the matter before the Permanent Court of International Justice under Article 402, *ibid.*, 306. Mr. Bevin (Workers' Adviser, British Empire) pointed out that the workers were in favor of the amended convention. Although "we have joined with our

sure that there would be no question of the legality of the revisory proceedings, the Conference decided to adopt a resolution offered by Mr. Yoshisaka which met his objections to the present proceedings safeguarding the future from such a deviation from prescribed practice.[138] This resolution asked for strict observance of Article 15 of the Constitution so as to enable distant states to make adequate preparation for conferences.[139] Following the settlement of this difficulty the amended convention was adopted with no opposing vote.[140]

---

coworkers against revision as a principle, we found that the international application of this Convention was such that the only way to make it really workable and applicable throughout the world was revision." He did not regard the question of legality as being important (308). See also favorable remarks of Mr. Jenkin Jones (Employers' Adviser, British Empire), 309, and Mr. Stiller (Government Adviser, Germany), 311.

[138] *Ibid.*, 326.

[139] This resolution was as follows: "Whereas the International Labor Organization should, in harmony with the spirit of Universality, embodied in Part XIII of the Peace Treaty, respect and safeguard the interests of Member States situated at long distances:

Whereas, in recent years criticisms have been raised at the Sessions of the International Labor Conference and on other occasions to the effect that the International Labor Organization had tended to lay undue emphasis on the European countries and had failed to pay proper attention to the interests of non-European countries:

Whereas any ground for such criticisms or allegations as above should be removed speedily with a view to insuring the maintenance of loyal collaboration of all the Member States far and near: and

Whereas, Article 401 of the Peace Treaty imposes specifically the obligation on the Director of the International Labor Office to transmit the Agenda so as to reach the Members four months before the meeting of the Conference in order to enable the distant countries to make adequate preparation and thus to contribute to the success of the work of the conference;

The sixteenth Session of the International Labor Conference draws the attention of the Governing Body to the necessity of a scrupulous respect for the interests of distant countries in the conduct of its functions and to the provisions of Article 401 of the Peace Treaty in fixing the Agenda for the International Labor Conference." *Ibid.*, Annex XI, 837-838.

Since the earliest Conference, dissatisfaction had been regularly expressed by extra-European states over the seeming lack of attention to their proper place in the Organization.

[140] *Ibid.*, 28. This adoption of the revised convention constituted the second convention on the subject, as the Irish Free State, Luxemburg, Nicaragua, and Spain had ratified the old convention. In accordance with Article 23, paragraph 2, of this convention, it ceased to be open for ratification by States Members from 30 October, 1934, on which date the new convention came into force. For a comparison of the original and the revised articles see Appendix I, *infra.*

The revision of this convention was successful in spite of the disregard for the letter of the stipulated procedure. This success was apparently due to the general recognition by the different groups in the Conference that revision would prove beneficial to all parties concerned. The acceptance of this amendment by the workers' group indicated that they recognized the necessity of revision under certain conditions. The adoption by the Conference of the resolution expressing the wishes of that body for stricter regard for Article 15 in the future will probably keep the substitute procedure, utilized in revising this convention, from becoming a precedent. For it is apparent that if revision is to be a desirable factor in the formulation of international standards of labor, the Organization must not resort to temporary expedients not making for a careful consideration of the objects of modification. With the exception of the legal procedural difficulties, the amendment of the Dockers Convention was a step forward in successful revision.[141]

Following the regular procedure, the Governing Body reported to the Seventeenth Session of the Conference (1933) on the working of eight conventions; but none of them was deemed in need of revision.[142]

The convention on Workmen's Compensation for Occupational Diseases adopted at the Seventh Session of the Conference, 1925,[143] had been ratified by a large number of countries,[144] but at various

[141] The Reporter of the committee on revision of this convention declared that if it set a precedent, it would be a most valuable one for all concerned, *I. L. C., Proceedings, Sixteenth Session,* 300.

[142] See *I. L. C.,* 1933, *Report of the Governing Body upon the Working of the Convention Fixing the Minimum Age for the Admission of Young Persons to Employment as Trimmers and Stokers; Weekly Rest; Compulsory Medical Examination of Children Employed at Sea; Rights of Association and Combination of Agricultural Workers; the Use of White Lead in Painting; Unemployment Indemnity in Case of Loss or Foundering of the Ship; the Age for Admission of Children to Employment in Agriculture,* and *Workmen's Compensation in Agriculture.*

[143] At the Conference which adopted the convention (1925), a recommendation was adopted which provided that each state was free to adopt by national legislation a more complete schedule of diseases, and the recommendation further proposed that where necessary a simple procedure be adopted for revision of the schedule of diseases. See *I. L. C., Seventh Session,* 1925, II, Third part, Appendix XII, 846-850, for text of convention, and 850-851 for text of the recommendation.

[144] Austria, Belgium, Bulgaria, Cuba, Czechoslovakia, Finland, France, Germany, Great Britain, Hungary, India, Irish Free State, Japan, Latvia, Luxem-

times the question of enlarging the schedule of diseases was discussed.[145] These discussions resulted in the placing of the question (of extending the schedule of occupational diseases) on the Conference agenda by the Sixty-first Session of the Governing Body. Instead of placing the question on the agenda in the usual way, "partial revision" was specified; thus the task of the Conference was less difficult than it might have been, as there was no need for revising the form and obligation of the existing convention. Yet this was a task of revision somewhat different from that with which the Conference had dealt in the past; for the proposal of revision did not originate either as a result of the Governing Body's examination of the decennial report or of the working of the convention in question.[146] This proposal was originated by the Governing Body in virtue of the powers given it under Article 14 of the Constitution. The Governing Body placed on the agenda items concerning minor details in respect to the subject matter of the convention and the question of the substitution of the new standard articles adopted in 1929 for those in the convention.[147] The Conference committee on occupational diseases gave a summary of the detailed report on the partial revision of the 1925 convention.[148] The Reporter of the committee prefaced his general remarks by an expression of satisfaction regarding the successful working of the revisory committee.[149] The discussion on the report was brief, as there

---

burg, Netherlands, Norway, Portugal, Spain, Sweden, Switzerland, and Yugoslavia. See *I. L. C., Eighteenth Session* (1934), Report V, *Workmen's Compensation for Occupational Diseases* (Introduction, vii).

[145] See particularly the discussion in the *Minutes of the Sixty-first Session of the Governing Body,* 1933, 74-80; and also work of the Committee on Industrial Hygiene, which compiled a proposal schedule, *I. L. C., Eighteenth Session,* Report V. See also in this Report, viii, record of resolutions of 1931 and 1932 Conferences.

[146] Report V, 1934, iv.

[147] These articles related to the regulation of ratifications, the coming into force of the convention, its denunciation and revision.

[148] See Report by Mr. Orenstein (Employers' Adviser, Union of South Africa), *I. L. C., Proceedings, Eighteenth Session,* 1934, 295.

[149] His statement was as follows: "Before proceeding with the presentation of the deliberations of the Committee, it is a pleasant duty to record the good will which prevailed throughout the discussions, and which is especially notable when we bear in mind that the task before the Committee was a very complex one, the subject matter being of a highly technical nature, with the intricacies of which a lay member must have had considerable difficulty in coping, particularly the workers' members who had not the advantage of technically qualified advisers." *Ibid.,* 639. See text of report, 639-646.

seemed to be general agreement as to the objectives outlined.[150] The Conference adopted the amendment convention without a dissenting vote.[151]

The revision of this convention demonstrated that when there is agreement among the groups represented in the Organization as to the need of modification, the efforts in that regard will probably be successful. This was true in this instance despite the inauguration of unprecedented procedure by the Governing Body in its revision of the convention before the Conference. This action by the Governing Body under the existing circumstances exhibited courage and resourcefulness in dealing with a pressing problem. As there was no definite question of a legal problem this method was of valuable assistance in formulating a procedure of revision flexible enough to be readily adaptable to unusual conditions.

The reasons for the failure in 1931 to revise the Convention Concerning the Employment of Women During the Night have been discussed in some detail.[152] In October, 1933, at its sixty-fourth session, the Governing Body decided to place again the question on the agenda with a view to overcoming the obstacles to revision encountered in the first attempt.[153] Following the first attempt at revision the Permanent Court of International Justice, at the request of the British and German governments, had handed down an advisory opinion which had cleared up some doubts concerning the scope of the convention.[154] This ruling facilitated a fresh consideration of the question of revision, as the Court held that the convention applied to all categories of female workers.[155]

---

[150] Mr. Cort van Der Linden (Employers' Delegate, Netherlands) opposed the wording of the convention which linked silicosis with tuberculosis as follows: "Silicosis with or without pulmonary tuberculosis, provided that silicosis is an essential factor in causing the resultant incapacity or death. Those industries or processes which are recognized in national laws or regulations as involving exposure to the risk of silicosis." *Ibid.*, 297.

[151] *Ibid.*, 298. See text of Draft Convention, no. 42, *Concerning Workmen's Compensation for Occupational Diseases* (*Revised 1934*), 669-673. For a comparison of the original and the revised articles see Appendix II, *infra*.

[152] See *supra*, pp. 57-59.

[153] See *Minutes of the Sixty-fourth session of the Governing Body*, October, 1933, 330-336.

[154] For a discussion of the Court opinion, see Chap. VI, pp. 157-164, *infra*.

[155] Advisory Opinion No. 50, *Publications of the Permanent Court of International Justice* (hereafter cited by *P. C. I. J.*, series number), Series A/B. See a complete discussion of this opinion in Chap. VI in the section on "Interpretation by the Permanent Court of International Justice," *infra*.

The observations received from governments which were parties to the convention, and also from those which had not yet ratified, in reply to the form questionnaire, were generally in favor of revision along the lines indicated by the Office.[156]

The expression in favor of revision of the scope of the convention was practically unanimous,[157] but one-half of the replies received gave no definite answer as to whether they specifically favored the suggested change in regard to hours.[158] The replies of some states indicated that they seemed to regard the insertion of a more flexible hour schedule as a means of evading the spirit of the convention, for they objected in their observations to the limits placed on the application of the suggested schedule.[159] These observations were very helpful in assisting the Governing Body in its formulating proposals for revision that would be as nearly as possible acceptable to all states and groups concerned.

The final decision of the Governing Body in this regard was made after considerable discussion, although most of the members favored revision.[160] The items to be placed on the agenda were three in number: The first, suggested by the British Government, stated that the convention should not apply to persons holding responsible positions of management not engaged in manual work;[161] the second, the Belgian Government proposed that the range of working hours be changed;[162] and the third, the Office

[156] This convention had been ratified by tweny-seven states up to October, 1933: Albania, Austria, Bulgaria, Chile, Colombia, Brazil, Greece, Cuba, Czechoslovakia, Estonia, France, Great Britain, Hungary, India, Ireland, Italy, Lithuania, Luxemburg, Netherlands, Portugal, Rumania, Spain, Switzerland, South Africa, Uruguay, Venezuela, Yugoslavia. Ten of this group did not reply to the questionnaire: Austria, Colombia, Cuba, Czechoslovakia, France, Greece, Luxemburg, Portugal, Uruguay, and Venezuela. Thirteen states not yet parties to the convention replied: Brazil, Canada, China, Denmark, Finland, Germany, Japan, New Zealand, Nicaragua, Norway, Poland, Siam, and Sweden. *I. L. C., Eighteenth Session*, Report VII, 1934, 9-19.

[157] Only Chile opposed. *Ibid.*, 13.

[158] *Ibid.*, 9-19.

[159] See opinion of Austria, *ibid.*, 10; Finland, 14; and the Province of Ontaria, 12. See also 24 for opinion of the Office.

[160] Mr. Hayday (British Workers' Delegate) was opposed to revision, as he feared the whole convention would be discussed. However, he voiced the only opposition, *Minutes of the Sixty-fourth Session of the Governing Body*, 1933, 332.

[161] *Ibid.*, 333.

[162] This amendment provided that under exceptional circumstances after consultation of employers' and workers' organizations, competent authorities might

proposed that the new formal standard articles be substituted for those in the original convention.[163]

When these proposals were discussed in the committee designated by the Conference to report on the subject, there was no opposition on the point relating to management, except by the British Workers' Delegate. There were, however, several attempts to amend the original suggestion on this point, all of which were unsuccessful.[164] When the question regarding the change of hours was discussed, the workers' representatives opposed the change, as they had done in the Governing Body; but the favorable vote of the government representatives and employers enabled the proposal to be accepted.[165]

The discussion in the Conference was of practically the same nature and by the same groups that defended or opposed the proposition in the bodies previously noted. Strong points both in favor and against the revision were stressed in the discussion.[166] The

---

substitute the hours of 11 p.m. to 6 a.m. for those in the original of 10 p.m. to 5 a.m. This item was opposed by the workers' representatives, *ibid.*, 334.

[163] *Ibid.*, 336. For the detailed facts concerning the entire proposals, see Appendix VI, 429-434.

[164] The Indian Government Representative, backed by the representative of the Danish Government, made a proposal which the workers' delegates and some government delegates opposed as widening the scope of exceptions to the convention in an undesirable fashion. See *I. L. C., Eighteenth Session, Proceedings*, 651-652.

[165] *Loc. cit.*, 652. The Swiss Government Representative attempted to get the committee to amend the wording so it would apply more specifically to a certain undertaking or industry, pp. 653-654. There was also an interesting suggestion in the committee meeting on which no action was taken. It was as follows: "The Convention is open to ratification by States that are not members of the International Labor Organization. Ratification by a State in accordance with this article will not entail the undertaking of any obligation other than those imposed by the terms of this convention," 654.

[166] A brief summary of these arguments follows. Those favoring revision gave four main points supporting this convention: (1) the revised article would be easier for governments to apply; (2) the proposed revision would meet the needs of certain industries by permitting two shifts and yet enable women workers to have a Saturday half holiday; (3) revision would facilitate ratification; (4) the Office text could be depended on to guarantee that exceptional circumstances and consultation of organizations would take place before action applying the provisions was effected. Arguments opposing revision were: (1) the demands were purely local in nature and not sufficient for revision; (2) revision as to hours would make the position of the workers more difficult; (3) the guarantees of the text were not sufficient; (4) revision would mean the increase rather than abolition of night work. See particularly remarks of Miss

point concerning the exception of women holding managerial positions from the provisions of the convention was adopted without considerable opposition.[167] The second point concerning the scope of hours of night work, aroused the vigorous opposition of the workers' group.[168] However, as the opposition was confined to one group, this item was retained in the revising convention in the form in which it was presented.[169] When the vote was taken on the final draft, the workers' group withdrew their opposition to the section they had opposed in order to make the Conference more harmonious, and the convention was adopted by an almost unanimous vote[170] in the same form as was originally proposed by the Office.[171] The successful revision of this convention seems to indicate that the errors made in the initial attempt could be satisfactorily avoided. In this instance the process was aided by the clarification of a proposal in question by the competent judicial body. The

---

Martindale (Government Adviser, British Empire) favoring revision and Miss Varley (Workers' Adviser, British Empire) opposing revision of the point concerning managerial positions, *ibid.*, 192-193.

[167] The vote on this section was eighty-five favoring the revision and one against, *ibid.*, 196. Mr. Mertens (Workers' Delegate, Belgium) explained the position of the workers' group on this clause as follows: "The Workers' Group thinks it its duty to make clear its position on this point, the question originally raised by the British Government later became the proposal of the Governing Body of the Office, and we are acting in the same spirit now in voting for that proposal as we acted three years ago when we voted against it, for the position has changed. The Permanent Court of International Justice has decided that the interpretation of the Convention given to it by us, and given to it by all countries which ratified, was wrong, and that these women in managerial positions are covered by the Convention.

"We have decided, therefore, that we cannot expect the twenty-seven countries which have ratified to change and remodel their legislation to suit this change in interpretation, and that we must bow to necessity and accept the proposed revision;" 195.

[168] See remarks of Miss Varley, *ibid.*, 196, and especially those of Mr. Mertens, p. 201, as he voices the unanimous opposition of his group to the "dangerous precedent" of revising a whole convention to remedy one local exception.

[169] The vote was 64-22, *ibid.*, 202.

[170] The vote was 120-1 in favor; Mr. Hayday, the British Workers' Delegate, cast the only opposing vote. *Ibid.*, 318. For an explanation of the workers' decision to vote in favor of the complete draft, see remarks of Mr. Mertens (Workers' Delegate, Belgium), 317.

[171] The proposal concerning the inclusion of the new standard articles was adopted without discussion. For text of final draft, see *ibid.*, Appendix XII, 665. For a comparison of the original and the revised articles see Appendix III, *infra.*

smooth functioning of the Organization during the various steps seemed to point to the possibility of a more satisfactory revisory process. The retreat of the workers' group from their usual position of opposition to revision in principle was an indication that they recognized that there are occasions when the revisory process is of value in furthering the progress of labor legislation.

The usual preliminary to an effort to revise a convention is the failure of a convention to receive widespread ratification. The *Hours of Work (Coal Mines) Convention* adopted in 1931 was a source of difficulty soon after its acceptance.[172] This convention was concerned with an important industry, and it contained a special provision stating that it should not come into force until ratified by certain states.[173] After non-official meetings of representatives of the principal states concerned in the ratification of the convention had failed to effect any solution of the difficulties, a proposal was made at the Seventeenth Session of the Conference for a tripartite meeting of the three representative groups.[174]

In the discussion of this proposal by the Governing Body, several differences of opinion were voiced as to whether it was a correct means of solving the difficulties. The workers' representatives were decidedly in favor of convening a tripartite conference.[175] The employers' representatives were greatly opposed to the suggested conference, as they feared that it would attempt to interpret the convention.[176] An alternate proposal to that of a

[172] On the invitation of the British Government an unofficial meeting of the representatives of seven states most concerned was held at Geneva, January 7, 1932. At this meeting the representatives agreed that they should all ratify at the same time but that they could not do so at present. This group met again February 20, 1933, without reaching an agreement. *I. L. C., Nineteenth Session,* 1935, Report VIII, *Partial Revision of Hours of Work* (Coal Mines) *Convention* (1931).

[173] Article 18 provides that two of the following states must ratify it before it will be effective: Belgium, Czechoslovakia, France, Germany, Great Britain, the Netherlands, and Poland. See text of the convention, *I. L. C., Fifteenth Session,* 1931, I, First and Second Parts, Appendix IX, pp. 748-757, and *Draft Conventions and Recommendations* (1919-1934), 203-211.

[174] This proposal was put in the form of a resolution. *I. L. C., Seventeenth Session, Proceedings,* 1933, 417; see text of resolution in Appendix XIV, 687.

[175] See the remarks of Mr. Mertens (Belgium), Mr. Hayday (Great Britain), and Mr. Jouhaux (France); *Minutes of the Sixty-fifth Session of the Governing Body,* 9-18.

[176] Mr. Oersted (Denmark) voiced the view of this group in declaring: "It

tripartite meeting was made by the French Government representative. This proposal favored revision on certain points, but pending such revision it suggested allowing the states concerned to make such interpretations as they deemed necessary to overcome difficulties.[177] As both the workers' and employers' groups opposed this suggestion, it was rejected by the Governing Body.[178] When a vote was taken on the tripartite conference, this proposal was supported by the government representatives and then adopted by the Governing Body.[179]

There was considerable delay in convening the tripartite conference.[180] This delay caused the Director to point out that in case of revision it would be impossible to get the points to be considered on the agenda according to the specified procedure.[181] Accordingly the Director suggested that a better solution would be to give "the officers of the Governing Body power to initiate the revision procedure by authorizing the Office to send the report of the Tripartite meeting to governments without first referring it to the Governing Body," so the time limit would be observed and the questions to be placed on the agenda would be defined.[182] However, there was a definite group division on the question; the mine owners favored revision of the convention, and the workers desired ratification of the existing convention. Four government delegates favored revision, two were opposed to it, and one state was not represented.[183] The final decision arrived at was to submit the records of the meeting to the Governing Body at its sixty-eighth meeting. Accordingly, with these efforts in mind, the Governing Body

---

could not recognize a Conference which was neither an International Labor Conference, nor a general preparatory Conference, but a limited Conference called to interpret a convention regularly adopted by the International Labor Conference." *Ibid.*, 10.

[177] See proposed resolution of Mr. Picquenard, *ibid.*, 20.

[178] *Ibid.*, 23.

[179] *Ibid.*, p. 29. See remarks of Mr. Mahaim (Belgium), 10, and the correspondence between the Office and governments, Appendix, 86-92.

[180] See remarks of Mr. Hayday and Mr. Jouhaux, workers' representatives, blaming the employers for the delay of the conference, *Minutes of the Sixty-sixth Session of the Governing Body*, 27-28.

[181] See report of the Director on the subject, *ibid.*, Appendix X, 68.

[182] See also two other alternate proposals, *ibid.*, 27.

[183] The delegates of Belgium, France, Great Britain, and The Netherlands favored revision; Czechoslovakia and Poland favored the present convention; Germany was not represented at the meeting. *I. L. C., Nineteenth Session* (1935), Report VIII, 8.

decided on partial revision of the convention and proceeded according to Section 7(a) of the Standing Orders.[184]

The governments' replies to the communication of the Office on the subject were generally in favor of discussing the amendment.[185] Three stated they did not suffer from difficulties which the proposed revision would attempt to overcome. On the basis of these replies the Governing Body definitely decided to put the question of revision on the agenda.[186]

Five points were to be considered in the revision of the convention limiting *Hours of Work in Coal Mines*. Four of these points related to technical provisions of the convention, which gave rise to difficulties of application in certain countries, thereby blocking ratification; the fifth related to the revision of the formal clause dealing with the revisory process.

The committee reporting to the 1935 Conference was composed of twenty-seven members (nine from each group). In reporting on the efforts of this body to reach a satisfactory agreement on the items considered for revision, the reporter, Mr. Parent (Employers' Adviser, France) emphasized the serious technical difficulties the committee had to overcome in order to reach any agreement.[187] The first point, which concerned the prohibition of work on Sundays and legal public holidays, was decided on without much disagreement.[188] The divergencies of opinion existed in respect to the points referring to the actual length of the extra time to be allowed.[189] The chief point of disagreement in the committee was whether a specific maximum of hours should be stated in the revised article, or whether the actual number of hours should be left to the administrative authorities. The committee could not reach a unanimous agreement on this point. The workers' representatives

---

[184] See *Minutes of the Sixty-eighth Session of the Governing Body.*

[185] Fourteen, answering, favored or offered no objections; Belgium, Czechoslovakia, Alberta (Canada), Great Britain, Finland, France, India, Luxemburg The Netherlands, Poland, Rumania, Spain, Sweden, and Yugoslavia. See Report VII (1935), *op. cit.*, 22-31.

[186] *Ibid.*, 10.

[187] See the preliminary statement in the committee report in *International Labor Conference, Provisional Record,* No. 22 (1935), 455.

[188] This point concerned the revision of Article 6 of the convention and the revised version stated that of "twenty-four consecutive hours eighteen at least shall fall on a Sunday or holiday."

[189] These items were listed as points two, three, and four, and are in Article 8, *Idem.*

and the British Government representatives favored a specific limitation, while the employers and the Belgian Government representative favored allowing the competent administrative authority to settle the number of hours.[190] When definite proposals were voted on, the point of view of the workers was rejected in part, and a compromise proposal adopted.[191] The formal article concerning revision was adopted without dissent. In conclusion, Mr. Parent (the Reporter) stated, "The work of the Committee has thus led to the removal of all the practical difficulties to which attention was drawn by Governments, and it may be said that there is no technical obstacle to the application of the 1931 convention if the Conference adopts the text proposed by the Committee." [192]

The Conference adopted this report without discussion, and it was referred to the Drafting Committee.[193] Yet, in spite of this agreement with the revision, statements made by several delegates indicated that ratifications might not be immediately forthcoming.[194] The value of the revision in facilitating ratification was attested by the favorable attitudes of the British and French governments toward the convention.[195]

The question of the general revision of the minimum age conventions was first raised by a resolution adopted by the Nineteenth Session (1935) of the conference.[196] Following this the Director

[190] *Ibid.*, 456.

[191] This provided in effect that pumpmen who were vital to the mine machinery could work only eight consecutive hours, while the hours of storemen could be fixed by the administrative authority. *Idem.*

[192] *Idem.*

[193] *Ibid.*, 462. See text of the revised convention in *Official Bulletin,* XX, no. 3 (1935), 62-71. For a comparison of the original and the revised articles see Appendix IV, *infra.*

[194] Mr. Parent (Employers' Adviser, France) in speaking as a representative of his group pointed out three difficulties existing in the convention in its revised form: (1) the existence of several different types of mines to which the provisions of the convention would apply unequally; (2) all competing states must ratify at the same time; (3) the attitude of some oversea states that were competitors might give rise to difficulties. Fear was also expressed by Mr. Legrand (Government Delegate, Belgium) that Belgium could not ratify the convention. *I. L. C., Provisional Record, op. cit.,* 458-460.

[195] See remarks of Mr. Legett (Government Delegate, British Empire), *ibid.,* 458. Also see statement favoring ratification and application by Mr. Blum-Picard (Government Delegate, France), 461.

[196] These conventions were the *Minimum Age Industry Convention,* 1919 (No. 5); *Minimum Age Sea Convention,* 1920 (No. 7); *Minimum Age (Agriculture) Convention,* 1921 (No. 10); and *Minimum Age Non-Industrial Employ-*

brought up for discussion in the Seventy-fourth Session of the Governing Body a proposal to place the revision of the four Minimum Age Conventions on the agenda of the 1938 conference.[197] During the discussion several members of the Governing Body insisted on placing this question on the 1937 Conference agenda as immediate action was urgent.[198] This viewpoint was linked with the proposal to revise all of the Minimum Age Conventions simultaneously. However, the Director of the Office and others pointed out the legal and practical difficulties involved in acting on all of these conventions at the same time.[199] The chief difficulty concerned the *Minimum Age (Agriculture) Convention,* 1921, which in spite of its title was not a convention concerning the admission to Agriculture, as no age was actually stated in the convention. The terms of this convention caused the Governing Body to eliminate it from the proposed revision until further study could be made. This left for immediate consideration the conventions on age of admission to sea, industrial and non-industrial employment.[200]

Some members of the Governing Body, particularly certain government and employers' representatives, protested the revision of any of the Minimum Age Conventions at such an early date as that contemplated.[201] But as this group represented a minority and it appeared that the practical difficulties, such as the short time elapsing between the date of the receipt of reports by governments and the time it would be necessary to take action were surmountable, their objections were not sustained.

The revision of the *Minimum Age (Sea) Convention,* 1920, was placed on the agenda of the Twenty-second Maritime Session by the Seventy-sixth Session of the Governing Body. In order to comply with the provisions of Article 15 of the constitution, which requires the Director to transmit the agenda of the Conference so

---

ment Convention, 1932 (No. 33). *International Labor Conference,* Twenty-second Session, 1936, *Partial Revision of the Minimum Age Sea Convention,* 1920 (No. 7), p. 5.

[197] *Minutes of the Seventy-fourth Session of the Governing Body,* Feb., 1936, 36.

[198] These members were Mertens (Belgium), Lubin (U. S.), and Jouhaux (France). Olivetti (Italy), was opposed to their proposal, *ibid.,* 36-37.

[199] *Minutes of the Seventy-sixth Session of the Governing Body,* 1936, 33.

[200] *Idem.*

[201] See the protests of Sir Bhupendra Nath Mitra (Indian Government Delegate) and others, *ibid.,* 37-43.

it will reach the States Members four months before the meeting of the Conference, it was decided that the Twenty-second (Maritime) Session should meet either after, or concurrently, with the Twenty-first (Maritime) Session.[202]

The questions as placed on the agenda concerned the following points:

(1) The raising of the minimum age from 14 to 15 years and any related revision of the exceptions provided in the convention.
(2) Substitution for Articles 5-12 of the 1920 Convention of the Standard Articles included in the Draft Conventions submitted to the Conference at its twenty-first session.[203]

When these proposals were submitted to the governments, thirty-seven replied. On the question of raising the minimum age to fifteen years, twelve replies were favorable.[204] Three governments favored the revision in principle, but reserved the right to express their views on the details.[205] Four other states were willing to consider the question.[206] Nine governments were opposed to the convention on the basis that it was unapplicable in their domains.[207] All of the states replying favored revision of the Convention on the question of the Standard Articles. In respect to these Articles the Office proposed that a special clause be inserted to the effect that the revised convention should not come into force until after the adoption by the Conference of draft conventions revising *Minimum Age (Industry)*, 1919, and *Minimum Age (Non-Industrial) Employment*, 1932.[208] When the Maritime Conference Committee studied the question, the employers' representatives expressed opposition to the revision of the maritime convention apart from the revision of the conventions concerning land industries.[209] Other members of the committee believed that there was no reason why in an individual country the raising of the minimum

[202] *Ibid.*, 7.

[203] *Ibid.*, 5.

[204] Bulgaria, Canada, Cuba, Czechoslovakia, France, Hungary, Mexico, Poland, Spain, Sweden, the United States, and Uruguay. *Ibid.*, 17.

[205] Argentina, Brazil, and Chile. *Idem.*

[206] Australia, Irish Free State, Japan, and Great Britain. The last named state insisted an exception be made in respect to hospital ships. *Idem.*

[207] Denmark, Ecuador, Estonia, Finland, Greece, Netherlands, Turkey, Union of South Africa, and Yugoslavia. *Idem.*

[208] *Ibid.*, 21.

[209] *I. L. C., Proceedings, Twenty-second Session*, Oct., 1936, 2.

age of employment at sea should be made dependent on the raising of the minimum age in other industries, as the conditions on board ship may differ considerably from conditions in the "shore industries." [210] After considerable discussion an amendment offered by Great Britain which would permit certificates to be issued to children in exceptional cases by "educational or other appropriate authority" was accepted by the Committee.[211]

The committee voted to substitute the new articles (5-12) concerning revision and the coming into effect of conventions for those in the Convention.[212] They also included in the standard articles the clause, proposed by the Office, providing that the convention should not come into force until after the adoption of draft conventions revising the *Minimum Age (Industry) Convention*, 1919, and the *Minimum Age (Non-Industrial Employment) Convention*, 1932.[213]

When the proper questions to be placed on the agenda, concerning the *Minimum Age Industry Convention*, were considered, the United States Government Delegate, Mr. Carter Goodrich, proposed that a wide change be made in the convention so that broad protection might be extended children in matters other than the age entrance in industry.[214] His proposals, which were approved by the Office, concerned the admission of children to industries which were dangerous to health, safety, and morals; and the compulsory registration of workers below a prescribed age.

---

[210] *Ibid.*, 13.

[211] The office text as modified by the adoption of the British Government amendment is as follows:

Article 2: (1) Children under the age of fifteen years shall not be employed or work on vessels, other than vessels upon which only members of the same family are employed.

(2) Provided that national laws or regulations may provide for the issue in respect of children of not less than fourteen years of age, of certificates permitting them to be employed in cases in which an educational or other appropriate authority designated by such laws or regulations is satisfied after having due regard to the health and physical condition of the child and to the prospective as well as the immediate benefit to the child of the employment proposed, that such employment will be beneficial to the child.

[212] *Ibid.*, *Committee for Partial Revision of the Minimum Age (Sea) Convention*, 1920, *Draft Report*, 4. Also see Appendix, VII-IX.

[213] *Ibid.*, *Minutes of the Committee for Partial Revision of the Minimum Age (Sea) Convention*, 14.

[214] *Minutes of the Seventy-seventh Session of the Governing Body*, 1936, 10. This convention had been ratified by 37 states.

The final form of the proposals for the Partial Revision of the Minimum Age (Industry) Convention, 1919 (No. 5) was as follows:

"(a) Revision of Article 2 so as to raise the minimum age from 14 to 15 years;
(b) Insertion of a provision raising the age laid down in Article 4 below which registration is compulsory;
(c) Insertion of a provision prescribing the age of admission to employment which is dangerous to life, health or morals;
(d) Revision of exceptions;
(e) Substitution for Articles 7 to 14 of the 1919 Convention of the Standard Articles in the form last approved by the Conference." [215]

The replies received on the questions to be placed on the agenda indicated that a majority of the states replying were in favor of raising the age-limits with reservations. The exception proposed by Great Britain in respect to children employed in vocational educational establishments caused the Office to put forward an article to meet this condition.[216]

When the items for revision were placed before the Conference, they were accepted with little opposition. All efforts to make changes were defeated.[217] The widespread approval of the convention was owing in part to the fact that the complete delegations of China, Cuba, Poland, Russia, and the United States voted in favor of the revision.[218]

[215] *International Labor Conference, Twenty-third Session,* Report VI, 1937, *Partial Revision of the Minimum Age (Industry) Convention,* 1919 (No. 5) (Sixth Item on the Agenda), 5.

[216] The article to be substituted for article 2 of the convention was as follows:

(1) Children under the age of fifteen years shall not be employed or work in any public or private industrial undertaking, or in any branch thereof, other than an undertaking in which only members of the same family are employed.

(2) Provided that national laws or regulations may provide for the issue in respect of children of not less than fourteen years of age of certificates permitting them to be employed in cases in which an educational or other appropriate authority designated by such laws or regulations is satisfied, after due regard to the health and physical condition of the child and to the prospective as well as immediate benefit to the child of the employment will be beneficial to the child. *Ibid.,* 21.

[217] See *I. L. C., Proceedings, Twenty-third Session,* 1937, 356-357.

[218] The final vote on the revision was 82 for and 18 against. *Ibid.,* 504.

As the convention on the admission of children to industrial and non-industrial employment were brought up at the same time, the action by the Governing Body in respect to it was similar.[219] The questions for revision concerned the exceptions and exemptions in respect to children between 14 to 15 years, the raising of the age for children doing light work from 12 to 13 years, insertion of a clause providing for registration below a prescribed age, deletion of article 9 which applied certain special provisions to India, and the substitution of the Standard Articles in the form last approved by the conference.[220]

The replies of the governments on the basic question of raising the age limit in regard to non-industrial employment indicated a variety of opinions. A large number opposed such action while some favored the specified change, others favored the principle of raising the age limit, a few expressed a desire to have the matter discussed before stating their position.[221]

The discussion of the revision of the convention in the Conference as well as the report of the committee indicated some of the delegates did not favor its acceptance in the form proposed.[222] The causes for this opposition varied considerably. The Swedish Government delegates feared it would be impossible for Sweden to apply the terms of the convention.[223] The Japanese Government Delegate felt he could not accept the clause which provided for no exemptions.[224] The British and Belgian employers' delegates opposed revision as detrimental to industry. The Belgian Employers' representative based his opposition partly on the theory that children should enter industry early to acquire skill and for competitive reasons.[225] These objections to the convention were met by speeches from M. Egorova, Russian Workers' representative[226] and Mr. Paul, American Employer's adviser.[227] The latter cited the beneficial effects of the National Industry Recovery Act in respect

---

[219] See *Minutes of the Seventy-sixth and Seventy-seventh Sessions of the Governing Body* cited above.

[220] *Report VII, I. L. C., Twenty-third Session, 1937, Partial Revision of the Minimum Age (Non-Industrial Employment) Convention,* 1932, 5.

[221] Of thirty-seven governments replying nine definitely favored raising the age limit, others favored it in principle, three were in favor of discussing it, fourteen opposed it, and nine expressed no opinion on the matter. *Ibid.,* 21-22.

[222] *I. L. C., Twenty-third Session, Proceedings,* 1931, 322-329.

[223] *Ibid.,* 324-325.

[224] Articles 5, 12, see Appendix.

[225] *I. L. C., Provisional Record,* 334.

[226] *Ibid.,* 332.

[227] *Ibid.,* 343.

to child labor and expressed the view that the determination of what was best for child welfare should be decided by the government and workers advisers.

Immediately following this discussion M. Justin Godart (French Government Delegate), and certain other government representatives submitted an amendment concerning article 2 which provided that if only members of a family were employed in an undertaking national laws might regulate the employment of children under such circumstances.[228] After a brief discussion this addition was adopted by a large majority.[229] Following its adoption, articles 2, 4, 5, and 6[230] and the new articles A, B, and C were adopted.[231] Then the revised articles were submitted as a whole and accepted by the members present.[232]

The attempts to deal with *Hours of Work in Coal Mines* Convention by the states concerned and the resulting resolution to consider revision afford many opportunities for speculation as to the possible part that may be played by groups outside the regular procedure of the Organization in bringing about the modification of conventions. Such action doubtless is an indication of the value of voluntary collaboration of states in an unofficial manner concerning a matter they desire to bring to the attention of the Organization.

The experience of the Organization in connection with revision has been varied, and it is difficult to draw specific conclusions that can be applied to the general problem. Several observations may

---

[228] This amendment was submitted by the following government delegates: M. Godart (France), Mahaim (Belgium), Phocas (Greece), Yermitch (Yugoslavia), Abbott (U. S.), and Palencia (Spain), *ibid.*, 347. Mr. Godart and his associates also urged the Conference to accept a draft Recommendation which they believed would be a step toward raising standards. The text of this Recommendation which was adopted by the Conference as the *Minimum Age* (*Family Undertakings*) *Recommendation*, 1937, is listed as: (5) *Recommendation* (*No. 52*) C (804).

[229] The amendment as finally adopted and incorporated in Article I of the revised Convention was as follows:

(a) Employment in establishments in which only members of the employer's family are employed, except employment which is harmful, prejudicial or dangerous within the meaning of articles 3 or 5 of this Convention, *ibid.*, 799.

[230] The vote was 84-4. *Ibid.*, 349.

[231] *Ibid.*, 350.

[232] The vote was 69-15, but as there was not a quorum it was necessary to delay the final vote until the next day. *Ibid.*, 350. The final vote was 81-22, 405.

be made. The first is that practice has shown that any working process of revision must be flexible enough to apply to emergency situations, and that, out of dealing with such situations, methods of value may be obtained for utilization in future modification procedure. The courage and resourcefulness of the Governing Body in meeting revision needs in a practical manner is proof of this. However, it is desirable to sound a note of caution in commending these emergency adaptations. They are valid and in most cases highly desirable in the formative period of a revisory process as long as they remain within the legal bounds of the Constitution. It is also encouraging to note the recent formulation of new techniques, adapted to individual conventions, which will facilitate future modification.

TECHNICAL QUESTIONS

It will not be the purpose of this exposition to explain the meaning of technical questions in relation to particular conventions, but rather to show the nature of the problem of technicalities in relation to the work of revision. There will be occasional references to actual detailed provisions of conventions in order to give a more realistic view of the subject matter involved.

Matters relating to a field as comprehensive and specialized as that of labor would necessarily require the consideration of experts. It has been said of the International Labor Conference that it is "to a large extent a Conference of technical experts bent on finding solutions for common technical problems."[233] Such a characterization is true to a more considerable extent of labor conferences than it is of diplomatic conferences. Since its beginning the Organization has recognized the need of the most expert technical assistance; accordingly, the Office has utilized specialists to prepare reports on particular subjects for each session of the Conference. The framers of the Constitution of the Organization were aware of the need of technical assistance at the periodical conferences and provided for such in two articles. The first, Article 3, which describes the details of conference procedure, states that: "Each Delegate may be accompanied by advisers, who shall not

[233] *The International Labor Organization: The First Decade,* preface by Albert Thomas, 311. This book was written by the members of the International Labor Office. An excellent statement of the role of technical experts is given by Director John G. Winant in "The International Labor Organization in Wartime and After," *Foreign Affairs,* XIX (April, 1941), 636.

exceed two in number for each item on the Agenda of the meeting."[234]

The provisions of Article 18 give the Conference competence to make use of expert assistance, saying that: "The Conference may add to any committee which it appoints technical experts, who shall be assessors without power to vote."

The extent to which technical aid is utilized by the Conference is illustrated by the number of advisers accompanying delegates at the second Conference. This Conference was a special meeting and considered only questions relating to seamen, so one hundred and fifty technical advisers assisted in the solution of these questions.[235]

In the opinion of the officials of the Labor Office, whose experience dates back to the first Conference, the work of formulating or revising a convention can best be accomplished by small, well-qualified committees; this belief is briefly expressed in these words:

> "It was found, and subsequent experience has confirmed the view, that a general debate on a technical subject which has been already thoroughly prepared throws little new light upon it. Hence immediate reference to a committee, where detailed negotiation can be undertaken, not only saves time, but may prevent the announcement of general theses from which retreat is subsequently difficult. In this respect . . . the Washington Conference set a precedent which has since become the general rule."[236]

One of the major causes of the demand for the revision of conventions has been due to the difficulty of applying technical provisions. The *Report of the Director to the 1921 Session* of the Conference suggested that a clause allowing amendments to provisions concerning points of detail, without changing essential articles, might be inserted in future conventions to facilitate rati-

---

[234] *Constitution and Standing Orders.* This article further provides in connection with technical advisers that, "When questions specially affecting women are to be considered by the Conference, one at least of the advisers should be a woman. . . . Advisers shall not speak except on a request made by the Delegate whom they accompany and by special authorisation by the President of the Conference, and may not vote. A Delegate may by notice in writing addressed to the President appoint one of his advisers to act as his deputy, and the adviser, while so acting, shall be allowed to speak and vote."

[235] See the list of the members of the delegations and their advisers, *I. L. C., Second Session, Geneva,* 1920 (xxi-xxxvi).

[236] *The International Labor Organization: The First Decade,* 328.

fications.[237] A few years later Mr. Molin and Mr. Ribbing (Swedish Government Delegates) sent to the Office a memorandum proposing a new type of draft convention:

> "Each Draft Convention would be drawn up in such a way that the international engagement inherent therein would only apply to matters of primary importance, it being open to the Members themselves to establish exceptions of minor significance from the point of view of the real effectiveness of the Convention." [238]

In spite of their timeliness, neither of these proposals found sufficient favor with the Conference for adoption.[239]

The difficulty of the general Conference in dealing with certain subject matter has caused the innovation of technical preparatory conferences,[240] in an effort to solve better special questions. The opinion of the Office on this matter is that:

> "Whether this attempt succeeds or not, the problem which it is sought to solve will have to be dealt with by the Organization in the next few years. Far from disappearing it is more likely to increase in importance. Maritime questions are not the only ones which have a highly technical character and must be studied by Conferences with special qualifications. In the early years, the Conference dealt with very general and purely universal problems; but since then there has been a tendency to submit to it questions affecting special industries, or special groups of countries, which cannot be dealt with by the ordinary methods of discussion at the Conference.[241]

Following the above consideration of the general aspects of the problem, it will be advisable to refer briefly to a few of the technical materials encountered in the actual revisory process. The first attempt at revision, which was that of the *Convention Concerning the Employment of Women at Night* (1919), did not en-

[237] *Ibid.,* 119. See also *Report on Amendment* (1923), 1.

[238] *Ibid.,* 7. This type of convention would have allowed the government ratifying to decide as to minor technicalities.

[239] *Loc. cit.*

[240] The following meetings of this nature have been held: Preparatory Technical Conference on Work in Coal Mines, 1930; Preparatory Technical Conference on Work in Coal Mines, 1931; Tripartite Preparatory Conference on Reduction of Hours of Work, 1933; and Tripartite Conference concerning Hours of Work in Coal Mines, 1934.

[241] *The International Labor Organization: The First Decade,* 83.

counter particularly technical subject matter;[242] notwithstanding, when the same convention was revised in 1934, there was a suggestion by one government that certain detailed regulations be included in the text. This suggestion was not acted upon favorably.[243]

The principal reason given for the revision of the *Convention Concerning the Protection against Accidents of Workers Employed in Loading or Unloading Ships* (*Protection against Accidents* (*Dockers*) *Convention,* 1929), was that the technical provisions were so inapplicable as to prevent ratification.[243a] When these points were considered by the Governing Body in 1932 it decided that, owing to the essentially technical nature of the proposals, it did not have the necessary competence to decide upon the substance of each proposal,[244] so that such decisions were left to the Conference. Twenty provisions for revision were placed on the agenda with the minor details to be decided at the Conference. The points to be considered were:

> "(1) Addition of a provision permitting the reduction by not more than 10 per cent of the measurement requirements of Article 2 (spaces and fencing of approaches and working places).
>
> "(2) Addition of a provision permitting the reduction by not more than 10 per cent of the measurement requirements of Article 3 (appliances for access).
>
> "(4) Modification of the requirements of Article 5, paragraph 2(a) (ladders giving access between deck and hold).
>
> "(5) Modification of the requirements of Article 5, paragraph 2(d) (ladders giving access between deck and hold).

[242] See *supra, "Modifications Accomplished."*

[243] This suggestion by Yugoslavia was that a list of the posts of management in connection with the employment of women at night be included in the revised convention. The Office replied to this proposal as follows: "The preparation of an internationally applicable list which would be neither too restricted nor too comprehensive would obviously present serious difficulties." The other governments appear to have regarded this as an unnecessary attempt to regulate the matter in detail. They were satisfied with the positive criterion of "holding responsible positions of management" and the negative criterion of "not ordinarily engaged in manual work" as furnishing a sufficiently strict definition; *I. L. C., Eighteenth Session,* 1934, Report VII, *Partial Revision of the Convention Concerning the Employment of Women During the Night,* 20.

[243a] *I. L. C., Sixteenth Session,* 1932, Report IV, *Partial Revision of the Convention Concerning the Protection against Accidents of Workers Employed in Loading or Unloading Ships,* 6.

[244] *Minutes of the Fifty-sixth Session of the Governing Body,* 1932, 74.

"(6) Modification of the provisions of Article 5, paragraph 5, concerning access ladders in the holds of vessels which are not decked.

"(7) Permanent exemption from the requirements of the Convention of ships existing or under construction at the date of ratification of the Convention (suppression of Article 5, paragraph 7, and modification of Article 16).

"(8) Modification of the safety requirements of Article 8, paragraph 2, or hatch coverings moved by mechanical power or of very light weight.

"(10) Insertion of a provision concerning the contents of the safe working load certificates contemplated by Article 9, paragraph 1.

"(11) Insertion of a provision for mutual recognition by members having ratified the Convention of the certificates provided for in Article 9 (supervision of loading and unloading machinery).

"(12) Modification of the requirements of Article 9, paragraph 3, concerning the annealing of chains and similar gear.

"(13) Insertion in Article 9, paragraph 4, of a provision that it shall not be necessary to furnish with brake cranes and winches moved by mechanical power and provided with a suitable valve and reversing gear.

"(14) Addition to Article 9 of a provision concerning measures to prevent the foot of a derrick being accidentally lifted out of a goose neck.

"(15) Insertion of a provision concerning the selection and supervision of the 'competent persons' referred to in paragraphs 1 and 3 of Article 9.

"(16) Modification of the provisions of Article 11, paragraph 44, concerning the removal of fastening of hatch beams.

"(17) Modification of Article 11, paragraph 7, with a view to permitting in certain cases the use of cant-hooks on barrels.

"(18) Modifications of the provisions of Article 11, paragraph 8, concerning the safe working load.

"(19) Addition of a provision for the mutual recognition by members having ratified the Convention of the validity of certificates issued by national authorities concerning compliance with the provisions of the Convention which are to be applied on board.

"(20) Exclusion of ships engaged in inland navigation from the scope of the Convention." [245]

The extremely technical nature of these provisions necessitated that special caution be exercised by every group that considered them. The revision of this convention was a function for experts in maritime matters to perform.

When the revision of the *Workmen's Compensation* (*Occupational Diseases*) *Convention*, 1925, was considered, it was recognized that most of the questions involved were essentially technical in nature, so they were referred to the Industrial Hygiene Committee of the Office, a group of specially chosen experts.[246] This body studied carefully the extension of the schedule of diseases, and its report furnished the Conference the necessary material to revise the convention.[247] The various delegations to the Conference included members competent to examine the report given by this committee.[248]

The report of the Industrial Hygiene Committee gave minute consideration to every phase of the occupational disease schedule. A considerable part of the first section of the report is devoted to a definition of occupational diseases.[249] The report goes into detail respecting the legislation on the subject in force in the different states,[250] and the part of medical experts in putting this legislation in effect.[251] The terms used in referring to the names of the various

[245] *I. L. C., Sixteenth Session* (1932), Report IV, 11-12. The above provisions do not include the minor technical details such as "cooming shall be fenced," p. 19; or "half-inch (12½ mm.) and smaller chains or gear in general use once at least in every six months," 18. For a careful explanation of each point on the agenda see 54-84 of the report cited.

[246] *I. L. C., Eighteenth Session*, Report V, *Workmen's Compensation for Occupational Diseases*, ix-x. See also *supra*, 63-65.

[247] *Ibid.*, 1-320.

[248] The Office was extremely desirous of having but one Conference session for the discussion of this topic, as it felt a second meeting would again require expert advisers with consequent extra expense to delegations, *ibid.*, x.

[249] *Ibid.*, 4-12. The difficulty and uncertainty of defining occupational diseases was pointed out by the reports as follows: "The incidence of forms of mixed poisoning is much greater than might be imagined, more especially under organization of the chemical industry. Cases of poisoning have been known to occur as the result of unforeseen reactions bearing no direct relationship to the industrial operations in question. There may be quoted in this connection those due to phosphorated hydrogen liberated from the residues of molten ore containing phosphorus, on which hot water has been poured," 9.

[250] *Ibid.*, 18. [251] *Ibid.*, 21-30.

diseases specified in legislative acts indicated that the laymen would not be expected to be familiar with the meaning of such words as "ankylostomissis," "Cachexia," "stomatitis," [252] and "suppurating callosities." [253] A large part of the report was devoted to "silicosis" as it was the main disease being considered for placement on the revised schedule of the convention.[254] This disease was defined *senso stricto* as a pathological condition of the lungs due to the inhalation of silica.[255]

The report of the Conference committee on the proposed revision indicated that in spite of the technicalities of the subject matter a satisfactory conclusion was arrived at in the committee meeting without great difficulty.[256]

On the basis of the report of the committee the Conference decided that silicosis should be added to the list of diseases of the convention in the following form:

> "Partial revision of the Convention concerning compensation for occupational diseases with a view to:
> A. Inclusion in the schedule appended to Article 2 of this Convention of the following occupational diseases:
> Silicosis—
> Poisoning by phosphorus and its compounds or its sequelae;
> Poisoning by arsenic and its compounds or its sequelae;
> Poisoning by benzene, its homologues and nitro and amido-derivatives or its sequalae.
> Poisoning of hydrocarbons of the aliphatic series and their chlorinated derivatives or its sequelae.
> Pathological manifestations due to:
> (a) Radium and other radio-active substances;
> (b) X-rays.
> Epitheliomatous cancer of the skin." [257]

The terms used in this convention make obvious the fact that in the process of revision technical questions frequently form a major part of the problem.

The work of the technical preparatory conference has been

---

[252] *Ibid.,* 18. [253] *Ibid.,* 29.

[254] *Ibid.,* 2-314. "Silicosis" was known before 1656 as "phthisis" and later as "byssinosis," 203.

[255] *Ibid.,* 209. English legislation defines silicosis as "fibrosis of the lungs due to silica dust"; French legislation as "pulmonary affection caused by absorbing siliceous, calcareous, or argilaceous dusts."

[256] See *supra,* 64-65.

[257] *I. L. C., Eighteenth Session,* 1934, Appendix X, 669-673.

referred to in a previous paragraph. The usefulness of such preparatory meetings was demonstrated by efforts to revise the *Hours of Work* (*Coal Mines*), 1931. This convention was not obtaining the necessary ratifications owing to the alleged technicalities which countries concerned believed they would encounter in applying certain subsidiary provisions of the convention.[258] After several unofficial meetings by the governments concerned,[259] the Governing Body convened a tripartite conference "with a view to the ratification of the Convention concerning hours of work in Coal mines." [260] The technical details of the convention were not considered at length by the Governing Body, but, as the Director of the Office stated, "The proposed Tripartite Conference would be one which would consider all methods of overcoming difficulties." [261]

Following the meeting of the tripartite conference, at which the technical difficulties which led to the proposals for revision were carefully considered,[262] the following questions were placed on the agenda of the nineteenth session of the Conference (1935) for partial revision of the *Hours of Work* (*coal mines*) *Convention*, 1931:

> "(1) The question of allowing a normal shift to work during certain hours on Sunday and legal public holidays, and the amount of the rest period for these workers which should fall within Sunday or legal public holiday.
>
> "(2) The question of extending the additional time allowed for workers employed on operations which by their nature must be carried on continuously, so as to enable the necessary work to be done by three shifts.
>
> "(3) The question of extending the additional time allowed for preparatory and complementary work, in the case of underground storemen, enginemen and drivers of locomotives,

---

[258] *I. L. C., Nineteenth Session* (1935), Report VII, 5-6, see *supra*, chapter III, 69-72, for a general description of the revisory process in connection with this convention.

[259] Article 18 of the convention provided that two of the following states must ratify before the convention would come into force: Belgium, Czechoslovakia, France, Germany, Great Britain, Netherlands, and Poland.

[260] See *Minutes of the Sixty-fifth Session of the Governing Body*, January, 1934, 23; also see general discussion of convocation of conference, 8-15.

[261] See remarks by Mr. Forbes-Watson (English Employers' Delegate) in explaining his lack of qualifications to enter into a discussion of the technicalities of the convention, *ibid.*, 14.

[262] For a statement of technical difficulties which led to revision see *I. L. C., Nineteenth Session* (1935), Report VII, 13-21.

so as to enable them to complete the work of this kind on which they are employed.

"(4) The question of allowing additional time to be worked on the day of periodical change-over of shifts of men (working on the three-shift system) in charge of main underground ventilation and pumping machinery which has to be operated continuously for seven days in the week." [263]

The revision of this convention was successfully completed in the 1935 Conference.

This brief survey of technical questions concerned in revision is no attempt to make a comprehensive treatment of the subject, yet perhaps an indication of the difficulties in this regard has been demonstrated. In the first place it is evident that the inapplicability of technical provisions to existing conditions in the states which are parties to agreements has been one of the chief reasons for the demand for amendment of conventions. Efforts by the Organization to meet this situation have been varied. Some provisions of the Constitution were of assistance in solving the problems. However, as the subject matter concerned in revision became more specialized, greater reliance was placed on small technical bodies for the formulation of more applicable provisions. This development was inevitable, as the layman delegates to the Conference were not competent to make a valid decision on the details of revision. To a degree which cannot be accurately determined at this early stage of development, technical advisers, special committees, the specially trained personnel of the Office, and preparatory technical conferences have dealt successfully with the problem of technical questions in revision.

[263] *Ibid.*, 11.

CHAPTER IV

LEGAL QUESTIONS IN REVISION

The solution of the legal questions involved has been one of the major problems of revision. Apparently the examination of conventions growing out of contemplated revision brought to light problems concerning the legal nature of conventions that had not previously been discussed. This lack of experience in dealing with such complex and difficult questions has meant that many of them have not yet been finally determined.

CONTRACTURAL NATURE OF CONVENTIONS

Before considering the contractural nature of labor conventions, it is necessary to refer briefly to the general contractural nature of multipartite agreements. International treaties are often spoken of as being a special kind of contract.[1] The extent to which an analogy may be made in applying private law contractual concepts to treaties is expressed by an authority on this subject in the following manner:

> "It is generally accepted that the fundamental condition of the validity of contracts in private law, i.e., the free concensus of parties, is not essential in international law, and that, as a result of the predominant conception of the *clausula*, the binding force of international contracts is not only weaker in degree but also different in kind from that of their counterpart in private law." [2]

Nevertheless, that the modern multipartite instrument has in three respects a similarity to a contract is asserted by a British authority on the topic as follows:

> "(a) In the matter of form, it is undeniably true; the nearest approach in private law to the treaty in point of form

[1] "Multilateral Conventions are after all only a form of contract in which the consideration for the acceptance of the contract by any one party is its acceptance by the others." Malkin, "Reservations to Multipartite Conventions," *British Yearbook of International Law,* VII (1926), 142.

[2] H. Lauterpacht, *Private Law Sources and Analogies of International Law,* 155; for an excellent discussion of "Treaties as Contracts" see 155-180 of this work.

is the contract; and (b) there is no sovereign body above the states, it is convenient to seek in the consent of the parties either the cause, a condition, of the binding force of a treaty though the effect of doing this may be at once to invest the treaty with the whole panoply of contractual notions; but (c) we must be on our guard against the assumption that, merely because treaties have borrowed from private law contracts their form and the source of their binding force all the rules as to formation, validity, interpretation and discharge of contracts are equally applicable to treaties."[3]

Many modern publicists agree on the distinction between the legal obligations of the old type of treaty which was concerned with the subjects of peace, alliance, and friendship and the new type which contains subject matter on a variety of technical topics. It has been asserted that the earlier treaty was a *Vertrag* (contract) while the new one is a *Vereinbarung* (agreement) raised to a higher power.[4] Included in this latter group of treaties are those termed "law making" treaties.[5] That international labor conventions are typical of this kind of agreement is suggested by the following statement:

> "We may point to the numerous Labour Conventions which have been negotiated by the International Labor Organization and are now in force between states which have adopted them. They seem to me to be typical Verinbarungen, their object being to secure identical rules upon the topics regulated by them in the different countries which adopt them."[6]

On the other hand an eminent legal publicist who has had an important part in the formation of "labor legislation" says, "It is

---

[3] Arnold McNair, "The Function and Differing Legal Character of Treaties," *loc. cit.*, 106. See also Harvard Research Draft on Treaties, *A. J. I. L.* (Supplement), July, 1935.

[4] *Ibid.*, 105. For a critical discussion of the validity of this distinction see H. Lauterpacht, *op. cit.*, 158-159; also see Paul de Auer, "Revision of Treaties," *Transactions of the Grotius Society*, XVIII (Problems of Peace and War), 155-175.

[5] Some examples of this type of agreement are: The Hague Convention for the Settlement of International Disputes, the Covenant of the League of Nations, the Statute of the Permanent Court of International Justice, and the Peace Pact of Paris. Arnold McNair, *op. cit.*, 107.

[6] *Ibid.*, 116.

not correct to say that all Labour Conventions are Vereinbarungen. Some of them are true Contracts (Verträge)." [7]

The wide difference of opinion on this subject is to some extent due to the difficulty of analyzing the contractual nature of agreements formulated by such unusual procedure as in the case of labor conventions. Generally, international treaties and conventions are negotiated by plenipotentiaries, who sign the agreements on their conclusion. A labor convention is not signed by diplomatic representatives. In addition to this difference, the act of ratification has a special significance in the case of labor conventions. For after the conclusion of a convention, it is obligatory that it be submitted by States Members to competent authorities for ratification.[8] In order to get a practical view of the contractual nature of conventions, it is desirable to consider the various opinions held by those who participate in the actual formulation of conventions.

The formal point of view of the Labor Office is expressed by Mr. Morellet (Legal Adviser of the Office). He asserts that while conventions "have a legal character of a special kind it cannot be maintained that they possess absolute legislative force"; rather they have a

> ". . . quasi-legislative character as texts adopted by a special authority distinct from the contracting States. On the other hand, it cannot be denied that they possess a contractual character in the sense that the mutual obligations which they lay down derive from the contracting States. In short, though it appears legitimate to regard international labor conventions as conventions of a special character involving a quasi-legislative element, there can be no doubt that they are nevertheless Conventions, that is to say that once ratified, they become actual contracts between states." [9]

It is to be noted that Mr. Morellet used the term "quasi-legislative" in reference to conventions, and that he avers that in spite of this they are contracts between states. According to Mr. Mahaim it does not matter whether the conventions are legislative or contractual treaties, as that distinction is one of content and does

[7] This point of view is ably defended by Mr. Ernest Mahaim in "Some Legal Questions Relating to International Labour Conventions," *loc. cit.*, 772.

[8] Article 405 of Part XIII.

[9] *I. L. C., Twelfth Session*, 1929, I, Third Part, Appendix I, 734.

not affect the contractual nature of the agreement.[9a] A point of view on the subject of the contractual nature of conventions that is in opposition to both of those previously referred to is held by Mr. Oersted, leader of the employers' group. First, he objects to the term "draft convention" and asserts the labor agreements are neither drafts nor conventions, for a convention is a contract between states, while a "draft convention" is not a contract. Rather, he says "draft conventions are conditional international laws" which may be accepted or rejected by the states members but not in any way changed by them.[10] Mr. Oersted says that no reciprocity exists in connection with these conventions.[11] This view is concurred in by another delegate experienced in the work of the Conference, who describes "draft conventions" as "mere understandings." [12] It can readily be seen that this point of view would place fewer obligations on states and probably would make the conventions unacceptable to the workers.

The position of those who hold that states are not obligated by labor conventions in the same sense they are by treaties is that the legal right of a state in respect to enforcement of obligations is not absolute. This, they assert, is demonstrated by the fact that any delegate may lodge a complaint concerning a convention whether his state has ratified the convention or not. Therefore, reciprocal rights do not spring from the convention, as it imposes no obligations on a state member with respect to other members.[13] Those accepting this view believe that a state is bound in virtue of the Peace Treaty and not owing to ratification of a convention.[14]

[9a] He further says: "Treaties are . . . acts involving . . . a concurrence of intention (accord de volontes)" and that the creation of the League of Nations bodies has not changed them in this respect. Mahaim, "Some Legal Questions Relating to International Labour Conventions," *loc. cit.*, 773.

[10] *I. L. C., Twelfth Session*, Appendix II, 763. Mr. Mahaim defends the term "draft convention" as a signed or initialed treaty awaiting ratification, *ibid.*, 767.

[11] *Ibid.*, 764.

[12] Mr. Olivetti, "Note on the Legal Effects of Revision," *ibid.*, Appendix III, 767.

[13] *Ibid.*, Appendix II, 674.

[14] It is instructive to note in this connection that when this question was being discussed in the Conference Mr. Paranjpye (Government Delegate, India) asked whether if all states ratified a new revising convention but one, would that one be bound by the old convention? Mr. Oersted stated the point of view just referred to and logically held the single state would be bound to the old convention. *I. L. C., Twelfth Session, Proceedings*, I, 357.

This position implies that a state is bound to the Organization rather than being a party to a contract with reciprocal obligations to other states. This unusual point of view was rejected by the Conference and the various units concerned in dealing with the legal problems of revision.[15]

It is evident in the case of some labor conventions that they clearly contain reciprocal obligations which are legally effective on the exchange of ratifications.[16]

The general view of the special group concerned with the manner in which states apply conventions[17] is that conventions are international treaties which the governments are bound to apply without restrictions.[18] This means that the state is obligated to bring its legislation into complete harmony with the convention.[19]

This variety of views on the subject indicates the difficulties attending legal problems in connection with "international legislation," [20] and particularly in connection with a new and complicated subject such as revision.

COMPETENCE OF REVISORY ORGANS

As there is no provision for revision in the Constitution of the Organization, the competence of the organs of revision had to be determined within the actual general limitations of the Constitution by an experimental process. These limitations concerned the adoption of a new convention, rather than any modification of an exist-

[15] The acceptance of this point of view would have meant the adoption of the proposal of the employers' group stipulating that conventions would not come into force until ratified by all states concerned.

[16] Article 1 of the *Convention Concerning Equality of Treatment of National and Foreign Workers as regards Workmen's Compensation for Accidents* (1925) is a typical illustration of this point: "Each member of the International Labour Organisation which ratifies this Convention undertakes to grant the national of any other member which shall have ratified the Convention, who suffers personal injury due to industrial accidents happening in its territory, or to their dependents, the same treatment in respect of workmen's compensation as it grants to its own nationals." See *Draft Conventions and Recommendations* (1919-1934), 104-108.

[17] Committee on Article 408. The work of this body is discussed in detail *supra*.

[18] *I. L. C., Eleventh Session,* 1928, *Proceedings,* I, 283.

[19] The competence of the Organization in this regard arises out of Article 408 of Part XIII or Article 22 of the Constitution.

[20] For a discussion of the inconsistencies in respect to parties to treaties, see Eagleton, International Legislation and the Drafting of Treaties," *Temple Law Quarterly,* VIII (1933-34), 220.

ing agreement. This situation doubtless was of significance in determining the competence of the various bodies concerned in revision.

The revisory article inserted in the conventions adopted at the Washington Conference stipulated in a general way the action to be taken by the bodies concerned in revision.[21] It required the Governing Body to make a report on each convention every ten years. The Governing Body must also consider whether or not revision is desirable. If it is, and the replies from the governments are favorable to the proposed modification, presumably the Conference takes action on the subject.[22] As this article is not so explicit as it might be, it is difficult to determine its implications.[23] The framers of the article evidently had difficulty in deciding on its contents, as the original draft gave the Conference the authority to revise a convention in five years after it came into force.[24] The terms of the first draft would indicate that the second adopted draft would allow revision before the convention had been in effect ten years; in fact, according to the Legal Adviser of the Conference, revision or modification could be undertaken by the Governing Body or Conference at any time.[25]

The competence of the Governing Body in deciding whether

---

[21] See *supra*, Chap. III, 44.

[22] The power to place items on the agenda is given the Governing Body and Conference in the following articles:

"Article 400. The agenda for all meetings of the Conference will be settled by the Governing Body, who shall consider any suggestion as to the agenda that may be made by the Government of any of the Members or by any representative organisation recognized for the purpose of Article 389.

"Article 402 (paragraph 3). If the Conference decides (otherwise than under the preceding paragraph) by two-thirds of the votes cast by the Delegates present that any subject shall be considered by the Conference, that subject shall be included in the agenda for the following meeting," Treaty of Versailles, *op. cit.* These articles correspond to Articles 14 and 16 of the Constitution.

[23] See comment of the Legal Adviser to the first Conference, *Proceedings, op. cit.*, 179.

[24] However, Mr. Manley O. Hudson, Legal Adviser, stated in reporting on the article: "Under the labor part of the treaty of peace, it is, of course, open to the Conference or the Governing Body to place any question on the agenda at any time," *loc. cit.*, 179.

[25] Possibly this opinion was influenced by discussions of the clause *rebus sic stantibus* just following the World War. For a general discussion on this point, see Mahaim, "Some Legal Questions Relating to International Labour Conventions," *loc. cit.*, 785-787.

revision shall be placed on the agenda was difficult to determine from the working of the first general revisory article. Nevertheless, the Governing Body has taken as being expressive of the intentions of the authors the words of the English text which states that the Governing Body "shall consider the desirability" of placing revision on the agenda.[26] According to the Director of the Office, the Governing Body is not obliged to propose revision but it must consider whether revision is desirable.[27]

No definite attempt further to define the competence of the Governing Body in respect to revision occurred until 1929, when the Organization was faced with actual revision. At this time a new procedure defining the action of the Governing Body on the topic of revision was included in the Governing Body's Standing Orders.[28] According to these provisions, when the Governing Body makes its decennial report on the working of a convention and following this considers its revision should take place, the Office must send the Governing Body's report to the governments for their examination.[29] Following this action the Governing Body shall, four months from the date it sent the report to governments and after considering the replies, "adopt the final report and define exactly the question or questions which it places on the agenda of the Conference."[30] These stipulations, which defined more exactly the place of the Governing Body in revision, were necessary before the actual revision of a convention could take place. The Governing Body may, according to this procedure, suggest total revision; but it may also decide that only partial revision is necessary. If it

[26] Although both texts are authenthic, the French text might be interpreted as compelling the Governing Body to place revision on the agenda, as it reads "decidera d'inscrire."

[27] *I. L. C., Eleventh Session,* 1928, *Report of the Director,* First Part, 22.

When the general problem of revision was being considered in 1929, the Office submitted a report to the Governing Body (Forty-third Session, March, 1929) which was in turn presented to the Conference. This report contained arguments for and against the suppression of the formal decennial revisory clause. The Office took the position that while the clause appeared unnecessary it obligated the Governing Body to consider in every case the desirability of revision. It regarded as weak the legal argument that, if this clause did not exist, it might be maintained that the Conference was not competent to modify a convention which the states had made their own property by ratification; see *I. L. C., Twelfth Session,* I, Third Part, Appendix II, 771-773.

[28] For the text of this procedure and a discussion of its formulation, see *supra,* Chap. III, 49, footnote 80 on Article 7(a) of the Standing Orders of the Governing Body.

[29] *Loc. cit.*

[30] *Loc. cit.*

decides on the latter, it must "define exactly" the provisions it proposes to revise, and the Conference may not discuss other provisions. This procedure definitely restricted the scope of the discussions of the Conference in regard to revisory efforts. The Conference could not open for discussion any question concerning a convention unless it had already been placed on the agenda by the Governing Body.[31]

In 1934 the Standing Orders Committee, reporting on questions relating to revision, made a proposal which aimed to facilitate the revisory process.[32] This suggestion was made in view of the fact that the Conference might occasionally have before it entirely distinct proposals for revision, which had been approved by the committee examining them, but which, owing to the opposition of those opposing each proposal, when combined in one text and submitted to the Conference for a final vote, caused the rejection of the entire revising convention by the Conference.[33] Accordingly, in case of such occurrence, it might be desirable that the Conference should have an opportunity to vote on a convention which included only one of the proposals made in the committee. This would keep a proposal for revision which was desired by a large majority from being defeated due to its connection with some article or group of articles that were unrelated to it in principle. The Standing Orders Committee discussed an article formulated to meet this situation,[34] but the proposal failed to obtain the necessary number of votes for adoption.[35]

[31] This limitation on the Conference was a point gained by those who were opposed to revision in principle, as it made for the greatest caution in the revisory process. The workers' group favored this limitation, as they feared that some of the provisions they had struggled to obtain would be sacrificed if open conference proposals were allowed. For an excellent discussion of this point, see F. G. Wilson, *op. cit.*, 255-256.

[32] *Minutes of the Sixty-fifth Session of the Governing Body*, 107.

[33] The above described situation actually existed when the attempt was made to revise the Convention on the Employment of Women at Night in 1931 and was one of the causes for the failure of the revisory effort. See Chap. III, pp. 57-59, *supra*.

[34] The text of the article was as follows: "If a Draft Convention providing for the revision of a previous Convention or more than one point fails on a final vote to obtain the necessary two-thirds majority, the Conference may, if it thinks fit, refer it back to the Drafting Committee with a request to lay before the Conference a Draft Convention providing for a more limited revision. In such cases a further final vote shall be taken before the end of the Session." See *Minutes of the Sixty-fifth Session, Governing Body*, 107.

[35] *Loc. cit.*

The practice of revision revealed the need of procedure for modification of some conventions prior to the expiration of the decennial period. Consequently, the Standing Orders of the Governing Body were amended in 1934 so as to allow the Governing Body to propose the revision "in whole or in part" of a convention at any time it deemed such action desirable.[36] This addition to the competence of the Governing Body was of value in facilitating revisory efforts.

The statement of the Legal Adviser of the Office concerning the legal problem of actual revision defines succinctly the constitutional limits:

> "Revision is the task of the Conference and must be effected in accordance with the rules of procedure laid down in the Treaties. The Conference cannot revise a Convention by means of a Recommendation. It cannot revise otherwise than by adopting a new Draft Convention." [37]

In 1929 the Conference adapted its Standing Orders to meet the need for revision procedure.[38] The only change in the standard articles that was necessary in case of revision was the adoption of single instead of "double-discussion procedure." [39] In the opinion of the Legal Adviser single discussion of revisory proposals was sufficient, as the purpose of the first discussion was to define the scope of the convention. In this case the Governing Body had already defined the scope of the question for revision.[40] In reply to the question of whether a revising convention which received a bare majority could become a rcommendation, the Legal Adviser was of the opinion that it could not do so as it would have no legal effect.[41] Mr. Morellet was also of the opinion that, although the Governing Body could limit the agenda, unquestionably the Conference could propose an item for revision at the next session.[42]

[36] See *supra,* Chap. III, 50. This action was taken particularly in view of the legal difficulties encountered in revising the Dockers Convention in 1932.

[37] Statement of Mr. Morellet, Legal Adviser to the Conference, *I. L. C., Fifteenth Session,* I, Third Part, Appendix I, 728.

[38] See Extract from Report Submitted by Mr. Mahaim on Behalf of Standing Orders Committee, *I. L. C., Twelfth Session,* I, Third Part, Appendix III, pp. 718-723; see also I, First and Second Parts, 341-345.

[39] See *supra,* Chap. I, 13-14, for a description of "double discussion procedure" in making conventions.

[40] *I. L. C., Twelfth Session,* 728-731.

[41] *Loc. cit.*

[42] In this connection the Legal Adviser states: "The procedure for the revision of Conventions is a question of so novel a character that there might be a danger

The question of the legal authority of the Conference in respect to adopted conventions was defined by the Legal Adviser, and this definition was accepted by the Conference. The Adviser stated that as the Constitution did not permit the Conference to adopt conventions binding on all states, *a fortiori* it could not repeal conventions it formulated, but which required ratification by states before they would come into effect. Consequently, the Conference cannot substitute a new convention for an old one.[43] This limitation on the power of the Conference was a logical one, as authority to impose a negative decision could not exist if a positive one could not be imposed.

A practical test of the competence of the bodies concerned in revision was met in the revision of the *Protection Against Accidents (Dockers)*, 1929.[44] In the first place, the convention had been adopted only two years before; and, according to the existing Standing Orders, its revision could be considered only at the end of the ten-year period. As the need for revision was considered pressing, the Governing Body decided to place the question on the agenda in virtue of its power to fix the latter.[45] This authority is granted in Article 14 of the Constitution:

> "The agenda for all meetings of the Conference will be settled by the Governing Body, who shall consider any suggestion as to the agenda that may be made by the Government of any of the Members or by any representative Organization recognized for the purpose in Article 389."

The Governing Body followed the regular procedure for revision with the exception of the consideration of the decennial report.[46]

In the preliminary preparation for revision, another legal difficulty was encountered in connection with the Dockers Convention. Owing to the short length of time prior to the 1932 Conference, the Office and Governing Body had failed to abide strictly by the

---

that constitutional principles might to some extent be lost sight of during the discussions of the Conference. The correct and regular application of revision procedure would no doubt be facilitated if a reference to those principles were inserted," *ibid.*, 733.

[43] *Ibid.*, 734. See also *I. L. C., Twelfth Session*, vol. II, *Report of the Director*, p. 21. This concept of the authority of the Conference was vigorously opposed by Mr. Oersted and his colleagues. See *I. L. C., Twelfth Session*, I, Appendix II, 765.

[44] For a discussion of this revision see *supra*, chapter III, 59-62.

[45] Chapter III, *supra*, 59.

[46] *Ibid.*

stipulations of Article 15 of the Constitution, which reads as follows:

> "The Director shall act as Secretary of the Conference, and shall transmit the Agenda so as to reach the Members four months before the meeting of the Conference, and through them, the non-Government Delegates when appointed." [47]

The agenda was not actually established and communicated in the time period this article provided. The Japanese Government Delegate made strong objections to this violation of the article. It was recognized that these objections were valid, and so the Conference passed a resolution to guarantee against future violations in order that the objector would not present his legal protest before the Permanent Court of International Justice.[48]

This brief survey of the competence of the revisory bodies has shown that the chief task in this connection has been the adjustment of their Standing Orders to the terms of the Constitution. This has been a difficult legal problem, as the specific point to be adjusted was not evident until a need for immediate revision had arisen. Consequently, the action taken has sometimes been of questionable validity. In addition to the necessity for *ad hoc* procedure of doubtful legality, the bodies concerned in revision have found it necessary to determine their respective competence in the revisory process. This has caused the adaptation of their Standing Orders to meet the need for revision.

THE STATUS OF ORIGINAL AND REVISED CONVENTIONS

When the International Labor Organization considered the legal consequences of revision, it was faced with the problem of determining the exact status of the old and the revised convention. The Organization had no precedent to assist in the solution of this problem. The early experience in respect to the Berne Convention on the *Employment of Women at Night* did not serve as a guide, for no revision had taken place; instead, an entirely new convention had taken the place of the one adopted in 1906.[49] The coexistence of these conventions had apparently given rise to no dif-

---

[47] *Constitution and Standing Orders.*

[48] Chap. III, *supra,* 61. The Japanese Delegate could have invoked Article 37. This difficulty led to the modification of the Standing Orders of the Governing Body noted above.

[49] See *supra,* Chap. I, 37-38.

ficulties, although some of the members of the Organization were parties to the Berne Convention and not to the new one adopted in 1919.[50] The discussion of the legal status of the original and revision convention revealed that a wide difference of opinion existed on the subject.

In 1929 the opinion of the Office was carefully presented by its Legal Adviser.[51] This opinion set forth three possible solutions to the problem. Before stating these tentative methods of dealing with the question, the Adviser discarded as legally impossible the idea that the Conference could substitute a new convention for the old one. He was of the opinion that such action would be contrary to both the general principles of international law and the Constitution of the Organization.[52] Consequently, this also involved the acceptance as the basic premise of the solution of the Office the adoption of a fresh convention as a means of accomplishing revision. This meant, of course, the co-existence of conventions, or a single combination of the new and old agreements.

The first proposal of the Office specified that the old unamended provisions and the new clauses constituting the revision were to be included in the same text.[53] This modified convention would consist of a single text containing all the contractual obligations. This was regarded as being satisfactory from the legal point of view, in so far as the convention itself was concerned. Nevertheless, there was a valid objection to this proposal; for, if the convention contained both the old and the new clauses, the Conference would have to take a final vote on its whole text. This would require the Conference to act on material that had not been placed on the agenda. In addition to this, the delegates might open discussion on these old texts, and, if allowed to do so, might go beyond the limits of the agenda. However, in spite of this objection, which is envisaged in a hypothetical situation, the incorporation of the text of the

[50] *Ibid., passim.* That is, the Labor Organization had experienced no difficulties from this situation as it was not connected with the old Berne Convention; however, as is pointed out above, contradictory legislation existed.

[51] Note by the Legal Adviser of the International Labor Office on the Legal Problems Connected with the Revision of International Labor Conventions, *I. L. C., Twelfth Session,* I, Third Part, Appendix I, 728-748. A view similar to that expressed by Mr. Morellet, Legal Adviser, is to be found in *The Report of the Director* to the *I. L. C., Eleventh Session* (1928), I, First Part, 22.

[52] See "Competence of Revisory Organs," and "The Contractual Nature of Conventions," *supra.*

[53] *I. L. C., Twelfth Session,* I, Appendix I, 735.

amendments in the old convention is extremely desirable from a legal point of view. In fact, ". . . the very notion of revision implies that the points to be discussed belong to a whole body of contractual provisions to which it is not merely permissible but necessary to attach them. The very term revision involves the idea of effecting a junction, so to speak, between the new provisions with which they are combined. There is ample legal justification for voting on the whole body of contractual provisions resulting from revision." [54]

The Adviser held that the only real disadvantage of the proposed procedure was the submission to the Conference of clauses of the convention not on the agenda.

The second system proposed by the Legal Adviser was to include in the revising convention only the new clauses constituting actual revision. According to this method there would be no legal connection between the old and new clauses, and a state that had not ratified the old convention but which wished to ratify the new one would be obliged to ratify both. Therefore, two sets of contractural relations would exist for the ratifying state. This would establish two régimes, and a state not willing to accept the old convention could not bind itself by the new one. In the opinion of the Adviser this would create an extremely complicated relationship that would be generally unsatisfactory.[55]

The third solution of the problem presented by the Office suggested that the revising convention should contain: (1) a new text of revised provisions, (2) reference to the old convention as to unrevised provisions. This proposal is half-way between the two listed above. It would require no double ratification. Notwithstanding, two systems of contractual obligations independent one of the other would be established. The objection to the first proposal in respect to the consideration by the Conference of items not regularly placed on the agenda would not arise in this procedure, as the text of the old convention would not be submitted.[56] The only disadvantage of the third solution is that it is less clear than the first one, and its workings are somewhat more complicated. In his closing statement in respect to the proposed solutions, the Legal Adviser expressed the opinion that any method adopted concerning revision in respect to the status of conventions would be imperfect and involve numerous difficulties.[57]

[54] Statement of Mr. Morellet, *ibid.*, 736.

[55] *Ibid.*, 738. [56] *Ibid.*, 740. [57] *Ibid.*, 741.

The legal interpretation of the relationship of conventions presented to the Conference by the Legal Adviser was not acceptable to many delegates. Mr. Oersted of the employers' group expressed their position on the subject. He believed the Conference was competent to abrogate the old convention.[58] From this point of view the contractual relation established on the ratification of a convention was between States Members and the Organization rather than between the individual members. This argument was supported by the fact that a member was obliged to submit a convention to the competent authority within a definite time, that there was no connection between the obligations of ratification and the action of other members, and that the denunciation of a convention by a state did not affect the ratification of the other states still bound by the convention. Furthermore, it was held that, when a new revised convention was drawn up, a state which had ratified the old convention could not be bound, unless it was provided that a convention should only come in force when all the old ratifying states had ratified the new document. This would mean that the new convention would be substituted, for the old one, and that it would contain provisions to preserve the results already obtained.[59]

Mr. Olivetti (Italian Employers' Delegate) presented a note on the legal effects of revision which was similar to the view of Mr. Oersted. He stated Mr. Morellet's note did not explain how a state's original obligation could be discharged upon the ratification of a revised convention. What if the state should ratify both the old and new conventions? He proposed the adoption of a "reglement type" revised convention as a substitute for a "reglement type" existing convention. Through the use of this device the Labor Organization would discharge the state from its former obligation.[60]

In presenting the report on behalf of the Standing Orders Committee, Mr. Mahaim pointed out that revising conventions possessed no obligatory force and came into effect only by the fact of ratification. So, if the old convention were automatically abrogated, as was suggested as desirable by the employers' group, ratification would be null and void and the entire structure of labor "legislation" would "crumble," to be replaced by a "mere draft." [61]

---

[58] *Ibid.*, 765-767. [59] *Loc. cit.* [60] *Ibid.*, 768.

[61] *Ibid.*, 769-771. Mr. Mahaim is of the opinion that two existing conventions on

These views on the subject of the effect of revision on the legal status of conventions indicate the great difference of opinion held by individuals and groups connected with the Organization. When the question came before the committee on Standing Orders, the view of those favoring the abrogation of conventions by the conference was rejected.[62] The final decision of the Conference based on the committee report indicated that it was better to risk the complications and inconsistencies of having two co-existing conventions than to suppress one of them automatically. The text adopted reads as follows:

> "Should the Conference adopt a new Convention revising this Convention in whole or in part, the ratification by a Member of the new revising Convention would, notwithstanding the periods of delay mentioned in the foregoing Article (d), involve the immediate denunciation of this Convention, provided that the new revising Convention has come into force.
>
> "As from the date of the coming into force of the new revising Convention, the present Convention would cease to be open to ratification by the Members.
>
> "Nevertheless, this Convention would remain in force in its actual form for those Members which had ratified it but had not ratified the revising Convention." [63]

What are the legal consequences of this revisory article, which is to be a part of each convention adopted by the Conference?[64]

---

the same subject create inconsistencies and difficulties; however, he further states, "it would be dangerous to abrogate the old Convention for the new revision convention may not receive many ratifications, and it will be remembered that the International Labour Organization cannot impose ratification on its Members. In particular, the new Convention may fail to be ratified by the Members that have ratified the first, and then what is the position? In those countries labour protection might be diminished or even withdrawn; the result of trying to improve the Convention would thus ultimately be to restrict its field of application." "Some Legal Questions Relating to International Labour Conventions," *loc. cit.*, 795.

[62] *I. L. C., Twelfth Session*, I, Third Part, Appendix III, 723.

[63] *I. L. C., Twelfth Session*, I, Third Part, Appendix XI, 811.

[64] In commenting on the article, Mr. Ernest Mahaim remarks: "The reservation at the end of the first paragraph provided that the new revising Convention has come into force will be observed. If, therefore, its coming into force depends on the ratification of two or more Members, the first Convention will remain in existence until the fulfillment of this condition. This explicit reservation is precisely that described above as implicit in Article 406. This Article applies not

The problem will perhaps be made more comprehensible if the existing denunciation clauses are taken into consideration. The old clause in vogue prior to 1928 provided that a state might denounce a convention ten years from the date on which it came into effect.[65] Thus as denunciation did not take effect until one year after its date, a state might denounce a convention from year to year following the termination of the ten-year period. In 1928 the denunciation article was changed to read as follows:

> "Each member which has ratified this Convention and which does not, within the year following the expiration of the period of ten years mentioned in the preceding paragraph, exercise the right of denunciation provided for in this Article, will be bound for another period of five years and, thereafter, may denounce this Convention at the expiration of each period of five years under the terms provided for in this Article." [66]

The denunciation clauses in the conventions adopted in 1929 and years following were not uniform. The convention concerning *Protection against Accidents* (Dockers) contained the same clause as the 1928 convention.[67] However, the denunciation clause of the convention on *Marking of Weight (Packages Transported by Vessels)* 1929, stipulated that:

> "Within the year following the expiration of the period of ten years mentioned in the preceding paragraph, a state failing to exercise the right of denunciation provided for in this Article, will be bound for another period of ten years, and

only to the ordinary, i.e., the original Convention, but also to a Convention revising it. There is in fact nothing to prevent the Conference from submitting a single Convention to several successive revisions. It will then be for the competent committee and for the Conference to determine carefully on which ratifications the coming into force of the second revision is to depend. If it is wished to avoid the co-existence of two Conventions, nothing could be easier. It will be sufficient to stipulate in the earlier Article, relating to the coming into force of the Convention, that all the contracting parties to the previous Convention should have ratified this new one." "Some Legal Questions Relating to Revision," *loc. cit.*, 795-796.

[65] In discussing the effects of revision, Mr. Mahaim expressed the fear that obligatory consideration of revision would destroy the stability of "international labor legislation" and stated that "if the period of denunciation is sufficient, I would be ready to suppress the clause providing for the revision of Conventions." *I. L. C., Eleventh Session, Proceedings*, I, 310.

[66] Article 9, *Minimum Wage-Fixing Machinery* (1928); *Draft Conventions and Recommendations*, 1919-1934.

[67] *Ibid.*, Article 21, 176.

thereafter, may denounce this convention at the expiration of each period of ten years under the terms provided for in this Article." [68]

The denunciatory clause in the *Sheet Glass Works Convention*, 1934, was similar to the one noted above.[69]

These examples of the lack of uniformity in denunciation clauses combined with the revisory article adopted in 1929 indicate how involved the problem of determining the period between the adoption of the revising convention and its coming into effect might become.

Taking all these factors into consideration, it appears, as Mr. Morellet, Legal Adviser of the Office, says, that the existence of "two such conventions would give rise to a rather complex legal situation." He further states concerning a proposed revision that the system adopted in 1929 would create the following legal status in respect to the existing conventions:

> "The new convention to be adopted this year will not bind the Members which have ratified the original Convention. It will constitute an entirely new juridical act, which will be subject to the procedure laid down in Article 405 of the Treaty of Versailles, and which must be brought by the States Members of the International Labour Organisation before their competent authorities with a view to a new ratification. In other words, the new Convention will require a new procedure for ratification in each state, even in those states which have ratified it, and it may even be ratified by the States which have not yet ratified it since it is not abrogated. But it can be denounced, for its Article 13 provides that, after the expiration of ten years from the date of its coming into force, the States may denounce it on one year's notice." [70]

In connection with Mr. Morellet's statement, the Office noted that a state could ratify both the original and the new conventions and that this would constitute a "difference" but not a "contradiction." [71]

In formulating a solution of the legal status of conventions, the Organization dealt with an extremely complex legal problem. The

---

[68] *Ibid.*, Article 5, 164. [69] *Ibid.*, Article 8, 313.

[70] *I. L. C., Fifteenth Session,* I, Third Part, 729. See also denunciation clause, Article 5, *Convention on Marking of Weight* (Packages Transported by Vessels) (1929), *Draft Conventions and Recommendations,* 1919-1934.

[71] *I. L. C., Fifteenth Session,* I, Third Part, 730.

argument advanced in some quarters, especially by the employers' group, that the Conference abrogate the original convention as a national legislative body repeals laws, could not logically be accepted; for, although conventions are laws, they are not binding until they receive the consent of States Members through ratification.[72] Consequently, the Conference would not have the competence automatically to release states from their obligations. In deciding that it was more desirable to have two conventions in existence on the same subject, the Conference made it possible for a situation to come about which might result in numerous inconsistencies. For example, in the case of two conventions in existence on the same subject the different states may be bound by two sets of regulations. Obviously, this makes a uniform application of standards impossible. Also another more complicated legal situation may arise if states which have ratified the original convention ratify the new one without denouncing the original.[73] Would these states be obliged to put into effect legislation in conformity with both conventions? A situation might exist which would make such action impossible. Or, are ratifying states bound to abide by the strictest regulations of the two conventions? It would seem that this would be the case, although it might bring about a contradictory situation.[74] The provisions of the convention last ratified would not be the only ones to be legally applied, as the obligations of the old convention are binding until denunciation takes place. Generally the method chosen by the Organization in 1929 to determine the legal position of the original and the revised convention failed to contribute to uniformity, which is one of the major aims of labor legislation.[75]

[72] Mr. Mahaim says these "laws" have a special character of their own as, "a law so described as conditional may be compared with the provision in social insurance laws that certain groups of persons may benefit by insurance without being compulsorily liable to it; e.g., employees earning more than the specified maximum salary. But the situation is not the same. In this case there is a genuine law, binding on certain groups of citizens, and such that its existence does not depend on the consent of all those to whom it applies." "Some Legal Questions Relating to Conventions," *loc. cit.,* 771, footnote 4.

[73] This actually happened in the case of the Berne Convention on the Employment of Women at Night. Thus Great Britain, the Netherlands, Switzerland, Italy, Austria, Belgium, France, Luxemburg, and Hungary are theoretically bound by both conventions.

[74] The position of the Office as noted above is that the regulations would be "difficult" but not "contradictory."

[75] The conclusions of Mr. Jenks, Assistant Legal Adviser of the Office, con-

The previous discussion emphasized the fact that the revisory article adopted in 1929 concerning the force and effect of revision on the original convention left a rather complicated legal situation. An attempt to remedy this condition resulted in the adoption by the Conference in 1933 of a number of minor changes in the standard articles of the conventions.[76]

The specific object of this slight modification was to leave to the session of the Conference discussing revision of a convention the decision as to whether a new revising convention should *ipso jure* involve denunciation of the earlier convention.[77] In the existing standard articles, no choice in this respect was left to the Conference. Consequently, if the Conference decided that denunciation *ipso jure* was not involved, ". . . the reciprocal obligations assumed by one State towards another under the terms of the earlier Convention would not lapse, owing to the ratification of the new revising Convention, and two States, only one of which had ratified the revising Convention, would still be bound as regards each other by the reciprocal terms of the earlier Convention."[78]

The Standing Orders Committee suggested that the following modified form of the standard article be inserted in the conventions of the Seventeenth Session, with the understanding that the Eighteenth Session of the Conference should decide whether it desired to make the modification permanent:

> "Should the Conference adopt a new Convention revising this Convention in whole or in part, then, unless the new Convention otherwise provides:

---

cerning this situation are valuable. He says: "It follows that while Conventions adopted in the years preceding and following 1929 are alike in not being subject to abrogation by a vote in the Conference, the rules on the other two points referred to differ according to whether a convention does or does not contain the new form of revision article approved by the Conference in that year. For Conventions containing this Article the position is clear. For earlier Conventions it would appear that, unless provision to the contrary is made at the time of revision, they will remain open to ratification despite the coming into force of a revising convention and continue to bind a Member until denounced as permitted by their terms after it has become bound by a revising convention. Whether it be competent for the Conference to make provision to the contrary when adopting a revising Convention cannot be considered a finally settled question." Jenks, "Revision of International Labour Conventions," *loc. cit.*, 58.

[76] *I. L. C., Seventeenth Session,* Appendix III, Report of the Committee on Standing Orders, 501.

[77] *Loc. cit.*

[78] *Loc. cit.*

(a) the ratification by a Member of the new revising Convention shall *ipso jure* involve the immediate denunciation of this Convention, notwithstanding the provisions of Article X above, if and when the new revising Convention shall come into force;
(b) as from the date when the new revising Convention comes into force, this Convention shall cease to be open to ratification by the Members.

This Convention shall in any case remain in force in its actual form and content for those Members which have not ratified the revising Convention." [79]

The 1934 Conference adopted this new article as a standard provision of all future conventions.[80]

This article made for more flexibility concerning the need of a particular convention. If the Conference should deem it necessary, the ratification of the new revising convention would involve the immediate denunciation of the old agreement. Thus, as the subject matter and circumstances surrounding a convention might necessitate the Conference's acting differently in respect to two different types of conventions this article would permit such action.

The great variety of denunciation and revisory clauses existing in conventions makes it impossible to formulate a uniform rule, under existing circumstances, determining the status of the old and the revising conventions. Nevertheless, it is possible to draw some conclusions. The exact obligations of the states parties to conventions adopted prior to 1929, which have since been revised, are in some cases difficult to define. The obligations of States Members parties to conventions containing the new (those formulated since 1928) revisory and denunciation articles can be more correctly evaluated. They vary, however, according to the stipulations contained in the respective conventions. It appears that the Organization is gradually developing methods which will make more exact the status of future original and revised conventions.

UNANIMITY RULE

The rule of conference procedure of the Constitution that allows conventions to be concluded by a two-thirds majority vote is an important factor in determining the nature of certain legal

---

[79] *Ibid.*, 502.

[80] *I. L. C., Seventeenth Session, Proceedings*, 52.

questions in revision. If instead of the specified two-thirds majority vote, unanimity had been required, the legal problems would have been of a different character.[81] For example, in a conference of the League of Nations all the delegates are governed by the policy of their respective states, and they vote as one unit. In the revision of a labor convention the interests of three groups—government, employers, and workers—must be considered. It is necessary in many instances that concessions be made to each of these groups before an agreement can be reached. As the convention being revised is often of technical subject matter, numerous compromises in matters of detail are necessary to obtain agreement between the points of view of the workers and employers. Generally, the opposition of workers to revision in principle would make revision almost impossible were more than a two-thirds vote required to adopt the revised convention. Nevertheless, the same rule that has facilitated the adoption of revising conventions has made the determination of their legal status more difficult.

The absence of an international legislature makes it necessary to consider "legislative" action by any international body with special care, particularly when legal questions arise. Some writers regard the absence of actual international legislative organs at the present time as an unfortunate feature in the international development of existing law.[82] National states have been extremely reluctant to surrender their sovereignty in order to further their collective ends.[83] Consequently, there has been in principle a strict

---

[81] It is difficult to envisage any method that could have been adopted by the Conference to circumvent the unanimity rule, in case of the adoption or revision of a convention. How the Assembly and Council of the League of Nations, particularly the former, has successfully evaded the unanimity rule in certain instances is demonstrated in detail by Cromwell A. Riches, *The Unanimity Rule and the League of Nations*, 1-217. The acquiescence of the smaller power to the will of the majority in the League units would hardly by analogy take place in respect to any of the three groups represented in the Labor Conference. As the delegations have no national solidarity, the situation is entirely different from that existing in the League.

[82] See H. Lauterpacht, "The Absence of an International Legislature and the Compulsory Jurisdiction of International Tribunals," *British Yearbook of International Law*, XI (1930), 136; also J. F. Williams, *Current International Law and the League of Nations*, 34-35. In his discussion of an international legislature, Lauterpacht infers that perhaps at the present stage of development the unanimity rule and the lack of an international legislature is a blessing in disguise for the purpose of keeping down disruption, 143.

[83] The opinion of one authority is that "all advance in the development of

adherence to the unanimity rule in international conferences.[84]

The attempt by the Organization to institute a procedure for the amendment of conventions encountered a serious legal question in connection with the unanimity rule.[85] The proposed procedure provided that all the government delegates should vote for an amendment before it could be adopted. Furthermore these national representatives should be "duly authorized to that effect." Those formulating the amendment procedure believed that these provisions would set at rest any objections to the lack of unanimity in sanctioning the modification.[86] Nevertheless, there were several objections to the proposed text. These objections chiefly concerned the constitutional difficulty of applying a system by which amendments might be made without the consent of legislatures to conventions on which legislation had been enacted at the time of ratification.[87] Some also doubted whether the amendment clause was within the limits specified in the Constitution.

Owing to these fears a committee of legal experts in consultation with legal authorities of a large number of the states concerned made a thorough examination of the constitutionality of the proposed procedure.[88] The general conclusion was that there were no real constitutional difficulties. This conclusion was based on the fact that consent to a convention containing an amendment would be "proceeding to a delegation of powers," a common practice

---

conventional international law, in the process of international organization, and in the promotion of the common interests of the community of states has come through mutual restraint and concession voluntarily imposed or granted by states. Particular states have often found that their own security and welfare could be better promoted by surrendering their sovereignty and uniting in federal unions rather than remaining independent." J. W. Garner, "Limitations on National Sovereignty in Interntional Relations," *American Political Science Review*, XIX, no. 1 (1933-34), 324.

[84] One writer believes that the results of the unanimity rule in international conferences have not been reassuring, for at times it has proved to be "highly dilatory" or "intolerably obstructive." However, "in public international unions the states of the world have been somewhat less hesitant to forsake the rule of unanimity than in international conferences. The numerous instances of the employment of the idea of majority control may be explained by the nature of the function of public international unions" . . . which is administrative "rather than policy forming." Norman L. Hill, "Unanimous Consent in International Organization," *A. J. I. L.*, XII, 319.

[85] See *Report on Amendment* (1923); also Chap. III, 39-43, *supra*, for a discussion of proposed amendment procedure.

[86] *Report on Amendment* (1923), *passim*.

[87] *Idem*.

[88] *Idem*.

in the law of most states.[89] According to this plan the executive power as represented by the government delegates at the Conference would be authorized in advance to signify state consent to amendments. However, this solution did not have the unconditional support of all the legal experts. The British representative feared that such a delegation of power as that proposed would be contrary to the spirit of the British Constitution.[90] Other delegates expressed the fear that some legislatures would be jealous of the executive power and would fail to make the necessary delegation. Nevertheless, none of these objectors challenged the legality of the procedure. Their chief fears were concerning political difficulties. The commission dealing with the subject of amendment believed these difficulties could be solved by adding the following paragraph:[91]

> "Nevertheless, if one of the members which has ratified the present convention should consider that the amendment adopted by the Conference is one requiring the approval of its legislative authorities, it shall within the above period of six months, inform the Secretary-General of the League of Nations, through the International Labor Organization, of this fact. In such case, the amendment will not be registered and put into force until it has been ratified by the said members.
>
> "A member shall give at least six months notice of such request to the International Labor Organization which shall forthwith inform other Members of the Organization." [92]

This paragraph allayed any doubt as to the lack of proper legal and political consent on the part of national authorities.[93]

---

[89] *Ibid.*, 3.

[90] This opinion was expressed especially in regard to war or other national emergencies, *loc. cit.*

[91] See Chap. III, 41-42, *supra,* for the original text of the amendment.

[92] *Report on Amendment* (1923), 6.

[93] In justifying the proposed procedure, the committee reporting cited the precedent of the Universal Postal Union. The convention of this union relating to the organization and the regulations concerning its application was concluded at Madrid in 1921, and contained amendment clauses (Article 28 of the Convention and Article 44 of the Regulations). These articles provide that the convention or regulations might be amended by unanimous consent, or the consent of a majority of the postal authorities concerned, without the approval of legislative bodies. The commission also cited the amendment to the last paragraph of Article 6 of the League Covenant adopted by the Second Assembly, which

The states not represented at the Conference would have an opportunity to approve the amendment. Thus the objection that an amendment by a two-thirds majority would limit the sovereignty of states was silenced.[94]

The commission on amendment procedure answered the objection that the proposed procedure might not be within the legal limits of the Constitution in a brief fashion. It stated that as the Constitution did not make any provision for the modification of conventions, there was no restriction on the sovereignty of states in this respect, and states were free in principle to amend as they might deem advisable. The commission was also of the opinion that the Conference was competent to suggest an amendment procedure. It further pointed out the fact that in applying Article 19 of the Constitution it was necessary to enact a general clause, as the Constitution did not specify any procedure.[95] Therefore, the formulation of a procedure of amendment was constitutional.

As the proposed amendment procedure was never adoped by the Conference, one can only speculate concerning its probable success. While doubtless the efforts to circumvent the rule of consent principle in international law were legally valid, it appears that the proposed procedure would have been very complicated.[96] The opinion that the need for some type of procedure was evident and that the method suggested was entirely valid is expressed by the Labor Office in the following terms:

> "There is admittedly no provision for amendment of conventions in the Treaty. In the absence of definite provisions, the conclusion may be drawn that the question should be solved according to the ordinary principles of international law, provided that the method selected is not contrary to the spirit of the Treaty of Peace. The Office does not propose to enter into a discussion on the foundation of this argument, but would merely point out that the amendment clause, as proposed, is entirely in accordance with the spirit of the Treaty. The two-thirds majority required for the amendment to be adopted must necessarily include the votes of non-Govern-

makes it possible to make changes in the distribution of League expenses simply by majority resolution of the executive assembly. *Ibid.,* 22-23.

[94] The commission pointed out that, if unanimity were required of states which had ratified, one state could always block amendment. *Ibid.,* 16.

[95] *Ibid.,* 19.

[96] The seemingly complicated nature of the procedure was the chief reason it was abandoned. See *Report on Amendment* (1924), 89.

mental Delegates, whose presence is one of the characteristic features of the International Labor Conference, and the one which differentiates it from the former meetings of plenipotentiaries to prepare agreements between states. In this way an international convention could no longer be modified except in agreement with the International Labour Conference and the Members which have ratified. States which have ratified a Convention would not be free to modify it among themselves even if they desired to do so, and no modification could be made without the consent of the employers, the workers and the States."[97]

In the formulation of a revisory procedure the question of the juridical nature of conventions is inexplicably connected with the manner in which they are concluded.[98] The fact that the revision of international labor conventions is concluded by a two-thirds vote in the Conference makes a special procedure necessary prior to their going into effect. In the first place, the effective date of a convention is not at the time of its adoption by the Conference, but according to the standard article adopted at the Washington Conference (1919):

> "As soon as the ratification of two members . . . have been registered with the Secretariat, the Secretary-General of the League of Nations shall so notify all the Members of the International Labour Organization. This convention shall come into force at the date on which such notification is issued by the Secretary-General of the League of Nations, but it shall then be binding only upon those Members which have registered their ratifications."[99]

This provision makes the legal date of the convention's coming into force later than would be the case in respect to an ordinary multipartite agreement.[100] Nevertheless, after a convention comes into effect there is no further connection between its legal force

---

[97] *Ibid.*, 86.

[98] See discussion, *supra*, "Contractual Nature of Conventions."

[99] See Articles 7 and 8 of *Washington* (*Hours*) *Convention, Draft Conventions and Recommendations*, 1919-1934. The Reporter of the committee, Mr. Manley O. Hudson, commented on this article as follows: "Clearly one country should not be bound internationally by a draft Convention unless it is ratified by other countries." *I. L. C., First Session*, 178.

[100] See remarks of Mr. Ernest Mahaim on the peculiarity of this procedure, in "Some Legal Questions Relating to Conventions," *loc. cit.*, 763.

and the fact that it was adopted by a two-thirds majority, for it then becomes a contract between states, not because of its conclusion by an international body of which the states are members, but due to their separate ratifications.[101]

If the International Labor Organization had been given legislative powers in the proper sense of the term, it would have been competent to repeal or revise a convention without obtaining the consent of individual members before any new provisions could go into effect in their respective territories.[102] The fact that the legal competence of the Organization is definitely limited in regard to its authority to change a ratified convention without the consent of the State Member concerned has been demonstrated in the previous discussion. The careful examination of the legal consequences of revision by the Organization made evident the legal limitations on the Labor Organization as a result of the two-thirds rule. In sacrificing the unanimity rule, the members of the International Labor Organization limit their sovereignty only in the sense that they oblige themselves to submit the draft conventions adopted by the Conference to the competent authorities.[103]

[101] Mr. A. Rapisardi Mirabelli comments on this legal phase of a convention in the following manner: "As to the provisions concerning the General Labour Conference (Article 405 of the Treaty of Versailles and the corresponding Articles of the other Peace Treaties), according to which the Conference may adopt Draft Conventions (by a two-thirds majority of the delegates present), these constitute innovations only so far as the ordinary conference of plenipotentiaries is replaced by a special body for the formulation of Draft Conventions. Besides, it is the separate States which conclude the Treaty, by means of ratifications, which they are always free to refuse." "Théorie générale des unions internationales," *Recueil des cours de l'Académie de Droit International,* II (1925), 371.

[102] The International Commission on Labor Legislation at Paris rejected the proposal of the Italian Delegation that conventions adopted by two-thirds should be given statutory effect after a lapse of one year, *Origins of the International Labor Organization,* I, 147.

[103] See Article 19 of the Constitution. The following pertinent comment in this regard is made by Mr. Ernest Mahaim: "Les obligations souscrites par les Etats adhérant à la partie XIII restreignent sérieusement leur souveraineté. Ils se sont engagé à se mettre d'accord avec des organisations patronales et ouvrières pour désigner les deux délégués non governmentaux à la conférrence et à laisser vérifier par celle-ci les pouvoirs de ces délégués (Art. 389). Ils se sont engagés à présenter à la parlement ou à tout autre autorité compétent les projets de conventions qui auraient été voté à la majorité des deux tiers des voix par la conférence" (Art. 405), "L'Organisation permanente du travail," *Recueil des cours de l'Académie de Droit International,* III, 1924, 73.

CONDITIONAL RATIFICATIONS

For various reasons, States Members of the Labor Organization have registered ratifications with the Secretariat of the League of Nations stipulating that they shall not come into force until certain other states have ratified the said convention. That such conditional ratification was envisaged at the time the first conventions were being drawn up is shown by the remarks of Mr. Manley O. Hudson (Legal Adviser to the Washington Conference, 1919) in reference to the effectiveness of this type of ratification:

> "It is possible that a Member may condition its ratification upon the ratifications of other Members of the labor organization. In such a case it is well understood that such a conditional ratification will become effective and should be registered by the secretary general only when the conditions are fulfilled." [104]

The type of ratification described by Mr. Hudson was put in practice by states early in the life of the Organization. The position of the Office has been that, although conditional ratification may be justified where great dangers result from non-ratification of competing states, such action should not be taken in respect to those conventions which do not affect commercial competition.[105] An instance of seeming abuse of the privilege of conditional ratification was the ratification by France of three Washington Conventions on condition that six other states ratify them.[106] Other states registered similar ratifications.[107]

Although the validity of ratification such as that of France has not been seriously questioned, proposed ratifications by Latvia and Estonia raised numerous legal doubts. The Washington Hours Convention was ratified by these two states with the conditional stipulation that it would not come into effect until the states within the meaning of Article 393 of the Peace Treaty had ratified

[104] *I. L. C., First Session Proceedings,* 178.

[105] See *The International Labor Organization: The First Decade,* 274.

[106] These conventions concerned the night work of women, night work of children, and unemployment; the states which were to ratify before the French ratification was effective were Czechoslovakia, Germany, Great Britain, Italy, Poland, and the United States. The Office deprecated this action as unnecessary. See *I. L. C., Sixth Session,* 1924, II, Third Part, 764. These conditional ratifications by France were made unconditional April 7, 1925. See *I. L. C., Seventh Session,* 1925, *Final Record,* II, Third Part, *Report of the Director,* 977.

[107] *I. L. C., Seventh Session, loc. cit.*

("states of chief industrial importance"). The Director pointed out to the Latvian government that it would be necessary to specify particular states to which the condition applied, as the states within the meaning of Article 393 varied.[108] A somewhat similar action was taken by the Latvian government in respect to the convention concerning unemployment indemnity in case of loss of the ship, for the condition provided that the ratification would become effective when "the principal maritime countries" had ratified.[109] The Director deplored this condition and pointed out that it was highly undesirable, and from the point of view of competition, unnecessary in the case of Latvia. He suggested that the clause be amended so as to state definitely the names of the states to which the condition applied.[110]

It is doubtful whether this type of conditional ratification is legally acceptable. Authoritative opinion has held the Latvian ratification in 1926 of the Maritime Convention (1920) is not a legal ratification.[111] The term "principal maritime countries" is meaningless without an authoritative definition and would lead to numerous complications. If states generally made such ratifications the result would be uncertainty concerning the status of States Members. Such ambiguous reservations are probably contrary to the purpose of the Constitution and without legal force. In respect to the use of the term "states of chief industrial importance" in conditional ratification, similar objections apply. The fact that these states vary over a period of years means that such a ratification would be too indefinite to be applied with certainty.[112]

What legal questions are involved in the type of conditional ratification practiced by the members of the Labor Organization? The Preamble of the Constitution states that it is to the special interest of States Members to further the adoption of international labor law, indicating that members should exhibit an individual as well as a collective interest.[113] In conditionally ratifying a con-

[108] *Loc. cit.* This article corresponds to Article 7 of the Constitution.

[109] *Loc. cit.* [110] *Ibid.*, 978. [111] F. G. Wilson, *op. cit.*, 247, note 2.

[112] Article 7 of the Constitution provides that "any question as to which are the members of chief industrial importance shall be decided by the Council of the League of Nations." Since Russia and the United States have joined the Organization, Belgium and Canada are no longer "states of chief industrial importance" within the meaning of the treaty.

[113] See Ernest Mahaim, "Some Legal Questions Relating to International Labour Conventions," *loc. cit.*, 772. An opinion slightly at variance with this

vention, with the ratification not going into effect until certain other states ratify, the state depositing the reservation is not acting individually. Rather the assumption of the obligation of the convention is explicitly bound up with the action of certain other States Members. In theory, this exceptional method of acceding to a convention is possibly at variance with the spirit of the Constitution.[114] In spite of this seeming contravention of the constitution, the position of the Office is that conditional ratification as exercised presents no real legal difficulties. This is well expressed in a note presented to a committee of the League of Nations on the general subject of validity of reservations:

> "It should, however, be explained that certain international labour conventions have been ratified subject to the specific condition that the ratification in question should only become operative when certain States named should also have ratified. These ratifications do not really contain any reservation, but merely a condition which suspends their effect; when they do come into force, their effect is quite normal and unrestricted. Such conditional ratifications are valid, and must not be confused with ratifications subject to reservations which modify the actual substance of conventions adopted by the International Labor Conference." [115]

This statement is a clear explanation of the effect of conditional ratifications, such as now may be deposited, which carry no reservations beyond their coming into effect. Obviously, after such ratifications come into effect, the same obligations are created as by an ordinary ratification.

Conditional ratification of a different nature from that described above has been seriously proposed to the Labor Organization. The legal questions raised by these proposals were of a more complex and disturbing character. The efforts of the Office to discover a

---

general view is expressed by F. G. Wilson, *op. cit.*, as follows: "Conditional ratification is a further application of one of the basic principles of the organization—the simultaneous action by the members in the protection of labor. Conditional ratification can be especially valuable in securing regional action in favor of high labor standards," 247, note 2.

[114] The Office takes this point of view of the subject and points out that conditional ratification hinders the progress of ratifications, *I. L. C., Sixth Session,* II, Third Part, 764.

[115] *Official Journal,* 1927, annex 967, p. 880; see also attached note on unacceptability of general reservations.

means of facilitating ratifications inspired the presentation of these new methods of "conditional" ratification.

The most far reaching of the reservation proposals was that of Mr. De Michelis, the Italian Government Representative, who suggested the amendment of Article 405 of the Versailles Treaty (article 19 of the Constitution) in the following manner:

> "Members of the International Labor Organization who, on account of particular circumstances of whatever kind, find themselves unable to ratify a Draft Convention adopted by the Conference, but whose internal legislation is at the same time almost identical with the text of the Convention adopted, are authorized to deposit a conditional ratification with the Secretary-General of the League of Nations, at the same time forwarding an explanation of that decision.
>
> "The annual Conference will examine each year the conditional ratification deposited by the different Members. After considering the explanations presented by the Members concerned and also a report which will be prepared by a special committee, the Conference will decide whether the conditional ratification can be admitted as satisfactory. No appeal from the decision of the Conference will be admitted." [116]

The other reservations proposed were to be allowed within the framework of the Constitution. The Netherlands Government suggested that the Governing Body might be authorized to give members the right to ratify a convention with reservations; and, on the request of one-third of the members of the Body, the proposed reservation would be brought before the Conference, whose decision would be final.[117] The Swedish Government was in favor of allowing the Governing Body to decide the acceptability of reservations.[118] Finland suggested that all reservations be approved by two-thirds of the Governing Body.[119]

In its report to the Conference on these variations of the general method of making reservations to a convention, the Office pointed out the many legal objections involved. One major objection was the fact that to allow governments to make such reservations would be unfair to the employers' and workers' groups which had participated in the forming of a convention on equal footing with the government representatives. Moreover, this procedure would

---

[116] *Report on Amendment* (1924), 29.

[117] *Ibid.*, 70. [118] *Loc. cit.* [119] *Loc. cit.*

be contrary to the special stipulations of the Constitution,[120] which provides that non-government representatives shall take part in deciding any exceptions to conventions.[121] Furthermore, the Office was of the opinion that such a multiplicity of reservations would make against the standardization which it is the purpose of the Organization to promote, as well as to make it impossible for governments to know their exact obligations.[122]

One argument that was put forward in favor of allowing reservations such as those described above is that there is no prohibition of reservations in the Peace Treaty. The Office reply to this point of view was that, although the Treaty does not prohibit reservations, neither does it authorize them, and the clauses of the Constitution must be interpreted strictly and scrupulously observed.[123]

The Office made an interesting and seemingly valid observation concerning the effect of reservations on a convention. It stated that in practice, if general reservations were allowed, almost every state would make reservations to conventions, which would mean the suppression of certain articles in the text. This would bring about no change from the present system in this respect, as the Conference may allow reservations within the text of the treaty. Accordingly, ratifications would not be made easier by this procedure.[124]

In connection with the "supervisory function" vested in the Conference by virtue of Article 408 (Article 22 of the Constitution), the Office considered this important provision would be rendered practically impotent, in view of the varied character of reservations that would inevitably be made.[125] Furthermore, the supervision of so many different reservations, creating such uncertain obligations, would be an impossible task.

In concluding its objection to the general reservations proposed,

---

[120] Article 19, paragraph 3. This article provides for reservations under certain conditions, which should provide sufficient elasticity. For example, the Washington (Hours) Convention made reservations in favor of Japan, India, Greece and Roumania. *Ibid.*, 74.

[121] *Ibid.*, 72.

[122] The uncertain status of the obligations of a State making no reservations to a convention, which all other states had ratified conditionally, was also noted by the Office. *Loc. cit.* An excellent analysis of the question of reservations is given by C. Wilfred Jenks in "The Significance for International Law of the Tripartite Character of the International Labour Organization," *Transactions of the Grotius Society*, XII (May, 1936), 45-81.

[123] *Ibid.*, 73. [124] *Loc. cit.* [125] *Loc. cit.*

the Office comments that, although some of the proposals stipulate that the Conference as a whole would approve of reservations before they are acceptable, such a proposal will remedy neither the disparity of obligations between states nor the difficulties which would embarrass the functions necessitated by Article 408 (22).[126] The Office further defends its specific and general objections to reservations by asserting that the Conference may include in a convention a clause which will allow members (not named) to make certain exceptions to be determined by themselves.[127]

The British Government made a most unusual suggestion which it believed would facilitate ratifications. This proposal called for the insertion of a clause in the body of conventions providing that they should come into operation among specified members only after certain states had ratified them. According to this system, ratification would be subject to a conditional period, which would not terminate until all the states named in the convention had ratified.[128]

In the opinion of the Office, this method would have serious consequences; for, if one state failed to ratify the convention, such a method would nullify all the other ratifications, as the convention could not come into force for any of the ratifying states. This would also cause other legal difficulties. With only the existing procedure for the enforcement of standards, as soon as a state outside of the conditional group ratified the convention, it would come into effect for the ratifying states in the conditional group, which would make these states subject to the supervision provided for in Article 408(22) and the sanctions to be applied in case of the non-application of the terms of the convention.[129] Thus the legal difficulties resulting from this proposed clause would make its adoption impossible.

It appears that, if the conditions are specific, there are no legal objections to the type of "conditional ratification" procedure now utilized by the States Members of the International Labor Organization. However, every attempt made to formulate a reservation procedure which might affect the substance of conventions, the obligations of members, the uniformity of labor legislation, or

[126] *Ibid.*, 74.

[127] For example, the *Weekly Rest (Industry) Convention* adopted by the Third Session allows members to make total or partial exceptions, *ibid.*, 75.

[128] *Ibid.*, 76.

[129] The sanctions specified in Article 409(23), Treaty of Versailles.

the effectiveness of the supervisory and enforcing functions of the Organization has met with serious legal objections and consequently has failed to be adopted.[130]

[130] In 1925 the Director of the Office explicitly stated that ratifications with reservations are not considered valid by the Office, *I. L. C., Seventh Session*, 1925, II, Third Part, *Report of the Director*, 978.

CHAPTER V

THE FUNCTION OF INTERPRETATION

THE APPLICATION OF INTERNATIONAL STANDARDS

The general function of interpretation is for the parties concerned, whether they are bound by the instrument or are endeavoring to decide the meaning of the text for parties so bound, to "discover and effectuate" the purpose of the treaty.[1] There is no set method which may be used as an infallible guide to a correct interpretation.[2] The use of exact rules might make a valid interpretation more difficult to be arrived at and result in a misconception of the function of interpretation.[3] The process of interpretation cannot properly be a mechanical action. In many cases the framers of the instrument never envisaged the situations that have arisen in connection with the application of the treaty. Consequently, interpretation involves "giving" to the text a meaning which is the most likely meaning in the proper effect to be given the clauses in question.[4] Interpretation is usually necessary as a

[1] A concise statement of a general rule of interpretation in the draft convention may be found in the Harvard Research Draft on Treaties, Article 19, as follows: "A treaty is to be interpreted in the light of the general purpose which it is intended to serve. The historical background of the treaty, *travaux preparatories,* the circumstances sought to be effected, the subsequent conduct of the parties in applying the provisions of the treaty, and the conditions prevailing at the time interpretation is being made, are to be considered in connection with the general purpose which the treaty is intended to serve." *A. J. I. L.,* XXIX, 937.

[2] *Loc. cit.* There is wide difference of opinion among authorities concerning the importance that should be attached to the intention of the parties to a treaty in arriving at an interpretation. Two noted British publicists express the opposing sides to this controversy. Mr. Alexander Fachiri is of the opinion that the Permanent Court of International Justice depends on the text of the agreement and that this is the proper course to pursue. See "Some Observations on the Interpretation of Treaties," *A. J. I. L.,* XXIII (1929), 752. Mr. H. Lauterpacht believes that an examination of the "common intentions" of parties is one of the chief means of fulfilling the purpose of the law. See "Interpretation of Treaties," *Harvard Law Review,* XLVIII (1935), 591.

[3] See *A. J. I. L.,* XXIX, 946. An excellent argument against the use of hard and fast rules in interpretation is given in Tsune-chi Yu, *The Interpretation of Treaties,* 28.

[4] The following differentiation may be made between interpretation and application: "Interpretation is the process of determining the meaning of a

result of differences in connection with the application of a treaty; abstract interpretation is rarely practiced.[5]

The application and the interpretation of treaties are closely connected.[6] Before a treaty can be put into effect provisions of the text must be translated into practical measures. Necessarily, this must involve some measure of interpretation by the authority applying the text or a reference of the provisions in doubt to a body competent to decide the meaning of these provisions.

In a realm as diverse as that of international labor regulations any effort to apply uniform standards is subject to grave complications. The problem of the application of the text of a convention to a variety of conditions in a large number of states necessitates among other things a flexible interpretation of the provisions of the convention. The application of any legislative standard to a variety of cases is a delicate judicial or political problem, but in the instances of the application of international labor standards the difficulties are multiplied. The complicative factors pertain to geographical environment; social, economic, and legal systems; racial characteristics; varying industrial development, and labor organization.

The proper method of effectuating an application of international labor standards has not been settled by theory or practice. At various stages of its growth the International Labor Organization has been spoken of as setting up a code of international labor standards.[7] Whether this work constitutes an actual progressive codification of international labor law may be a matter of debate; nevertheless, the fact that efforts to apply general standards are being made is evidence of the practical significance of standardized application.[8]

---

text; application is the process of determining the consequences which, according to the text, should follow in a given situation." Comment on the Draft Convention of Treaties, *A. J. I. L.*, 29, 938.

[5] *Ibid.*, 939.

[6] *Ibid.*, 938. It has been stated in this connection that "Closely connected with the enforcement of treaties is their interpretation, often, in fact, to interpret is the very act of enforcement." J. M. Mathews, *American Foreign Relations*, 476.

[7] See *I. L. C.*, I (1920), 166; *International Labor Review*, I (1921), p. 17; *Official Bulletin*, I (1923), 282; and *I. L. C.*, I, *Proceedings* (1930), 15.

[8] See a complete discussion of this question by F. G. Wilson, *Labor in the League System*, 163-191, and by the same author in "The Enforcement of International Labor Standards," *Annals*, CLXVI (1935), 95-101.

The machinery for the enforcement of the provisions of ratified conventions is both political and judicial. The international judicial body acting in this regard is the Permanent Court of International Justice.[9] National courts in the states parties to labor agreements also apply interpretative rules to conventions.[10] The international political machinery for this purpose consists of the Governing Body, Office, and Conference of the Labor Organization and the Secretary-General of the League of Nations. The national bodies carrying these provisions into effect are the political departments of the various States Members of the Organization. The work of the Governing Body and the Conference in providing machinery for the discussion and coöperation necessary for the application of standards deserves special attention.

The Constitution provides ample machinery for the enforcement of the provisions of conventions;[11] nevertheless, in practice the only method employed to date is the requirement that members report the steps they have taken to fulfill their obligations. This procedure is set forth in Article 22:

> "Each of the Members agrees to make an annual report to the International Labour Office on the measures which it has taken to give effect to the provision of the conventions to which it is a party. These reports shall be made in such form and shall contain such particulars as the Governing Body may request. The Director shall lay a summary of these reports before the next meeting of the Conference."[12]

So far the annual reports have been a means of observing the application of conventions in the states that have ratified them; notwithstanding, the Organization has failed to take any positive action on the basis of ineffectual application as indicated by some reports.[13]

A recent indication of the growing interest in interpretation as a means of furthering the effective application of international standards is shown by the attention given the subject by the

---

[9] See *infra.*, Chap. VI, 150-155, for a discussion of the jurisdiction and practice of the Court.

[10] See *infra.*, Chap. VII, for a comparison of the practice in national courts.

[11] See Articles 22-34 of the Constitution; also see Chap. VIII, 206-211, *infra.*, for a more detailed discussion of application.

[12] *Constitution and Standing Orders.*

[13] See instances cited in chapter VIII, 207, *infra.*

Governing Body in 1933.[14] At this meeting the Governing Body requested the Committee of Experts (a special group which examines the reports made in compliance with Article 22) to prepare a statement showing the interpretation given to the scope of all conventions applying in a general way to workers in industrial undertakings. Whether this effort will be productive of results can only be determined in the future. At least it is a definite attempt to connect interpretation and application in a manner conducive to uniformity.

It appears that interpretation is essential to any valid application of a treaty. Without the proper interpretation a convention might possibly become something altogether different from what the makers of the instrument intended.

UNIFORMITY AS AN OBJECTIVE

The interpretation of conventions for the purpose of bringing about uniform application would seem to be a justifiable objective in respect to international labor legislation. The purpose of such legislation as seen particularly by the employers' group is to equalize competitive conditions among industrial states. While this view does not coincide with that of the workers, which is that the purpose of international labor legislation is to further social progress, both groups agree that a degree of uniformity is necessary before desirable results may be attained. The provisions of the Constitution concerning the application of conventions demonstrate the desires of the framers in this regard.[15] The efforts of the Organization in the general direction of uniformity are shown by the constant pleas of the workers and the Office for the cooperation of States Members toward this end.

In the beginning the prime purpose of the Organization was to bring about uniformity by securing a widespread ratification of the conventions drawn up by the Conference. It would appear that this objective has to some extent been modified. Modification has come about possibly in view of the fact that the States Members of the Organization have been less ready to ratify the agreements formulated than was at first anticipated.[16] It would also follow

---

[14] See *Minutes of the Sixty-fourth Session of the Governing Body* (1933), 338-339.

[15] See Article 22, *Constitution and Standing Orders.*

[16] In the first twenty-four sessions of the Conference a total of sixty-three conventions received eight hundred sixty-nine ratifications, March, 1940.

that the reluctance of states in ratifying conventions has slowed up the process of forming new conventions.[17] The result of this slackening of the "legislative" activity of the Conference has caused the Organization to devote more effort toward raising labor standards internationally through less tangible methods. One method used to bring about this end has been the emphasis of the Organization on the general raising of the standards of backward members to the level of those of the more progressive members.[18] At first the Organization made special recognition of conditions in states of retarded industrial development.[19] However, since 1921 these states have been unwilling to admit their backward condition, and the workers' group has opposed the placing of special arrangements for this purpose in conventions. This development has tended to further the uniformity of the provisions of conventions to which states may become parties. The experience of the committee on Article 22 has caused this body to state that "no ratification at all is better than a ratification which remains ineffective." [20] The point of view which supports this position is that whereas more "platonic" ratifications might result in a slight increase in moral prestige, the value of such acts is small in comparison with the "discredit" which they might bring on the general work of the Organization in the regard of those states which apply conventions "scrupulously." [21]

The valuable assistance which can be given toward assuring uniformity of international labor standards by interpretation is easily comprehensible. Any attempt to allow the application of a convention by a heterogeneous group of states without some interpretation of its provisions might possibly result in a different application in some essential respect in each ratifying state.

[17] An indication of this is shown by the fact that sixteen conventions were formulated at the first three conferences, while scarcely three times that number, forty-four, were agreed to at the next fifteen conferences. See a discussion of this aspect of the development by F. G. Wilson, *op. cit.*, 215.

[18] See remarks by members of the Governing Body in *Minutes of the Sixty-sixth Session of the Governing Body* (1934), *passim.*

[19] Provision for such exceptions is made in Article 19, paragraph 3, and Article 35 of the Constitution. For example, the *Hours Convention* made special provision for Japan, India, China, Persia, and Siam; see Articles 9, 10, and 11, *Draft Conventions and Recommendations*, 1919-1934.

[20] *I. L. C., Proceedings, Fifteenth Session,* 1931, I, Third Part (Appendices), 615.

[21] *Idem.* See also remarks of Mgr. Nolens (Netherlands), *I. L. C., Proceedings, Eleventh Session,* 1928, I, 291ff.

The desire to promote uniform interpretation has frequently been expressed by the units of the International Labor Organization concerned with problems of raising international labor standards. The great need of such uniformity has repeatedly been demonstrated by the reports of states on Article 408. Nevertheless, there has been some doubt as to the proper body to give the uniform meaning of conventions for this purpose.[22] The Conference has been generally held to be unqualified to give an opinion on questions of law. It has been suggested that the authority to give interpretations be delegated to the Committee of Experts, as they are qualified to render such service.[23] As yet this suggestion has met with little favor, and no action has been taken on the subject.[24] The Committee on Article 408 (22), in connection with its reports in 1933, stressed the necessity of uniform interpretation in connection with the proper application of a convention.[25] They were of the opinion that the proper application of a convention rested on the condition that the provisions which have to be applied are properly interpreted. If the meaning of the provisions is found to be different by the ratifying states, then the application of the convention will not be uniform, but will be to some extent contrary to the real intention of its provisions.[26] As a step toward overcoming the discrepancies of interpretation the committee on interpretation suggests the preparation of ". . . a simple statement, if possible in a tabular form, showing the interpretation given to the scope of all conventions applying in a general way to workers in industrial undertakings." [27]

The work of the Committee of Experts which functions in connection with the reports under Article 22 has tended to work toward uniformity of the application of conventions. The Governing Body appears to have generally favored a strict interpretation of

[22] See *I. L. C., Proceedings, Fifteenth Session,* I, 618; also II, *Report of the Director,* 5.

[23] *I. L. C., Fifteenth Session,* I, 619. The function of the Committee of Experts is to note the differences in interpretation without deciding what the right interpretation is. *I. L. C., Eleventh Session,* 1928, II, *Report of the Director,* 278.

[24] See *Report of the Director,* 1930, for a discussion of the function of the Committee of Experts. The Governing Body stressed the need of uniform interpretation in 1931, asserting that it was not competent to interpret but that the Conference was competent. *Minutes of the Fify-fifth Session of the Governing Body,* 1931, 181.

[25] See *Minutes of the Governing Body, Sixty-fourth Session,* 1933, 451.

[26] *Idem.*

[27] *Ibid.,* 452.

the Constitution, which has meant that the terms of Article 22 which only provide for a consideration of the reports of States Members cannot be made the basis of extending the functions of the investigation committee to the actual enforcement of conventions.

ADAPTATION AS AN OBJECTIVE

In the matter of setting up international standards that will be to some degree uniform as a means of furthering the social conditions of labor, the function of interpretation should serve to a great extent as a means of adapting the provisions of conventions to the circumstances in individual states. Without interpretation, efforts to adapt the terms of treaties to the particular situation might fail to satisfy the real purpose of the instruments. Such lack of the proper application of conventions would constitute a serious handicap to future international labor standards. In applying the provisions of bipartite instruments, it is essential that the parties concerned have an understanding of the principles involved and of the application of the provisions to be applied. The problem in respect to multipartite agreements is similar and consequently more intricate. In the formulation and conclusion of multipartite conventions differences of opinion often necessitate compromises which make obscure the meaning of the final text. This obscurity can be dispelled only by the *interpretive* opinion of some qualified body.

One problem in the adaptation of labor conventions may often arise which will make interpretation imperative. In the domain of labor regulation in states with varied degrees of development, conditions exist that make an exact application of the provisions of a convention impossible. The text provides no means for a more practical interpretation. The only resort in regard to the matter lies in the consultation of the body qualified to give an interpretation. Unless this is done the state in doubt in respect to the matter, if wishing to clear up the question in order to further ratification, will be unable to ratify; or, if desiring to apply the ratified convention, will be unable to do so in a manner conducive to any degree of uniformity. So it is evident that interpretation may substantially further both ratification and application.[28]

The International Labor Organization may learn of the failure of the adaptation of national legislation to the provisions of con-

[28] For examples of the opinions of the Office which have assisted ratification, see *infra.,* Chap. VI, 136-143.

ventions by a number of methods. An invocation of the investigatory machinery provided by the Constitution is one method[29] which has never been used. Another is by recourse to the Permanent Court of International Justice, a method so far utilized in but one instance.[30] The unofficial interpretations rendered by the Office do not serve in any way as authoritative precedents, but they point the way for proper state action.[31] In addition to these methods, the form reports handed in by States Members each year in compliance with Article (22) give some indication of what is actually being done to put legislation into effect.[32] The examination of these reports by both a general committee for the purpose and a committee of experts indicates a definite effort to attain a general idea of the manner in which conventions are being adapted.[33] The Committee of Experts which has been functioning since 1926 has no real power to interpret conventions or to criticize constructively their application; rather, its jurisdiction seems to extend only to an evaluation of the conformity between legislation and conventions.[34] In spite of the lack of authority of the committee in making forceful recommendations, its suggestions are in effect interpretive and possibly are instrumental in causing States Members to pass the proper legislation to make their obligations effective or to be more punctual in observing regulations already existing.[35]

---

[29] See Articles 23-24.

[30] See *infra,* Chap. VI, 157-164.

[31] See *ibid.,* 136-149.

[32] See Treaty of Versailles.

[33] The importance of the reports on Article 408 (22) was attested in 1931 by the following statement: "The Committee considers it desirable once more to call the attention of the Conference to the importance of the Annual reports supplied by the Governments. These reports are absolutely indispensable to enable the International Labor Organization to ascertain whether the states which have ratified conventions are effectively discharging the obligations incumbent upon them under these conventions." *I. L. C., Proceedings, Fifteenth Session,* I, Third Part, 614.

[34] The question of the competency of the Committee of Experts to interpret conventions was brought before the Governing Body in 1931. See *Minutes of Fifty-fifth Session of the Governing Body,* 182.

The Committee of Experts expressed its opinion on the adjustment of the work of the Labor Organization as follows: "This great advance in social solidarity and humanitarian ideals is not yet adjusted to the national consciousness of individual nations. The Committee confirms the opinion of the Committee on Article 408 to the Conference at its last two sessions, concerning the exact obligations resulting from the ratification of conventions. We are, however, working through a living international organism, founded on a spirit of active and voluntary collaboration," 672.

[35] Obviously, there is no method by which the influence of this group may be

The question of the extent to which labor conventions can be adjusted to the economic and social conditions of totalitarian states through interpretation is a matter of speculation.[36] However, if such adaptation can possibly be furthered by this method it will be of considerable value. The fact that with Russia's membership in the Labor Organization the problem of adaptation may become more difficult may cause the function of interpretation to be of greater importance. Yet it is doubtful whether the existing process of interpretation will be capable of rendering the contemplated service without a significant extension of the powers of the units concerned or the granting of sufficient authority to official bodies so that they may give the necessary interpretations.

SPECIAL CONSIDERATIONS IN THE LABOR FIELD

The place of interpretation in the realm of labor has been uncertain owing to the experimental nature of many phases of the work of the Organization. The developing concept of its work and the state of flux in which many of the agencies exist render any meticulous evaluation of the function of interpretation impossible. In spite of the impossibility of exactly determining the importance of interpretation to international labor regulations, the need of proper interpretive processes is possibly greater in this field than in any other.

One reason the function of interpretation has been of an indeterminate character in respect to international labor conventions has been due to doubt as to the bodies with the proper authority to give interpretations.[37] Obviously, there has been no doubt as to the competency of the Permanent Court of International Justice, as that is clearly stated in the Constitution.[38] Nevertheless, the States Members of the Organization have been hesitant in bringing matters in need of interpretation before the Court. Possibly this has been due to some extent to the formal proceedings incident to Court action. In view of the frequent need of the interpretation of some minor point of a convention, the

---

measured. See *Annual Reports,* under Article 408, of 1930, in which the Committee suggested that greater attention should be given to the practical application of national laws. *I. L. C., Proceedings, Fourteenth Session,* 1930, I, Third Part.

[36] At present, no totalitarian state is a member of the organization. However, as long as this type of state exists, it will be necessary to consider its role in reference to international labor standards.

[37] See *supra,* Chap. I, "Bodies Competent to Interpret."

[38] *Loc. cit.*

Permanent Court is scarcely the most convenient organization to which an ordinary appeal should be made. Some believe that the Governing Body should give interpretations, others the Conference or the Committee of Experts which reviews the reports under Article 408 (22). None of these views has been received with sufficient favor to be put into practice. In a measure, this need for interpretation has been filled by the unofficial statements by the Office concerning the provisions in question.[39] Yet, as the opinion is unofficial, its value is not equal to that of a body qualified to give authoritative interpretations. However, it appears that as long as the Governing Body adheres to the point of view that no unit of the Organization may make interpretations (as the Constitution does not give them specific authority to do so), the function of interpretation will be as limited as it is at present.

In the interpretation of some treaties the ratifying states often reach agreements between themselves as to the meaning of provisions in doubt. This simple method of clarification may not be utilized for this purpose by members of the International Labor Organization, as labor conventions are not the result of state action. In the making of conventions representatives of employers and workers share equally with state representatives in arriving at the final decisions. Accordingly, if the states were given the sole authority to reach agreements as to interpretation, the result would be to give them more power than they should legally have.[40] This unusual character of labor conventions makes the process of interpretation a difficult one.

Another special factor in the field of labor is the action of national courts in the interpretation of conventions. Unlike the subject matter of some international instruments, labor questions are universally subject to many different types of courts.[41] Thus labor matters may come before administrative officials, conciliatory bodies, special industrial courts, or the regular courts of law. For example, in Germany (under the Weimar Constitution) the position of the Federal Minister of Labour in respect to applying

[39] See *infra,* Chap. VI, "Interpretation by the Office."

[40] It appears that a method of interpretation along these lines might be feasible. Such a procedure would provide for a decision concerning agreements of individual states on interpretations to be arrived at after consultation and approval of the most representative employers' and workers' group.

[41] See *International Survey of Legal Decisions on Labour Laws* (hereafter cited as *International Survey*), 1926. Introduction.

labor law was of special importance.[42] He might issue administrative orders or decrees which had the force of law. Of course, his application of labor laws was only a part of the machinery of interpretation,[43] as there are numerous types of courts which interpret.[44] Boards of conciliation, which settle some labor questions in England, use methods of procedure which are quite different from those followed in the regular law courts.[45] In France there is as yet no clear distinction between industrial law and other types of law. This means that the bodies which interpret may apply a variety of principles.[46] This diversified treatment is necessarily the cause of many conflicting opinions arrived at by so many different methods. One result of this variance is the complication of the function of interpretation.

The interpretation of conventions is possibly of greater importance in bringing about the ratification of international labor conventions than it is in the field of ordinary treaties. In the instance of the usual multilateral instrument, the signatory states

---

[42] The following statement attests the position of administrative authorities in Germany: "Administrative authorities of the Reich and of the States come in contact in different respects with questions of labour law. This relates in particular to the authorities of industrial police and supervision. The position of the Federal Minister of Labour is of special importance. He supervises the execution by the States of the labour laws enacted by the Reich. His instructions and directions are decisive for the administrative practice of the Federal authorities placed under him. Numerous laws of the Reich delegate to him the right to issue executory decrees having the force of law. He has the right to declare collective agreements binding. He has a dominating position in conciliation procedure." See *International Survey,* 1932, xxx. The important changes occurring in the administration of labor law under the Third Reich are described by Taylor Cole, "National Socialism and the German Courts," *Journal of Politics,* III (May, 1941), 169-197.

[43] See an instructive discussion of "The Administration of Labour Law in Germany," by Hugo Siefart, *International Labor Review,* XV (May, 1927), 684-708.

[44] See *supra,* Chap. I, 17-18.

[45] In north England boards exist under the Arbitration Act of 1889. They are composed of employers and workmen. H. C. Gutteridge, "The Interpretation and Administration of Labour Laws in England," *International Labor Review,* X, no. 2 (August, 1924), 229.

[46] For example, in France trade union self-government is not protected from judicial interference as it is in England. However, collective agreements are protected and treated as judicially enforceable contracts. "The Sources and Interpretation of Labour Law in France," by Paul Pic, P. Garraud, and Edouard Lambert, *International Labor Review,* XIV, no. 1 (July, 1926), 9.

ratify on the recommendation of their representatives without any great need for any opinion as to the meaning of the provisions by any international authority. Also in many cases resort to external authorities for an interpreation is impossible, as such authorities do not exist. A different situation exists in regard to the submission of conventions adopted by the International Labor Conference to the competent national authority, for this act is compulsory, and the States Members often desire an interpretation of the text of agreements prior to taking action. They may wish an explanation of the meaning of a passage in order to see whether their existing legislation will conform to the international instrument. If the national legislation is in accordance with the terms of the convention, immediate ratification will follow; otherwise, ratification may be delayed until legislation can be passed to conform to the convention.[47] An additional cause for a need of interpretation of labor conventions prior to ratification lies in the fact that a state considering action in regard to a convention may not have been present at the Conference when the agreement was formulated and therefore may not be aware of the meaning of the convention in the minds of the framers. These conditions concerning ratification give an added importance to the function of interpretation in the labor field.[48]

The nature of the subject matter of labor conventions often necessitates a careful interpretation of their provisions. This is due to the fact that many conventions contain technical stipulations which may be difficult to adjust to the conditions in certain circumstances.[49] The existence of technical terms usually indicates that a careful application is desired. If more general terms are used, the party to the instrument might feel authorized to proceed in a discretionary manner. Consequently, as there seems to be no opportunity for the state to make an exception unless it is explic-

[47] Some states ratify prior to the passage of suitable legislation, hoping that the necessary legislation will soon follow. These states have been severely criticised by the committee on Article 22: See *I. L. C., Proceedings, Seventeenth Session,* 519. See also condemnation by committee on Article 22 (408) of "window dressing" and emphasis on strictly legal character of conventions, *I. L. C., Proceedings, Fifteenth Session* (1931), 615.

[48] See the large number of requests for interpretations for the purpose of ratifying conventions in chapter VI, "Interpretations by the Office," *infra.* It should be noted at this point that interpretation may likewise serve a similar purpose in respect to certain other conventions which contain technical subject matter.

[49] See Chap. III, "Technical Questions," *supra.*

itly granted in the terms of the convention, it is necessary that an interpretation be requested of the proper authority. Thus the need for such interpretations often occurs in connection with international labor regulations.

The special recognition given by the International Labor Organization to the industrial conditions in backward regions may make the function of interpretation of labor agreements more difficult than it would otherwise be.[50] This recognition is in the form of the non-application of some of the provisions of conventions to stated areas, or the extension of the length of time when the provisions of conventions may come into effect.[51] The existence of these exceptions means that the problem of interpretation is likely to become extremely complicated. In general, the workers' groups deny that any necessity for such exceptions exists. Consequently, they press for the discarding of the special conditions at the earliest possible moment. In addition to this factor, the Asiatic States have refused to admit that their industrial conditions are in a backward state as compared with those of other States Members. These attitudes, coupled with the lack of definite attempts by the Organization to enforce the obligations of conventions, makes satisfactory interpretation a difficult task.

The application of conventions to colonies constitutes a problem somewhat similar to that just previously considered. No adequate method of measuring application exists. In the future there may possibly be an increasing demand for the raising of standards in respect to these areas either through interpretation or by new agreements concerning the special conditions.

The need in respect to interpretation in the field of labor has not changed appreciably since it was clearly stated in 1921 by Mr. Albert Thomas, the Director of the Office, as follows:

> "The articles of a convention are drafted with the intention on the one hand, of securing an equivalent standard and on the other of allowing for national differences of industrial organization and method. It is therefore necessary that there should be some means whereby the elasticity which is properly allowed by any given Article can be authoritatively defined. Any such

[50] Article 19, paragraph 3, and Article 35 of the Constitution state that exceptions shall be made in the instance of backward regions.

[51] For example, the hours convention of 1919 makes special provision for Japan and India, and does not apply to China, Persia, and Siam. *Draft Conventions and Recommendations.*

definition of application which is permissible as regards any given Article cannot, however, be regarded as a question for one country only. The convention as a whole and each Article of it is negotiated by the International Labor Conference and is the joint product of its effort. The whole of the International Labor Organization therefore is interested in and may be affected by the interpretations which are given to the instrument which it has created. The intentions of the Conference might be entirely falsified if each country were obliged to interpret the Articles of the convention for itself because there was no authority whose advice it could seek." [52]

[52] See *I. L. C., Third Session*, 1921, *Report of Director*, 117. At that same time the Director believed that the Governing Body should create a "body of jurisprudence," and that it should interpret, 118.

Chapter VI

INTERPRETATION BY INTERNATIONAL BODIES

INTERPRETATION BY THE OFFICE

THE NEED for some method of assisting states in arriving at a uniform interpretation and application of certain indefinite provisions in the texts of conventions and recommendations has been obvious since the first Conference of the International Labor Organization. The only method provided for in Part XIII of the Peace Treaty (the Constitution) was that of last resort to the Permanent Court of International Justice. The use of this legal method was too complicated and too far removed from the needs of practical situations to be utilized in meeting the numerous requests for the clarification of texts of conventions.[1] The refusal of the Governing Body to lend its services in this regard left the burden of responsibility with the Office. The Office has taken the position that, although it does not have the authority to give official interpretation to agreements made by the Conference, it is in a position to examine the records and documents of the meetings of the Conference and of its various commissions, and is thereby frequently able to assist governments in the elucidation of doubtful points.[1a] In giving this unofficial interpretation the Office early pointed out that it could not change the significance or scope of decisions of the Conference. This viewpoint was expressed in the Official Bulletin as follows:

> "These decisions are the result of prolonged discussions among the three groups of interests represented, and from the agreement in which these exchanges of opinion have resulted it does not appertain to the International Labor Organization to depart by either weakening or strengthening the texts. Its only function must be to furnish every explanation as to the real sense of these texts, and, when there is room for doubt, to give an interpretation by making use of every indication which may help."[2]

[1] One reason for the failure of states to utilize the court is the fear of endangering relations with states cited for violations.

[1a] See *Official Bulletin,* III, no. 13 (1921), 7.

[2] *Ibid.,* 389; see also *Report of the Director,* 1921, 56-57, and *Report of the Director,* 1925, 978.

A recent examination of the method of unofficial interpretation by the Office resulted in the approval by the Governing Body of the recommendation of the Standing Orders Committee to the effect that no change should be made in the present exercise of this function.[3] This action apparently evidences the usefulness of the service rendered by the Office.[4]

In forming an opinion as to the application of a convention the Office has generally proceeded according to the following lines: first, the Conference proceedings in which the convention in question was framed are examined, and secondly, the records of the commission or committee which reported on the subject of the convention are examined.[5]

LIBERAL INTERPRETATIONS FAVORABLE TO STATES MEMBERS

In advancing its unofficial opinion in respect to passages of conventions referred to by states in their requests the Office has exercised due caution. The general position it has taken has been referred to above. In rendering interpretative advice on a convention the Office has recognized its limitations and has been careful not to overstep its bounds.

A number of governments have expressed doubts as to the proper interpretation of the draft convention on *Hours of Work (Industry)* adopted in 1919. In 1920 the Swiss Government requested an opinion of the International Labor Office as to the application of the operative provisions of the convention to small trades and industries in "rural and mountainous" districts.[6] In the request for assistance from the Office the Swiss Government expressed the belief that a liberal interpretation would be of assistance in the application of the convention. The Office gave a careful, detailed reply to this request. This reply was based on the text of the convention, the discussions at the Conference, the preparatory work of the Organizing Committee, and the decision of the Committee on Hours of Labor.[7] As a result of this examination the Office found that most of the exceptions desired by the Swiss Gov-

---

[3] *Official Bulletin,* XVII, no. 4 (1932), 156.

[4] See argument in support of this method of interpretation in *Official Bulletin,* XII, no. 1 (1927), 38.

[5] See *Official Bulletin,* VI, no. 7 (August 16, 1922).

[6] See letter from Swiss Department of Public Economy, March 6, 1920, in *Official Bulletin,* III, no. 13 (1921), 387.

[7] *Ibid.,* 388.

ernment could be allowed, although, where possible, the government should endeavor to make the hours in the small industries in the regions referred to conform with the terms of the convention.[8]

At approximately the same time the Swiss communication was received by the Office the German Government asked the Office whether the term in the Hours Convention "work essentially intermittent" applied to certain groups of workers, i.e., porters, foundry workers, and seasonal workers.[9] The German Government wished to have the point in question clarified before the convention was brought before the competent legislative authorities for consideration. The reply of the Office indicated that it was the term in question applied to the categories of workers listed above but that the use of this method of application was discretionary and should not be abused.[10]

In 1928 the Office again interpreted the *Hours of Work (Industry)* Convention, 1919, so as to allow the inquiring state discretion in determining its application. In this instance certain owners of confectioneries and tea rooms in Luxemburg contended that their establishments were not covered by the term "industrial undertakings" but that they were commercial in nature.[11] The government of Luxemburg was not sure of the proper classification of the establishments in question. In replying to the communication on this matter the Office pointed out that the last paragraph of Article 1 of the convention provided that "the competent authority in each country shall define the line of division which separates industry from commerce and agriculture." Accordingly, Luxemburg could decide as it desired in this matter.[12]

---

[8] This was true of Articles 1, 2, 3, 4, 5, 8, 10 of the agreement; however, Article 6, concerning transportation and communication, could not be exempt as continuous operations, and Article 9 was given no exact interpretation. *Ibid.*, 399-404.

[9] See letter of Ministry of Labour, Germany, to Director, *ibid.*, 405.

[10] *Ibid.*, 406. During this same year the German Government made another request concerning the spread-over of the weekly shift in the Hours Convention, to which the Office replied by citing tables of detailed statistics to illustrate the shift spread. See *Official Bulletin*, III, no. 14 (1921).

[11] See letter of the Director-General of Social Welfare and Labour, Luxemburg, to Director of the International Labor Organization, *Official Bulletin*, XIV, no. 2 (1929), 58.

[12] *Ibid.*, 59. The Office also referred to legislation in effect in neighboring states which followed this provision.

It is instructive to note that the Office held that the *Recommendation concerning the Limitation of Hours in the Fishing Industry* did not apply to fish

The extent to which the proper application of a convention may be determined by a State Member was indicated by the Office in its answer to a query of the Norwegian Government concerning whether a government should have freedom of judgment in hiring personnel for maritime employment offices.[13] The Office believed that the government might have a certain freedom in deciding whether an individual was qualified, although his training did not exactly correspond to that provided for in the convention.[14]

The conventions on the employment of young persons were the source of a variety of requests. In 1921 the Office, in reply to a letter from the German Ministry of Labor asking whether there should be a "widening or limiting" interpretation of certain exceptions in the draft convention concerning the *Night Work (Young Persons) Employed in Industry* (1919), stated that a "widening" interpretation should be applied.[15] This interpretation applied particularly to continuous processes in connection with the manufacture of iron and steel.[16]

The Netherlands Government addressed a communication to the Office concerning the *Minimum Age (Industry) Convention*, 1919.[17] The substance of this request was as to the applicability of the term "work done in technical schools," [18] to work performed in actual industry as complementary to theoretical instruction. The Office replied that the term "technical schools" had been given no definition, but rather that ". . . the persons responsible for drafting the convention left their meaning to be interpreted by each State Member in the manner which might appear to it to be the most suitable—but the education must be equivalent—approved and supervised by public authority." [19] Consequently, if the Netherlands Government decides that children under the age limit pro-

---

preserving in the unorganized fish industry. See *Official Bulletin,* III, no. 18, 1-4.

[13] The convention in question, which was concluded at Genoa in 1920, concerned the establishment of facilities for finding employment for seamen. See *ibid.,* no. 21, 14-15.

[14] *Loc. cit.*

[15] See *ibid.,* no. 23, 26-28.

[16] *Loc. cit.* This decision was reached only after careful consideration of the record of the preparatory work.

[17] See *Official Bulletin,* XII, no. 1 (1927), 35-36.

[18] Article 3 of convention, *loc. cit.*

[19] *Ibid.,* 39. The Office explained that this view was confirmed by certain annual reports under Article 408 (22). See *I. L. C.,* II (1924), 1076.

vided for in the convention may receive training in industry, such action is not a contravention of the terms of the agreement.

In 1926 the Netherlands Government informed the Office that it could not ratify the convention concerning the age for the admission of children to employment in agriculture, as it was not certain that the section questioned applied only to children obliged to attend school under national laws.[20] The Office was of the opinion that the convention applied only to children who came under the compulsory school age.[21] This interpretation made the convention dependent on the application of national laws.

The ratification of the convention fixing the minimum age of admission of children to employment at sea was delayed by the French Government until the Labor Office interpreted certain articles of the convention to determine whether they applied to fishing vessels.[22] The reply of the Office was to the effect that the convention did not apply to fishing vessels. This conclusion was directly based on resolutions of the Conference adopting the convention and the Conference held the year following its adoption.[23] Thus according to this opinion there was no obstacle in the path of ratification by the French Government.

The convention concerning *Night Work (Women)*, 1919, which was interpreted in such a varied manner that it was finally necessary to revise it, was the source of a request by a representative of the Finnish Government as to the possibility of working two shifts in the hours prescribed by the convention.[24] The Office was

[20] *Official Bulletin,* XII, no. 2 (1927), 90-94. Article 1, to which the Netherlands Government referred, was as follows: "Children under the age of 14 years may not be employed or work in public or private agricultural undertaking, or in any branch thereof, save outside the hours of school attendance, and this employment shall not be such as to prejudice their attendance at school."

[21] Reports under Article 408 (22) were cited by the Office to prove this contention, *loc. cit.*

[22] Article 2 of the convention states: "Children under the age of 14 years shall not be employed or work on vessels other than vessels upon which only members of the same family are employed." Article 1 of the convention says this covers all craft excluding ships of war; see *Official Bulletin,* XIII, no. 2 (1928), 69.

[23] A resolution adopted at the Genoa Conference (Fourth Sitting) stated "that fishing vessels shall not be dealt with by this conference, and that it be a recommendation that each nation shall legislate nationally for men employed in the fishing industry and that each Government call into consultation representatives of employers and workers." *Ibid.,* 72. The same view was taken by the 1921 Labor Conference. See *Proceedings,* 73.

[24] *Official Bulletin,* XIII, no. 1 (1928), 19-21. The hours were 6 a.m. to 11 p.m.

of the opinion that the preparatory work in connection with the convention indicated that two shifts should not be allowed.[25]

The manner in which the Office indicates some conventions are intended, in so far as possible, to harmonize with the general spirit of national legislation is demonstrated by its reply in regard to the scope of the convention concerning *Workmen's Compensation (Occupational Diseases)*, 1925.[26] The government of South Africa was uncertain as to the application of the phrase "work in connection with animals infected with anthrax." Did this apply to agricultural workers who burned the dead bodies of such animals? The Office answered this question in the negative for two reasons: (1) since South African legislation does not cover agriculture, the workers would be excluded from the convention's scope, for the general obligation is that compensation is payable "in accordance with the general principles of the national legislation relating to compensation for industrial accidents"; (2) Article 2 of the convention provides that only occupations covered by national legislation are under the convention.[27]

The subject of the regulation of the use of white lead in painting to avoid poisoning has been difficult to apply. In 1927 the Swiss Government wrote to the Office to get an opinion on what seemed to be a discrepancy between the French and English texts.[28] The Office reconciled the seeming inconsistency by explaining that the use of the term "*peinture decorative*" in the French text meant the same as "artistic painting" in English and that such work was excepted from the prohibition concerning white lead.[29] The Office also held in a later interpretation that the scope of the convention did not apply to pottery works.[30]

The interpretation by the Office of the convention concerning *Night Work (Bakeries)*, 1925, following a request by the govern-

---

[25] *Loc. cit.* Two shifts were not sanctioned by the office, as an amendment allowing such was defeated by the conference committee.

[26] See *ibid.*, no. 2, 73-74.

[27] *Loc. cit.*

[28] See *ibid.*, no. 1, 29.

[29] The Office referred to its Blue Report no. XI, 1921, on the subject which defined the scope of the articles in question, 1, 11, and 111, *ibid.*, 30.

[30] See *Official Bulletin*, XV, no. 2 (1930), 34-36, in which request of the Italian Government and the reply of the Director is given. See also comment on the application of the convention in *Official Bulletin*, VI, nos. 8-9, 327-333. For liberal interpretations of the *Recommendation concerning the Protection of Women and Children against Lead Poisoning*, see *Official Bulletin*, III, no. 16 (1921), 15-18, and no. 17, p. 14.

ment of South Africa is evidence of its desire to see conventions applied in a practical fashion.[31] Article 3(b) of the convention allowed exceptions to the provisions of the convention in "tropical countries" for climatic reasons. The Secretary of Labour of South Africa believed that the article providing for such exceptions was justified in some parts of South Africa. In replying to the request on this matter the Office discovered that the term "tropical countries" had not been used in a strict sense when this convention or other conventions concerning hours were framed. Therefore, it held that the proper course would be to allow exceptions where the climate is hot and the benefits from night work will accrue to the workers.[32] Another question which arose in connection with this convention concerned the determination of the proper employers' and workers' organizations to be consulted in case of exceptions to the convention. Also, the question was brought up whether the agreement between these two representative groups need be unanimous.[33] The opinion of the Office was that the governments must decide the representative groups on the basis of existing facts, and the same method must be followed in respect to unanimity or majority decisions.[34]

The interpretation of the *Minimum Wage Fixing Machinery Convention*, 1928, in 1929 exhibited the extent to which a liberal, practical application of an agreement could make it possible for a state to ratify it.[35] The Secretary for Labor of South Africa was in doubt as to whether his government could ratify the convention mentioned above, as no legislative provisions were in force concerning compulsory associations of employees and employers.[36] In the absence of such legislation the Secretary stated that the authority of the executive would be exercised. The Office replied to

[31] See *Official Bulletin*, XIII, no. 2 (1928), 75-78.

[32] *Loc. cit.* It is pointed out by the Office that in discussing the convention on *Night Work of Young Persons Employed in Industry* Brazil and India were regarded as "tropical," although in the strictest sense they are not.

[33] *Official Bulletin*, XIV, no. 2 (1929), request of Czechoslovakia, 60-61.

[34] The Office stated that the general rule was "that decisions are valid if they are adopted by a majority"; the reply of the Office also pointed out that the preparatory work of the convention offered no solution. *Ibid.*, 62-63.

[35] See *ibid.*, 64-65.

[36] Article 3, section 2, of the convention provided: "The employers and workers concerned shall be associated in the operation of the machinery in such manner and to such extent, but in any case in equal numbers and on equal terms, as may be determined by national laws and regulations."

this communication by pointing out that the term "in such manner and to such extent" would permit ratification without legislative regulations.[37]

The provisions in some conventions could be interpreted in such a manner that they would cause considerable difficulty, delay, and general inconvenience to the state applying them. It has not been the practice of the Office to interpret conventions in a manner that would so inconvenience states. The convention concerning the *Equality of Treatment of National and Foreign Workers as Regards Workmen's Compensation for Accidents* is an agreement which, if given a technical interpretation, would bring about unnecessary complications.[38] In 1928 the Minister of Social Welfare of Czechoslovakia requested the opinion of the Office concerning the use of the term "special arrangements" in the convention.[39] The representative of the government of Czechoslovakia did not believe that a special convention was necessary to carry out the provisions of the convention, but rather that if a special arrangement could be made to facilitate the transfer of funds the purpose of the convention would be fulfilled. The Labor Office supported this interpretation, noting that the purpose of the use of the term "special arrangements" in the convention was only to deal with the difficulties in the transfer of funds.[40]

In 1931 the Polish Government prepared to ratify the convention concerning *Hours of Work (Commerce and Offices)*, 1930, but hesitated until it could get an unofficial interpretation of Article 10 of the convention.[41] The sections in question were, first, that nothing in the convention ". . . shall affect any custom or agreement whereby shorter hours are worked or higher rates of remuneration are paid than those provided by this convention," and that "Any restrictions imposed by this Convention shall be in

[37] *Loc. cit.*

[38] See *Official Bulletin*, XIII, no. 1 (1928), 24. The official short title of this convention is *Equality of Treatment (Accident Compensation) Convention*, 1925.

[39] Article 1 of the convention provided that: "This equality of treatment shall be guaranteed to foreign workers, and their dependents without any condition as to residence. With regard to the payments which a Member or its Nationals would have to make outside that Member's territory in the application of this principle, the measures to be adopted shall be regulated, if necessary by special arrangements between the Members concerned," *loc. cit.*

[40] *Ibid.*, 24-25. The Director of the Office referred to preparatory work of the Conference in support of this view. See *I. L. C.*, 1924, II, 564-571.

[41] See the letter of the representative of the Polish Government accredited to the League of Nations in *Official Bulletin*, XVIII, no. 1 (1932), 48-49.

addition to and not in derogation of any other restrictions imposed by any law, order, or regulation which fixes a lower maximum number of hours of employment or a higher rate of remuneration than those provided by this convention." [42]

The Polish Government believed that two interpretations of this section were possible. The first interpretation would require the ratifying state to alter shorter hours or higher rates in force. The second interpretation would make Article 10 an interpretative rather than an operative clause.[43] The Office interpretation coincided with the second view of the Polish Government, holding that the article should be applied so as not to impose upon states an obligation to maintain conditions superior to those for which the convention calls.[44] This decision on the matter made the application of the convention possible for the ratifying state.

The practical value of unofficial interpretation by the Office is demonstrated by the method used by the Irish Free State in 1929 to determine whether its existing practice in respect to the convention concerning the *Application of the Weekly Rest in Industrial Undertakings* fulfilled the provisions of the convention.[45] The Irish Minister of Industry and Commerce presented a memorandum to the Office showing the regulations in force in regard to the subject. The Office was of the opinion that the exceptions allowed by the Irish Free State were valid, as such exceptions could be allowed according to the provisions of the convention if governments made them after consultation with workers' and employers' organizations.[46]

STRICT INTERPRETATION LIMITING STATES

In giving unofficial interpretations concerning the meaning of conventions the International Labor Office has not hesistated to construe the texts of conventions in such a manner that the discretion of the state has been limited.

An early interpretation by the Office regarding the convention concerning *Unemployment*[47] was requested by the Norwegian Gov-

---

[42] *Loc. cit.* [43] *Ibid.*, 50-52.

[44] The Office letter cited discussions in *I. L. C., Fourteenth Session*, I, 458-459, to support this interpretation, *ibid.*, 50-52.

[45] *Official Bulletin*, XIV, no. 9 (1929), 124.

[46] *Ibid.*, 125.

[47] See letter from the Royal Department for Social Affairs, Norway, to the International Labor Organization, November 18, 1920, *Official Bulletin*, III, no. 14, 9.

ernment. The inquiring state believed the reciprocity provisions pertaining to unemployment insurance should apply only to certain aliens whose parent states granted like reciprocity to Norwegian nationals. According to this interpretation the local authorities should be allowed to decide the specific application in particular cases. In the reply of the Office, the opinion was expressed that any discriminatory practice in respect to any nationals should be abolished. The Office held that the chief purpose of the convention was to provide for reciprocity agreements between member states in order to facilitate payments for insurance.[48]

In 1930 the convention concerning the *Marking of Weight (Packages Transported by Vessels)*, 1929, was the subject of a restrictive interpretation by the Office.[49] The Swiss Government was in doubt as to the meaning of the term "the country from which the package or object is consigned." [50] The doubt concerned whether the original state alone consigned the package or whether it was reconsigned by the state through whose territory the package was passing. In reply to this inquiry the Director of the Office stated that it was ". . . clear that this obligation can be assumed only by the State in the territory of which the consignment is made —the obligation to see that this requirement is observed shall rest solely upon the Government of the country from which the package or object is consigned, and not on the Government of a country through which it passes on the way to its destination." [51] This interpretation of the text of the convention left no choice to the states concerned.

The difficulty encountered by the Swedish Government in the proper application of Article 6 of the convention concerning *Workmen's Compensation (Accidents)*, 1925, is illustrative of the different interpretations that may be placed on a convention in the absence of specific stipulations.[52] The Swedish Government representative gave three possible interpretations as to the time of the payment of compensation: (1) compensation due as from the fifth day after the accident, the day of the accident not included; or (2) at the latest as from the sixth day after, the day not included; or (3) at the latest as from the fifth day, the sixth

[48] *Ibid.,* 10. See also interpretation of Hours Convention by the Office by reference to statistical tables in *ibid.,* 4-7.

[49] See *Official Bulletin,* XV, no. 4 (1930), 153.

[50] Article 1 of this convention.

[51] *Ibid.,* 154-156.

[52] See *Official Bulletin,* XV, no. 4 (1930), 150.

day included.[53] In reply to these projected interpretations the Office set aside No. (2) as the text used the term fifth day in a restrictive sense. However, the Office was of the opinion that the preparatory work of the convention offered no solution or exact definition as to whether the day of the accident should be included in the payment of compensation. Neverthless, the Office concluded that while the first interpretation would be legally passable the third would be more desirable as the term "not later than" would seem to indicate that the fifth day should be included in the payment of compensation.[54] This interpretation meant that the text of the convention was to be applied restrictively.

Mr. de Michelis, Italian Government Representative, addressed a letter to the Office in 1930 requesting an interpretation of the terms "poisoning" and "sequelae" as used in Article 2 of the convention concerning *Workmen's Compensation (Occupational Diseases)*, 1925.[55] He wished to know whether these terms covered only "clinical forms" or all diseases. In the reply of the Director of the Office it was pointed out that the French definition of "sequelae" in preparation of the convention would not apply to indirect consequences. However, it would cover clinical forms and morbid developments which might arise as the direct consequence of poisoning.[56]

In interpreting the word "woman" as used in Article 2 of the convention concerning the *Employment of Women Before and After Childbirth*,[57] the Office declared that ". . . reference to the text of the Convention reveals no mention of the exclusion of women whose salaries exceed a certain figure." [58] This left no discretion in the matter to the states party to the convention.

In reply to the question of whether or not exceptions could be permitted in undertakings not concerned with iron and steel with a different type of furnace than that stipulated in the convention concerning the *Night Work (Young Persons)*, 1919,[59] the Office

[53] *Loc. cit.* [54] *Ibid.*, 150-151.

[55] See *Official Bulletin*, XV, no. 2 (1930), 36-38. [56] *Loc. cit.*

[57] See letter from Mr. de Michelis, representative of the Italian Government on the Governing Body of the International Labor Office, to the Director of the International Labor Office, Rome, January 12, 1930, *Official Bulletin*, XII, no. 2 (1930), 31.

[58] The Director stated that the preparatory work did not refer to salary, *ibid.*, 32.

[59] See request of the Belgian Minister of Labor and Social Welfare, *Official Bulletin*, XVI, no. 1 (1930), 30-31.

10

stated that the exceptions which may be permitted are enumerated in the second paragraph of Article 2 and consequently, "According to the principles which should underlie all correct legal interpretation, any enumeration of exceptions to the general rule is always limitative and must be interpreted restrictively." [60]

The German Government delayed submitting the convention concerning the *Hours of Work* (*Commerce and Offices*), 1930, for ratification by the competent legislative body owing to doubt in respect to a certain provision in the convention.[61] The section in question was Article 1, paragraph 3, which states, "It shall be open to the competent authority to exempt from the application of the Convention . . . (b) Offices in which the staff is engaged in connection with the administration of public authority." The position of the German Government was that all civil service workers were in the above-mentioned category. The interpretation of the Office was contrary to this position; it held that the term "public authority" referred to those "engaged in the administration of public authority," or to those entitled to give orders in the name of the state.[62] The Office was of the opinion that the duties of the position and not the function should determine the line which should be drawn. This opinion further pointed out that according to the German interpretation whole public staffs would be excluded from the application of the convention, and this would obviously be contrary to the scope of the convention.[63]

---

[60] To support this contention the Director cited a passage from a report in the preparatory work on the convention as an example, *ibid.*, 32-33.

[61] See letter from Minister of Labor of the Reich to the Director, August 29, 1932, *Official Bulletin*, XVII, no. 3 (1932), 118.

[62] The view of the Office was supported by the definition of the scope of Article 1, which is as follows: "(1) This convention shall apply to persons employed in the following establishments, whether public or private:

(a) Commercial or trading establishments including postal, telegraph and telephone services, and commercial and trading branches of any other establishments;

(b) establishments and administrative services in which persons employed are mainly engaged in office work;

(c) Mixed commercial and industrial establishments, unless they are deemed to be industrial establishments.

The competent authority in each country shall define the line which separates commercial and trading establishments, and establishments in which the persons employed are mainly engaged in office work, from industrial and agricultural establishments."

[63] In this connection the Office pointed out that in the 1930 Conference an

The convention concerning the *Employment of Women Before and After Childbirth* stipulates that women within the scope of the convention "as an additional benefit shall be entitled to free attendance by a doctor or certified mid-wife." [64] The French Government requested the opinion of the Office as to whether their existing social insurance legislation would satisfy this requirement. This legislation provided for maternity benefits which amounted to less than free medical attendance.[65] In answer to the request the Director of the Office pointed out that there could be no exceptions or reservations to the convention and that the existence of a system of social insurance did not in any way diminish the "very definite obligation" of free attendance of doctor and mid-wife.[66]

CLAUSES OF DOUBTFUL MEANING

For various reasons the Office has occasionally declined to give any unofficial interpretation to certain clauses. In a request made by the Swiss Government and discussed above, the Office replied that it would not give an opinion in regard to Article 9 of the convention on the *Hours of Work (Industry)*, 1919, as it had no exact information on the subject matter on which to base an opinion.[67]

In other instances the Office has declined to give definite interpretations to certain clauses of conventions. This position was taken by the Director following a request by the Finnish Government in 1928.[68] This request concerned the *Seamen's Articles of Agreement Convention*, 1926. Finnish legislation stated that an agreement could only be terminated in a port of Finland if the seamen were nationals. The convention provided for termination in any port where the vessel loads or unloads.[69] Hence there appeared to be a definite discrepancy between the convention and the legislative provision. The Office noted this difference and referred to Article 405 of the Constitution of the International Labor Or-

---

amendment was proposed that would include the staff of certain public services in the list of exceptions, but it was defeated. *Ibid.*, 123.

[64] Article 3(c).

[65] See *Official Bulletin*, XVII, no. 1 (1932), 39-40.

[66] *Ibid.*, 40-42. The Office reply also noted that other states allow free service.

[67] *Official Bulletin*, III, no. 13 (1921), 17.

[68] See *Official Bulletin*, XIII, no. 1 (1928), 27.

[69] *Loc. cit.* Finnish legislation conflicted with Article 9, paragraph 3, of the convention.

ganization, which provides that a convention shall not lessen protection.[70] Nevertheless, the Office believed that the question was difficult and delicate for it to decide.[71]

In interpreting doubtful texts of conventions the Office has in each case prefaced its opinion with an emphatic explanation of its position as an interpreter. This explanation has made clear the fact that any opinion rendered by the Office is distinctly unofficial and has no legal force.

Generally, the purpose of the requests for interpretation received by the Office from States Members has been of a two-fold nature. A large number of the requests were for clarification of particular clauses in order that ratification might be facilitated. Many other opinions were asked of the Office to assist the states in the application of conventions to the circumstances in their respective jurisdictions.

The majority of the opinions expressed in the replies of the Office have been construed liberally in respect to the obligations of the requesting state. This construction has allowed the States Members to proceed in the ratification or application of the convention. In reading the texts of conventions in a liberal manner the Office has supported this point of view by the existing practice in other states, the preparatory work in framing the convention, and the general purpose of the document. Whether or not the abundance of liberal interpretations has to any extent resulted from a desire for more widespread ratification is difficult to determine from the evidence. It appears, however, that the Office has supported its point of view in each case with substantial evidence.

In giving interpretations which limit the discretionary application of conventions by States Members, the Labor Office has attempted to avoid lessening the protection of workers. In instances where the phraseology is explicit and where the exceptions are enumerated, the Office has not hesitated to give a limitative reading of the text.

There have been only a few cases in which the Office has refused to express an opinion on the text of a convention. The examples

---

[70] This section of the article, which is the final paragraph, states: "In no case shall any member be asked or required, as a result of the adoption of any recommendation or draft convention by the conference, to lessen the protection afforded by its existing legislation to the workers concerned."

[71] *Ibid.*, 28.

concerned clauses of doubtful meaning owing to ambiguity or to inexact information on the subject concerned.

THE GOVERNING BODY

Early in the history of the International Labor Organization certain States Members, desiring to know to what extent they were bound by certain clauses and how existing legislation would meet the provisions of conventions, applied to the Office for interpretations. The Director replied that he was not authorized to give official interpretations,[72] but that possibly the Governing Body could give authoritative, official opinions.[73] This suggestion by the Director was not acted on by the Governing Body, and the interpretation of conventions has been limited to unofficial opinions by the Office.

In 1923, when efforts were being made to formulate a plan whereby the ratification of conventions could be facilitated, certain states proposed that the Governing Body be authorized to interpret conventions.[74] One suggestion stipulated that the only appeal from a decision by the Governing Body should be to the Conference.[75] The Belgian Government made a vigorous objection to this proposal. This objection was based on the belief that no proper procedure of interpretation by the Governing Body could be instituted.[76] Any official interpretation, in the opinion of the Belgian Government, should be made by the Conference, as there were not a sufficient number of jurists on the Governing Body to render a valid interpretation.[77]

The point of view of the Office on the subject of interpretation by the Governing Body was expressed in 1924 as favorable to such action. The Office was of the opinion that under the authority of the Constitution the Governing Body might make decisions corresponding to those which would be taken by a legal body.[78] These decisions, according to the Office, would not be handed down in cases where an actual dispute had arisen, but would rather,

[72] See *supra.*

[73] *I. L. C., Third Session,* 1921, *Report of the Director,* 57.

[74] These states were Japan, Netherlands, Norway, Sweden, and Switzerland; see *I. L. C., Sixth Session,* 1924, *Report on Amendment,* 77.

[75] See suggestion of the Netherlands Government that the Governing Body be allowed broad judicial powers, *ibid.*

[76] *Ibid.,* 80.

[77] *Loc. cit.*

[78] This opinion is based on the provisions of Articles 23, 24, and 25. *Ibid.,* 81.

"only have the weight of an advisory opinion."[79] This opinion could be based partly on the various opinions of States Members, and it would express the general opinion of the Organization on the subject in question.[80]

The desire of the Office for official interpretation by the Governing Body was not fulfilled. After a decade of abstention from giving official opinions, the position of the Governing Body has remained unchanged. In 1931 the Director stated that there was "still some uncertainty as to the competent body for giving authentic interpretations," and that "it is now being generally recognized that only the Permanent Court is competent to give an official interpretation of conventions."[81]

There is no accurate way of determining whether or not the lack of official interpretations has been detrimental to the progress of international labor legislation. Nevertheless, it appears that some of the uncertainty surrounding the meaning of some conventions could have been mitigated by an official interpretation from a body to which access could have been obtained without great difficulty.[82]

THE PERMANENT COURT OF INTERNATIONAL JUSTICE

The Constitution of the International Labor Organization, (Part XIII of the Treaty of Versailles and corresponding articles in the other treaties of peace) provides that the Permanent Court of International Justice shall determine questions concerning labor conventions, in the following words:

---

[79] *Ibid.*, 82.

[80] *Loc. cit.*

[81] *I. L. C., Fifteenth Session*, 1931, II, *Report of the Director*, 5. See also *Minutes of the Fifty-second Session of the Governing Body*, 1931, 443, in which unofficial interpretation by the Office is approved.

[82] This point of view is expressed as follows by Mr. Kaufmann (Government Adviser, Switzerland), Reporter on Article 408 (22): "A third very important point considered by the Committee is the question of interpretation. The committee points out that the legal situation is quite clear, in view of the terms of Article 423 of the Treaty of Versailles, which provides for the possibility of resort to the Permanent Court, but from the practical point of view the position is not so satisfactory because we still find that certain provisions of conventions are differently interpreted in different countries. In cases of this kind the Committee can merely discuss the question, and has no power to impose solutions. It is therefore necessary to find some way of overcoming the persistent discrepancies between legislation and conventions." *I. L. C., Proceedings*, 1933, 411.

> "Any question or dispute relating to the interpretation of this Part of the present Treaty or of any subsequent convention concluded by the members in pursuance of the provisions of this Part of the present Treaty shall be referred for decision to the Permanent Court of International Justice." [83]

This stipulation definitely places international labor conventions within the jurisdiction of the Court. Nevertheless, there are certain limitations on the jurisdiction of the Court in respect to international bodies. Article 34 of the Statute of the Court states that "only States or members of the League of Nations can be parties in cases before the Court." [84] International organizations may not be parties to a dispute before the Court. The Court may allow such organizations to furnish information under Article 73 of the rules of the Court.[85]

As to the access of parties to the Court,[86] it would appear that any state may probably have access.[87] The parties eligible to present questions to the Court may do so in virtue of provisions in the League Covenant and the Revised Statute of the Permanent Court. It is provided in Article 14 of the Covenant that a dispute of an international character may be submitted to the Court; or there may be a reference by the Council or by the Assembly of a dispute or questions for an advisory opinion.[88] Article 36 of the Statute of the Court provides four sources of the Court's jurisdic-

[83] Article 37. In case States Members fail to put into effect the provisions of conventions to which they have agreed under Article 405 the question involved may be referred to the Permanent Court for final decision under Articles 29 and 30.

[84] *P. C. I. J.*, Series D, no. 1.

[85] See *ibid.*, 1931 Rules, Article 73. The text as adopted in 1922 provided for notice to Members of the League and "to the States mentioned in the Annex to the Covenant." *P. C. I. J.*, Series E, no. 1, 250, 263. In 1926 this phrase was changed to "any States entitled to appear before the Court." The 1922 text contained a second paragraph: "Notice of such request shall also be given to any international organizations which are likely to be able to furnish information on the question." This paragraph was suppressed in 1926; at that time there was some discussion as to the nature of the "international organizations" which might be considered, but as the Court could decide the proper bodies when the occasion to do so arose, there appeared to be no need for a specific definition. See *P. C. I. J.*, Series D, no. 2, 224-225, 237; also Series E, no. 8, 273-274. See also Manley O. Hudson, *The Permanent Court of International Justice*, 287.

[86] The term "parties" refers to recognized states. See Hudson, *op. cit.*, 354, for a discussion of eligible states.

[87] *Loc. cit.*

[88] Treaty of Versailles.

tion: (1) reference by parties; (2) special provisions in "treaties and conventions in force"; (3) declarations recognizing jurisdiction "as compulsory *ipso facto* and without special agreement"; and (4) the section which gives the Court competence to decide disputes of its own jurisdiction. Article 37 further provides that "when a treaty or convention in force provides for the reference of a matter to a tribunal to be instituted by the League of Nations the Court will be such tribunal." [89]

We are particularly concerned here with the advisory opinions of the Permanent Court, as they represent the only form of interpretation so far recorded in respect to the International Labor Organization.

The basis of the advisory jurisdicion of the Permanent Court is Article 1 of the Court Statute, which in effect is incorporated in the provision of Article 14 of the Covenant.[90] The nature of advisory jurisdiction was provided for in the revision of the statute under the Revision Protocol of September 14, 1929. This revision incorporated into the statute the procedural provisions already existing in the Rules of the Court, and Article 68 stipulated that "in the exercise of its advisory functions, the Court shall further be guided by the provisions of the Statute which apply in contentious cases to the extent to which it recognizes them to be applicable." [91]

A request for an advisory opinion may be presented to the Court either by the Council or the Assembly of the League of Nations. The usual channel for the request is the Council.[92] This request

---

[89] This provision is of special importance to labor conventions, as they contain such a stipulation. For a discussion of the general limits on the Court's jurisdiction, see Hudson, *op. cit.*, 364-368.

[90] See *P. C. I. J.*, Series A, no. 6, 21, and Hudson, *op. cit.*, 433. For a general survey of the question of advisory opinions, see M. O. Hudson, "Advisory Opinions of National and International Courts," *Harvard Law Review* CXXXVII (1930), 475. A special treatment of the subject is given in Hudson, "The Advisory Opinions of the Permanent Court of International Justice," *International Conciliation Bulletin*, no. 214 (1925), 321-375.

[91] See Statute of the Court. In respect to the nature of advisory opinions Hudson says: "Whatever course might have been taken, the actual discharge of its advisory functions by the court has always been kept within limits which characterize it as a judicial function, and the court itself has conceived of the function as a judicial one." *The Permanent Court of International Justice*, 435. See also *P. C. I. J.*, Series B, no. 13, 23.

[92] An attempt was made in 1920 to procure for the Governing Body and the

may, according to Article 14 of the Covenant of the League, be "upon any dispute or question." [93]

The Director of the International Labor Office attempted early in the life of the Organization to get special arrangements for disputes before the Court in connection with labor conventions.[94] He was in favor of the election of certain judges who were experts on labor legislation and the representation of workmen and employers on the Court when labor cases were heard. Another proposal before the League Committee considering the subject provided for a special chamber of five judges to be assisted by four assessors who should act in an advisory capacity.[95] The article finally adopted provided for a small chamber of judges and assessors:

> "Labour cases, particularly cases referred to in Part XIII (Labour) of the Treaty of Versailles and the corresponding portions of the other Treaties of Peace, shall be heard and determined by the Court under the following conditions:
>
> "The Court will appoint every three years a special chamber of five judges, selected so far as possible with due regard to the provisions of Article 9. In addition, two judges shall be selected for the purpose of replacing a judge who finds it impossible to sit. If the parties so demand, cases will be heard and determined by this Chamber. In the absence of such demand, the Court will sit with the number of judges provided for in Article 25. On all occasions the judges will be assisted by four technical assessors sitting with them, but without the right to vote, and chosen with a view to ensuring a just representation of the competing interests.
>
> "If there is a national of one only of the parties sitting as a judge in the Chambers referred to in the preceding paragraph, the President will invite one of the other judges to retire in favor of a judge chosen by the other party in accordance with Article 31.

Conference of the International Labor Organization the right to request an opinion from the Court; this effort failed. Hudson, *The Permanent Court,* 436.

[93] See the following pages, *ibid.,* for further discussion of advisory opinions: necessity for the Court to comply with a request for an opinion, 446-447; form of requests provided for in Article 72, 448-449; composition of the Court in advisory proceedings, 454; legal force of advisory opinions, 455-456.

[94] See *Records of First Assembly of the League of Nations,* Committee I, 557-565.

[95] See *ibid.,* 361, 394, 398. The statement was made in the committee that labor disputes might present features "not of an exclusively legal character."

"The technical assessors shall be chosen for each particular case in accordance with rules of procedure under Article 30 from a list of 'Assessors for Labour Cases' composed of two persons nominated by each member of the League of Nations and an equivalent number nominated by the Governing Body of the Labour Office. The Governing Body will nominate, as to one-half, representatives of the workers, and, as to one-half, representatives of employers from the list referred to in Article 412 of the Treaty of Versailles and the corresponding articles of the Treaties of Peace.

"In Labour cases the International Labour Organization shall be at liberty to furnish the Court with all relevant information, and for this purpose the Director of that Office shall receive copies of all written proceedings." [96]

The special chamber provided for in this article has been regularly constituted and assessors have been named.[97] As no case has been tried before the special chamber so far, its effectiveness cannot be gauged.[98]

In rendering the numerous decisions and advisory opinions during its brief history, the Permanent Court has formulated a number of general canons of interpretation. The Court defines its duty as being ". . . . to interpret the text as it stands, taking into consideration all the materials at the Court's disposal." [99]

---

[96] Article 36, *P. C. I. J.*, Series D, no. 1.

[97] For a general comment on this article and the appropriate action to be taken by the Labor Organization, see *I. L. C., Fourth Session*, 1922, II, *Report of Director*, 744-745. In this report a list of the assessors to participate in Labor Cases is given, 745-749. See also a memorandum presented by Sir Montague Barlow on the views of the British Government on representations before the Court, 750. The special labor chamber appointed at the first meetings of the Court consisted of Lord Finlay, President; MM. de Bustamente, Altamira, Anzilotti, and Huber, Judges; MM. Nyholm and Moore, Deputy Judges.

[98] See request sent to League Members asking nomination of assessors, *Official Bulletin*, IV, no. 14 (October, 1921), 278. Shortly after this request the Council asked the Court to give an opinion as to the rules in choosing assessors, *Official Bulletin*, IV, no. 26 (December, 1921), 542. For an excellent discussion of the problems that might arise in the choice of assessors, see Hudson, *The Permanent Court*, 328.

The record of the appointment of the members of the chamber for labor disputes for the period beginning January 1, 1934, and ending December 31, 1936, is given in *Minutes of the Sixty-fifth Session of the Governing Body*, 1934, 119.

[99] *P. C. I. J.*, Series A/B, no. 44, 40. The extent to which the Court has filled its proper function is attested by one writer as follows: "The members have

In interpreting conventions the Court has placed emphasis on the "plain," "clear," or "natural" meaning of texts.[100] Generally, the Court has held that if the text is sufficiently clear it will not consider preparatory work.[101] In instances where the text is not clear, the Court has relied on the aim and spirit of the convention.[102] The Court has not hesitated to interpret agreements in a sense that would restrict the sovereignty of states.[103]

The Permanent Court has given six advisory opinions concerning the International Labor Organization. These opinions have constituted the sum of the Court's interpretations in regard to the work of the Labor organization, as no contentious case has yet come before the Court.[104] Four of the Court's opinions have involved an interpretation of the Constitution (Part XIII of the Treaty of Versailles); the sixth and last alone concerns a con-

---

recognized their true function not as the application of principles of general justice, nor the discussion of theories, but the more properly judicial function of finding what the treaty makers have actually done." R. R. Wilson, "The Interpretation of Treaties" (Contributions of the Permanent Court of International Justice to the Development of International Law), *Proceedings of the American Society of International Law*, 1930, 45.

[100] See comments by Yi Ting Chang, *The Interpretation of Treaties by Judicial Tribunals*, 29-39; C. C. Hyde, "The Interpretation of Treaties by the Permanent Court of International Justice," *A. J. I. L.*, XXIV, no. 1, 1-19; R. R. Wilson, "The Interpretation of Treaties," *loc. cit.* See also oral argument in *P. C. I. J.*, Series C, no. 3, I, 197-198.

[101] See A. Fachiri, "The Interpretation of Treaties," *A. J. I. L.*, XXIII (1929), 745-752.

[102] This was the decision in connection with the *Thirteenth Advisory Opinion*, Series A/B, no. 19; in this case the Court referred to the object of the International Labor Organization as stated in the preamble. See also *P. C. I. J., Eighth Judgment*, Series A, no. 9.

[103] See *P. C. I. J., Sixteenth Judgment*, Series A, no. 23; see also Series B, *Advisory Opinion*, no. 10.

[104] The opinions are as follows: *Nomination of Netherlands Delegate at the Third Session of the International Labor Conference, P. C. I. J.*, Series B, *Advisory Opinion*, no. 1, July, 1922 (see also Series C, no. 1); *Competence of the International Labor Organization as to Agricultural Labor*, no. 2, August 12, 1922; *Competence of the International Labor Organization as to Methods of Agricultural Production*, no. 2, August 12, 1922; *Competence of the International Labor Organization to Regulate, Incidentally, the Personal Work of the Employer*, no. 13, July 23, 1926 (see also Series C, no. 12); *Free City of Danzig and International Labor Organization*, no. 18, August 26, 1930 (see also Series C, no. 18); *Interpretation of the Convention of 1919 concerning Employment of Women During the Night*, no. 50, November 15, 1932 (see also Series C, no. 60).

vention brought into force by the International Labor Organization.

The first question before the Court in regard to labor related to the interpretation of Article 389 (3) of the Constitution. This article states the conditions under which delegates may be nominated to the Labor Conference.[105] The Court held that the word "representative" as used in Article 389 did not necessarily refer to a single organization. Rather it was of the opinion that the most representative body might be the most numerous group of workers who were members of several labor organizations. The Court was also of the opinion that the duty of deciding which group should send a delegate to the Conference was the function of the government.[106]

The second and third advisory opinions handed down by the Court pertained to the competence of the International Labor Organization in respect to agriculture. The Court stated in the second opinion that, although Part XIII did not refer to agriculture as such, the treaty should properly be read as a whole, and its meaning should not be determined merely from particular phrases, which, if detached, might be interpreted in more than one sense.[107] Consequently, it found the relevant portions of the treaty clear enough to establish the competency of the Labor Organization in regard to agricultural workers.[108] In the third advisory opinion, which concerned the subject of production in agriculture, the Court held that the competence of the Organization did not extend to such a general economic question.[109] The Court based

[105] The section of this article (paragraph 3) which was questioned is as follows: "The members undertake to nominate Non-Government Delegates and advisers chosen in agreement with the industrial organizations, if such organizations exist, which are most representative of employers or workpeople, as the case may be, in their respective countries." Article 389, Treaty of Versailles.

[106] *P. C. I. J.*, Series B, no. 1, 9-27. For details concerning the opinion see *Official Bulletin*, VI, no. 7, 291ff.

[107] See *P. C. I. J.*, Series B, no. 2. The Court held that the word "industriel" might be applied to agriculture, 35. For a detailed discussion of the subject see "Agriculture and the International Labor Organization," *The International Labour Review*, VII, no. 4 (April, 1923), 642-648.

[108] The Court was of the opinion that "construction of text itself" fixed the competence of the Organization and that there was no need of referring to the preparatory work, as the text was clear. See in this connection "Additional Observations," by M. de Lapradelle, *P. C. I. J.*, Series C, no. 1, 182, 187-189.

[109] *P. C. I. J.*, Series B, no. 3. The question before the Court was, "Does exami-

this opinion on the rule that it must depend on the construction to be given treaty provisions.[110] In the words of the Court, "the organization and development of the means of production are not committed to the Organization," but rather only the incidental effect on production is within the competence of the International Labor Organization.[111]

The Thirteenth Advisory Opinion of the Permanent Court also related to the competency of the International Labor Organization. It concerned the incidental regulation of the work of the employer by the Organization. The Court took a position in regard to the matter similar to that taken in the Second Advisory Opinion, interpreting the text of the treaty (Part XIII) in the light of the whole instrument. The conclusion of the Court was that the competence of the Organization did extend to the question involved.[112]

The opinion requested of the Court by the International Labor Office as to whether or not the Free City of Danzig was eligible to membership in the Labor Organization laid down no new principles of interpretation.[113]

The first interpretation of an international labor convention was in regard to the convention of 1919 concerning *Night Work (Women)*.[114] This convention had been the source of much discussion and criticism prior to the advisory opinion of the Court. In 1931 an attempt to revise the section causing the difficulty resulted in failure.[115] The passage which aroused the controversy was Article 3: which is as follows:

---

nation of proposals for the Organization and development of methods of agricultural and of other questions of like character fall within the competence of the International Labor Organization?" (49).

[110] *Ibid.*, 53. Mr. C. Wilfred Jenks, assistant legal adviser, carefully examines the opinions presented before the court and concludes that the argument of M. de Lapradelle, representing the French Government, was historically unsound. See "La Competence de L'Organisation Internationale du Travail examen de quatre avis consultatifs rendus par La Cour Permanente de Justice Internationale," *Revue de droit international et de legislation comparée,* XVIII, Troisième Serie, no. 1 (1937), 166.

[111] *P. C. I. J.*, Series B, no. 3, 53.

[112] *P. C. I. J.*, Series B, no. 13, 22.

[113] *Ibid.*, no. 18. The decision was that Danzig was not eligible to membership.

[114] *P. C. I. J.*, Series A/B, no. 50, November 15, 1932.

[115] See *supra,* 57-59, for a description of the background of the convention, see also *P. C. I. J.*, Series C, no 60, 161-182.

> Women without distinction of age shall not be employed during the night in any public or private industry, or in any branch thereof, other than in an undertaking in which only members of the same family are employed.

The British Government interpreted this article as meaning that women could not be employed in positions of supervision or management. Other states believed that the article applied only to manual workers. Consequently, His Majesty's Government suggested to the Governing Body that the section in question be referred to the Permanent Court for an advisory opinion.[116] After much discussion of the question the Governing Body decided to forward to the Council of the League of Nations a request for an opinion on the question raised by the British communication.[117] In accordance with this letter the Secretary-General of the League of Nations sent an official request to the Registrar of the Permanent Court.[118]

Following the receipt of the request the Court asked four international organizations to furnish relevant information on the subject in question.[119]

---

[116] See letter of British Government to the chairman of the Governing Body for an advisory opinion in *Minutes of the Fifty-seventh Session of the Governing Body,* April, 1932, 349; also see comment of the Office, 350. See text of the convention in *Draft Conventions and Recommendations* (1919-1934), 24-33.

[117] *Ibid.,* 216. See letter from Director of International Labor Office to Secretary-General of League, *P. C. I. J.,* Series C, no. 60, 11. At this meeting of the Governing Body a request for an opinion by the Court on the question of whether the convention applied to salaried employees was presented by the German Government (see 215). This request was delayed until the Fifty-eighth sitting, and at that time was set aside for more careful study. The result was that no ultimate action was taken to bring the question before the Court; see *Minutes of the Fifty-eighth Session of the Governing Body,* April, 1932, 395-401. For a complete statement of the request see Appendix III, 406-407.

[118] *P. C. I. J.,* Series C, no. 60, 9.

[119] These organizations were the International Labor Organization, International Federation of Trades Unions, International Organization of Industrial Employers, and International Confederation of Christian Trades Unions, *P. C. I. J.,* Series A/B, no. 50, 369. In Series C, no. 60, the written statements of the interested groups are given as follows: the statement of the International Labor Office in which the Office assumes a neutral position in regard to the question, 161-182; the written statement of His Majesty's Government (under Article 73 of the Rules of the Court) giving its position and the positive opinion that the convention applies to workers in "supervisory" positions, 182-187; the exposition of the German Government which sets forth its position on the matter, 187-189; the opinion of the International Confederation of

On October 14, 1932, oral statements were heard before the Court.[120] The first statement was that of Mr. Phelan, representing the International Labor Organization.[121] He stated that the Organization approached the subject impartially; noting ". . . the existence of differing interpretations of the convention . . . it deplores these differences . . . and it appears before the Court with the one object of facilitating the adoption of a solution of the problem which will be legally satisfactory." [122]

The Labor Office representative called attention to the significance of the precedent which the decision in the case would create. He examined in detail the different groups of conventions and estimated the effect of a decision in this case on each group. The basis of this grouping was the definite nature of the convention.[123] The conventions that contained references to persons who were incapable of being defined exactly would, in the opinion of Mr. Phelan, fail to be affected by any opinion the Court might render in the present case.[124] The second type of agreements were those in which the field of application was defined with precision.[125] The definiteness of the terms of this group makes it extremely unlikely that difficulties of interpretation similar to those in regard to the convention being considered will arise. Nevertheless, Mr. Phelan pointed out that the majority of conventions were in the same group as that of the agreement being considered. The scope of the conventions of this class is defined in a more or less general way, and so difficulties of interpretation are liable to arise frequently.[126] Mr. Phelan called the attention of the Court to the

---

Christian Trade Unions, 189-196; and the memoirs of the International Federation of Trade Unions, 196-198.

[120] The members of the Court were as follows: MM. Adatci, President; Guerreo, Vice-President; Baron Rolin-Jacquemyns, Count Rostworowski, MM. Fromageot, Anziolotti, Urrutia, Sir Cecil Hurst, MM. Shücking, Negulesco, Jhr. Van Eysinga, Judges, *P. C. I. J.*, Series A/B, no. 50, 365.

[121] See *ibid.*, 207-215.

[122] *Ibid.*, 208.

[123] He was of the opinion that if the text contained no detailed definition (most conventions do) that "it will be legitimate to consider the purpose of a convention in order to determine its scope," *ibid.*, 212.

[124] He pointed out that there were only a few conventions in this class, and that the convention on the subject of the marking of weight on heavy packages was an example. *Ibid.*, 213.

[125] This group is composed of less than ten conventions: an example of the type is the seamen's articles of agreement, *loc. cit.*

[126] According to Mr. Phelan, *loc. cit.*, this group contained twenty conventions.

large number of conventions in the last group which would be affected by the opinion in the present case. In this connection, he stated that "A mechanical uniformity of interpretation is neither necessary nor desirable, but the opinions of the court carry such weight that the decision given in this particular case is certain to have a very definite influence upon the interpretation of all Labour Conventions." [127] In his final remarks to the Court of Mr. Phelan recalled that in interpreting conventions the International Labor Office had always attempted to observe two principles, "(1) That of not stretching the scope of a convention beyond the limits set by the text and by common sense; and (2) that of taking care not to diminish, by admitting unnecessary qualifications, the benefits which the workers are entitled to expect the convention to secure for them." [128]

Following this excellent presentation of the circumstances concerned in the case by Mr. Phelan, Mr. Alexander Fachiri, counsel for the British Government, gave an exposition of the position of His Majesty's Government.[129] He pointed out in the beginning of his discourse that following the present interpretation of the convention by his government, women managers and supervisors could not work in England.[130] In addition to this existing difficulty the British counsel made reference to three allegedly more serious dangers that might arise. The first of these was the fear that, if conventions were differently interpreted and applied by States Members, the purpose of the Constitution, Part XIII, which he said was the uniform application of labor standards, would be defeated. Secondly, if this convention was not held to apply to women in positions of supervision and management, other exceptions might be expected in regard to labor conventions generally. Lastly, if the principles applied to the construction of this convention favored exceptions to the text, this would have an undesirable effect on the construction of all labor conventions and other international agreements.[131]

In regard to the actual interpretation of the convention, Mr. Fachiri stated that the relevant article (Article 3) was "absolutely plain, clear, and free from ambiguity." [132] He asserted that those

[127] *Ibid.*, 214.

[128] *Ibid.*, 215.

[129] See *ibid.*, 215-237.

[130] *Ibid.*, 216.

[131] *Loc. cit.*

[132] *Ibid.*, 218. Mr. Fachiri read from various articles of the convention to demonstrate the text was not inconsistent. See 217.

who believe the convention does not apply to supervisors and managers base their view on the historical interpretation, holding that the Berne Conventions apply only to manual workers and that by the principle of succession the Washington Convention should do likewise.[133] Mr. Fachiri stated that his government did not depend on "extraneous documents" in interpreting conventions but rather was governed by the text of the convention. He was of the opinion that unless this course were followed the door would be left open "to every kind of inequality and evasion." [134] Furthermore, Mr. Fachiri regarded preparatory work as incapable of consideration, when the text was clear, although in the preparation, of the convention in question the subject under consideration had not been directly mentioned.[135] The British counsel rested his appeal with the Court by predicting that all treaties would be adversely affected if the Court decided contrary to the position of the British Government.[136]

The point of view of Mr. Fachiri was supported by other oral arguments before the Court.[137]

The Permanent Court made clear in the beginning of its advisory opinion that ". . . the wording of Article 3, considered by itself, gives rise to no difficulty; it is general in its terms and free from ambiguity or obscurity." [138] The Court further stated that there was nothing in Article 3 which was inconsistent with the preamble or other provisions of the convention.[139] Therefore, it con-

[133] *Loc. cit.*

[134] *Ibid.*, 219-220. The British counsel refers to the case above relating to the Territorial Jurisdiction of the International Commission of the River Oder. *P. C. I. J.*, Series A, no. 23, 19-22.

[135] He cites in support of this statement the *Mosul Case, P. C. I. J.*, Series B, no. 12, 22-23; the *Lotus Case*, Series A, no. 9, 16; and the *Danube Case*, Series D, no. 14, 31. See *P. C. I. J.*, Series A/B, no. 50, 221.

[136] *Ibid.*, 236.

[137] Dr. Feig, representing the German Government, presented difficulties similar to those of Great Britain. Also, respect for the actual text of the convention was demanded by Mr. Serrarens, representing the Confederation of International Christian Syndicates.

[138] Series A/B, no. 50, 372. The exact question presented to the Court was: Does the Draft Convention Concerning the Employment of Women During the Night, Adopted in 1919 by the International Labor Conference, apply in the industrial undertakings covered by the said Convention, to women who held positions of supervision or management and are not ordinarily engaged in manual work?" 373.

[139] *Loc. cit.*

cluded that the proper question to be considered was whether there were other grounds for restricting Article 3 to manual workers. After examination of the possibilities of restrictions in Part XIII (the Constitution), the Court concluded that it was not the purpose of the authors to limit conventions so as to apply to manual workers alone.[140] In this connection the Court cited other advisory opinions on the competency of the Labor Organization which demonstrate the breadth of its authority.[141] Accordingly, the Court was of the opinion that "To justify the adoption of a rule for the interpretation of Labour conventions to the effect that words describing general categories of human beings such as 'persons' or 'women' must *prima facie* be regarded as referring only to manual workers it would be necessary to show that it was only with manual workers that the Labor Organization was intended to concern itself." [142]

The Permanent Court discarded as invalid the contention that the convenion in question was intimately connected with the Berne Conventions.[143] After emphatically stating that in examining the preparatory work of the convention it was not deviating from its adopted rule of not considering such evidence when the text is clear, the Court declared that its examination disclosed no facts that would lead to a conclusion contrary to the plain text of the convention.[144] The opinion of the Court likewise referred to the specific provision in which the *Hours of Work (Industry) Convention,* 1919, adopted at the same time as the agreement in question which stipulated that it should not apply to supervision, management, or confidential capacity. The Court believed that if a limitation had been intended in the convention being considered it would have been provided for in the text.[145]

The final decision was:

> "For these reasons the court by six votes to five, is of opinion that the convention concerning the Employment of Women During the Night, adopted in 1919 by the Interna-

[140] *Ibid.,* 374.

[141] The advisory opinions cited are Nos. 2 and 3 of August 12, 1922, and no. 13 of July 25, 1926.

[142] *P. C. I. J.,* Series A/B, no. 50, 375. The Court cites the use of different terms in the preamble: "travailleurs," "workers," "work people," "travailleurs salaries," and "wage earners."

[143] *Ibid.,* 377. See comment of Hudson, *The Permanent Court,* 554.

[144] *Ibid.,* 379-380.

[145] *Ibid.,* 381.

tional Labor Conference, applies, in industrial undertakings covered by the said convention, to women who hold positions of supervision and management and are not ordinarily engaged in manual work." [146]

One of the dissenting judges, M. Anzilotti, rendered a vigorous opinion. In his opinion the chief thesis of the majority opinion was unfounded in view of the fact that Article 3 was not clear, for "the subject and aim of the convention" had to be ascertained before the text could be considered in its true relation.[147] Mr. Anzilotti stressed the allegation that Part XIII had for its object the regulation of the employment of "manual workers" (ouvriers), and that the task of regulating the work of "travailleurs" was "secondary" and "incidental." [148] He further cited sections from the Peace Treaty which would seem to prove this contention.[149] To Judge Anzilotti the express purpose of Part XIII was the regulation of the work of manual laborers, and any inference extending this purpose must be proved.[150] Accordingly, that purpose linked with the aim of the Berne Convention and the intention of the authors of the 1919 convention as evidenced by the preparatory work formed the basis of the vigorous dissent.[151]

The decision of the Court in this opinion was rendered on grounds that were arrived at by the general canons followed by the Court in its preceding interpretations. The caution of the Court in relying on the preparatory work relevant to the subject being considered was characteristic of its attitude when it believes a text is clear.

The advisory opinion on *Night Work (Women) Convention, 1919*, assisted in the clarification of a passage which was the source of conflicting interpretations. The legal interpretation by

[146] *Ibid.*, 382. Four of the five dissenting judges, Baron Rolin-Jacquemyns, Count Rostworowski, MM. Fromageot and Shücking declared that "in their opinion, the agenda, documents and Minutes of the Washington Conference . . . do not permit them to subscribe to the grounds and conclusions of the present opinion."

[147] *Ibid.*, 383; Mr. Anzilotti placed great weight on the "intention of the parties."

[148] He based this contention on the purpose of the early international labor movement. *Ibid.*, 385.

[149] *Ibid.*, 386.

[150] *Ibid.*, 387.

[151] *Ibid.*, 388. For a discussion of the possible significance of this dissent to the future interpretations of the Court see C. C. Hyde, "Judge Anzilotti on the Interpretation of Treaties." *A. J. I. L.*, XXVII (July, 1933), 502-506.

the Court compelled a revision of the convention in question. This revision resulted in the ultimate formulation of a more practical agreement.

The advisory opinions delivered by the Permanent Court on questions presented by the International Labor Organization have been of great assistance in the functioning of that organization.[152] The series of opinions given by the Court have stated a consistent view of the functions of the Organization.[153] The effect of the advisory opinion of the Court on the one convention considered possibly may indicate that when other conventions require legal interpretation the Court will give an opinion which will be of assistance in adjusting the difficulties arising from the question concerned.

---

[152] The purposes served by these opinions are described by Manley O. Hudson as follows: "Advisory opinions have facilitated the efficient functioning of various international institutions other than the Council. International bodies do not operate automatically, and many legal questions may arise to condition their action. In numerous instances authoritative answers to such questions have been obtained from the Court through the medium of the Council." *The Permanent Court,* 467.

[153] In this connection, see *ibid.,* 538.

CHAPTER VII

INTERPRETATIONS IN NATIONAL COURTS

GENERAL LEGISLATIVE APPLICATIONS

THE ACTUAL application of the principles and provisions of international labor conventions depends upon national action. First of all, the national states must take appropriate steps to put into effect the provisions of the convention which they ratify. Following this, the measures applying the convention nationally must be enforced by judicial or administrative orders. Although the measures by which conventions are applied are wholly governmental, the work of the representatives of the employers and the workers is not ended when the conventions are adopted. The successful application of the conventions may depend to a considerable extent on the coöperation of organized workers and employers. This coöperation may be effected through the administration of conciliatory commissions or boards on which employers and workers are members; or there may be an unofficial coöperation of organized groups in the enforcement and enactment of legislative provisions.

The International Labor Organization has not consistently followed a definite policy of advocating any particular type of national legislation in the application of conventions. The Organization has generally favored the establishment of national codes in regard to particular subjects.[1] On two occasions the Office has suggested that national codes be adopted in respect to a given subject.[2] As the Conference has failed to act on either of these suggestions, no convention providing for codification has been adopted. Since the efforts to provide for national codes in international agreements have been unsuccessful, the Office has apparently ceased trying to raise standards by this method. Instead it has merely attempted to encourage national codification, and it

[1] Professor F. G. Wilson is of the opinion that the marked tendency of the Organization toward codification is due to the influence of the first director, Mr. Albert Thomas, who, being a Frenchman, was more interested in codes than Anglo-Saxons are. *Labor in the League System,* 167.

[2] The first attempt concerned the codification of the law relating to seamen, which occurred in 1926. The second was the Office proposal in 1928 of a codification of laws relating to safety and industrial hygiene.

appears that its indirect efforts have had a definite effect on the formulation of national codes.[3]

The Labor Organization is able to determine how a state is applying the conventions it has ratified by the reports received under Article 408 (22) of the Constitution.[4] These reports are made annually and contain a record of the measures which have been taken to give effect to the provisions of conventions to which they are parties. This method of checking on the application of conventions by states is as effective as the members make it. Some states do not file their reports with the Office within the specified period; other reports are incomplete.[5] However, most of the states do fulfill their obligations in regard to reporting the measures taken to put conventions in effect.[6]

The form of the report which stipulates the measures adopted in national territory is prescribed by the Governing Body. The

---

[3] See *I. L. C., Report of the Director*, 1930, Section 186. The following legislative acts in regard to the *Unemployment Indemnity* (*Shipwreck*) *Convention* are evidences of codes that have been enacted in recent years:

France: Act of December 13, 1926, to issue a Seaman's Code. *Recueil générals des Lois*, 1927, part II, 78-80; see also *Legislative Series* 1926, France, 13.

Italy: Act of December 31, 1928, respecting the mercantile marine code, *Italia, Leggi e Decreti* I, no. 3055 (1929), 312-313.

Poland: Seaman's Code of June 2, 1902, *Studies and Reports*, Series P, no. 1.

Spain: Labour Code of August 23, 1926, *Boletin de la Revista general de Legislacion y Jurisprudence*, ser. II (Leg.), CCIII (August, 1926), 593-731.

[4] This article is as follows: "Each of the Members agrees to make an annual report to the International Labor Office on the measures which it has taken to give effect to the provisions of Conventions to which it is a party. These reports shall be made in such form and shall contain such particulars as the Governing Body may request. The Director shall lay a summary of these reports before the next meeting of the Conference."

[5] A recent report of the Committee of Experts appointed to examine the annual reports made under Article 408 contained the following statement: "The number of annual reports which the different Governments were called upon to supply, under Article 408 of the Treaty of Versailles and the corresponding Articles of the other Treaties of Peace, for the period 1 October 1933 to 30 September 1934, was 601, of which, by the time that the committee concluded its work, the office had received 521. The corresponding figures for the previous year were 522 reports, of which 436 arrived in time to be examined by the Committee." *International Labour Conference: Summary of Annual Reports under Articles* 408, (1935), 273 (hereafter cited *Summary of Annual Reports under Article 408*).

[6] The states that fail to make reports are usually those of little industrial importance. The Central American republics have generally been lax in sending in their reports when due.

first request is for a list of the legislation, administrative regulations, or other provisions which apply in the convention and for a copy of the same.[7] These legislative measures are published by the Office annually and are entitled *Legislative Series.* As a means of making the information received more useful in measuring the actual effect of conventions, the States are asked to indicate where the national law is not in harmony with the provisions of the ratified convention. Furthermore, they are asked whether the ratification of the convention had any legal effect and to what extent the mere act of ratification is considered as having modified previously existing legislation. The second request is for a detailed indication for each article of the convention of the measures taken under which the article is applied.[8]

The reports filed by the members indicate in a comparative fashion to what extent they are applying legislation. The filing of these reports gives the Office the actual legislative or administrative measures that have been enacted. The form of these acts within the different states varies. The application of conventions in states with advanced labor legislation may depend in part on legislation passed before the convention was ratified.[9]

All conventions ratified by Great Britain are put in force by appropriate acts of Parliament, which usually adhere rather closely to the form of the international agreement. Sometimes the new law bringing the convention into effect is a supplementary act to legislation in existence prior to the ratification of the agreement.[10] Frequently a series of legislative acts apply the provisions of the conventions.[11] The convention on *Equality of Treat-*

[7] See *Summary of Annual Reports under Article 408,* 1936.

[8] *Idem.*

[9] This is true in respect to the *Unemployment Indemnity (Shipwreck) Convention* (1919), which is applied in Great Britain to some extent by the Merchant Shipping Acts, 1894 to 1923. See *Great Britain: General Public Acts,* for legislative references cited.

[10] As is pointed out above, this is the case in respect to the Merchant Shipping (International Labour Conventions) Act, 1925. See 15 and 16 Geo. 5, c. 42; see also *International Legislative Series* (hereafter cited *Legislative Series*), 1925, Great Britain, 5. This act is the only statute which schedules a convention without specifically giving the force of law to any of its provisions; see C. W. Jenks "The Authority of English Courts of Decisions of the Permanent Court of International Justice," *British Yearbook of International Law 1939,* XX, 22.

[11] The numerous parliamentary acts relating to the convention on unemployment reflect an adaptation of legislation owing to national conditions; during the period of 1920-1931 a new act was passed for each year, the final act being

ment (*Accident Compensation*), 1925, is applied in Great Britain as a part of the general and well-recognized law of workmen's compensation. British legislation in regard to this convention applies to foreigners in the same manner that it applies to British subjects.[12] This legislation applies both to accidents and occupational diseases.[13] In some cases one general parliamentary act is broad enough to apply the provisions of a convention for a number of years without any supplementary legislation. This was true in regard to the convention fixing the *Minimum Age* (*Sea*), 1920.[14]

Legislative application of international labor conventions in France takes the form of general acts of Parliament and decrees of administrative bodies which put in force the legislative acts. The unemployment convention of 1919 has been put into effect to date by three acts and a number of decrees.[15]

---

the National Economy Act, 1931, 21 and 22 Geo. 5, c. 48; see also *Summary of Annual Reports under Article 408*, 1935, 21.

[12] See statement in *Summary* cited, 180.

[13] The following acts which relate to this convention have been passed:

Workmen's Compensation (Transfer of Funds) Act, 1927. 17 and 18 Geo. 5, c. 15.

Workmen's Compensation (Silicosis and Asbestosis) Act, 1930. 20 and 21 Geo. 5, c. 24.

Workmen's Compensation Act, 1931, amending section 9(4) of the Workmen's Compensation Act of 1925, 20 and 21 Geo. 5, c. 29; see also *Legislative Series*, 1931, Great Britain, 4.

[14] This convention was adopted at Genoa in 1920 and was ratified by Great Britain in 1921. The legislation putting the convention into effect was entitled, "Employment of Children, Young Persons, and Women Act of 20 May 1924."

[15] This convention was ratified by France, August 25, 1925, and the following measures have been adopted (or were already on the statute books), putting it into effect:

Act of March 14, 1904, concerning the finding of employment for employees and workers of both sexes and in all occupations: Book 1, Part IV, of the Labour Code. *Recueil général des lois*, 1904, 90-92 see also *Journal Officiel*, 17 Mars 1904.

Act of February 2, 1925, to amend section 85 of Book 1, Part IV, of the Code of Labour and Social Welfare with regard to employment exchanges and departmental employment offices. *Recueil général des lois*, 1925, part II, 78-80.

Decree of March 9, 1926, to issue public administrative regulations to enforce the Act of February 2, 1925. *Ibid.*, 1926, part II, 137-139.

Act of July 19, 1928, to amend sections 79, 81, 82, 83, 88, and 102 of Book 1 of the Labour Code. *Ibid.*, 1928, part II, 500-502.

Decree of March 28, 1922, concerning grants to public employment exchanges. *Journal Officiel*, 30 Mars 1922, 3445ff.

Decree of December 28, 1926, as amended by a series of decrees concerning

In contrast to the mass of regulations necessary to give the unemployment convention effect in France, the convention concerning the *Night Work (Women)*, 1919, has required only two legislative acts and one decree to give it force.[16] These measures have for the most part been supplementary or amendatory to legislation already existing.

The *Unemployment Indemnity (Shipwreck) Convention*, 1920, has been put into force in France by two major acts which appear to meet the necessary requirements laid down in the convention.[17] The terms of this act seem to apply the convention in a non-restrictive manner.[18]

The French application of the *Workmen's Compensation (occupational diseases) Convention*, 1925, consists of two acts and two decrees.[19]

---

the conditions to be fulfilled by municipal or departmental unemployment funds which grant subsidies to workers wholly unemployed, in order to obtain grants from the national fund. *Recueil général des lois*, 1927, part II, 166-167.

Decree of September 9, 1905, as amended, concerning subventions for unemployment societies. *Ibid.*, 1906, 234-236.

[16] These provisions are:

Act of January 24, 1925, to amend sections 20 to 28 and 96 of Book II of the Code of Labour and Social Welfare. *Ibid.*, 1925, part II, 73-75.

Decree of May 5, 1928, defining the allowances and exceptions contained in sections 17, 24, 25, and 26 of Book II of the Labour Code. *Ibid.*, 1928, part II, 380-381.

Act of April 23, 1919, respecting the eight-hour day. *Ibid.*, part II, 258-259.

[17] These two acts are: Act of December 13, 1926, to issue a Seaman's Code, document cited; Act of February 15, 1929, providing for payment of an unemployment indemnity to seamen in case of capture, wreck, or declaration of unseaworthiness of a vessel. *Ibid.*, 1929, part II, 66.

[18] For example, where the British courts (see "Croxeth Hall," *infra*) held that a seaman may ask for "money wages" alone for the specified two months' period, the French administrative interpretation (which is not binding) would include an additional allowance of food.

[19] The Act of January 1, 1931, to amend and to supplement the Act of October 25, 1919, to extend to industrial diseases the Act of April 9, 1898, respecting industrial accidents. *Recueil général des lois*, 1931, part II, 1-3.

The Act of July 15, 1926, to extend the time limit fixed in the second paragraph of section 7 of the Act of October 25, 1919. *Ibid.*, part II, 354; see also *Legislative Series*, 1926, France, 7.

The decree of December 31, 1920, issuing public administrative regulations for the application of the Act of October 25, 1919. *Recueil général des lois*, 1921, part II, 20.

The decree of November 16, 1929, respecting the compulsory declaration of occupational diseases under section 12 of the Act of October 25, 1919. *Ibid.*, part II, 417-418.

The convention on unemployment was given effect in Germany by a series of acts and orders.[20] The method of application followed was the legislative enactment of a basic act followed by specific amendments when the necessity for change arose.

The convention fixing the *Minimum Age (Sea)*, 1920, is applied in Germany by one general act and augmented by a special code for seamen.[21] The German authorities report that this convention is being applied both in the spirit and the letter.[22]

In states with advanced social legislation new legislative acts may not be necessary to put a convention in effect following ratification. This was the case in Germany when the *Unemployment Indemnity (Shipwreck) Convention*, 1920, was ratified.[23] The ratification of this convention was of no value in so far as stimulating new legislation was concerned. The adherence to the convention by Germany might aid as an example to other States Members. It might also be viewed as a guarantee that existing legislation would be kept in force.

The convention on *Workmen's Compensation (Occupational Diseases)*, 1925, was ratified by Germany in 1928. The provisions applying the principles of this convention are based on the Federal

---

[20] These acts were:

Act of July 16, 1927, respecting employment exchanges and unemployment insurance. *Reichesgesetzblatt*, part I, no. 32, 187; successively amended by various acts and orders, particularly by Act of May 12, 1933, to exempt women domestics from compulsory unemployment insurance; Act of May 26, 1933, to amend certain penal provisions, 265, 293, respectively; Act of September 22, 1933, to amend assistance for unemployment, 656; and order of December 11, 1933, reducing the waiting period in unemployment insurance.

[21] This act is the Act of May 30, 1929, concerning the international conventions fixing the minimum age for admission of young persons to employment as trimmers or stokers and concerning the compulsory medical examination of children and young persons employed at sea. *Ibid.*, part II, 383. The code referred to is the Seaman's Code of June 2, 1902. See *Studies and Reports*, Series P, no. 1, *op. cit.*, 100.

[22] See *Summary of Annual Reports under Article 408*, 1935, 81.

[23] This convention was ratified April 3, 1930. Legislation already existing apparently provided sufficient guarantees to apply the provisions of the convention. The legislation consisted of the following acts: Act of December 24, 1929, respecting the international convention concerning unemployment indemnity in case of loss or foundering of the ship (1929), *Reichesgesetzblatt*, December 24, 1929, part II, 759. Seaman's Code of June 2, 1902, Vol. XXVII, act 2871, 175-211.

Insurance code, a decree, and three administrative orders.[24] These acts coördinate the regulations concerning accident insurance with the new measures applying to occupational diseases.

Labor legislation in Italy is quite frequently put in force by decrees. These are termed sometimes legislative decrees, in other instances codes,[25] and in some cases Royal Legislative Decrees.[26]

Chile has ratified a large number of labor conventions.[27] In addition to the leadership in ratifications, this South American state has apparently been prompt in fulfilling the obligations incurred under the conventions ratified. Legislative decrees are the most common method of applying the principles of conventions,[28] although administrative regulations are sometimes issued.[29]

Parliamentary acts, legislative decrees, and administrative orders have been used to put labor conventions into effect. In some instances a convention has been put in force by one act; in other cases a series of orders has been necessary. The variety of methods used would appear to add to the complexity of uniform legislative application.

---

[24] These acts are as follows:

Federal Insurance Code, *Legislative Service,* 1928, 3.

Second Decree of February 11, 1929, part 1, 27.

Fourth Order of the President of the Federation of December 8, 1931, part 1, 699.

Order of the President of the Federation of June 14, 1932, part 1, 273.

Order of October 19, 1932, part 1, 499.

[25] In connection with the application of the convention on *Unemployment Indemnity* (*shipwreck*), a decree was issued which was termed: "Legislative Decree of December 27, 1925." *Italia Leggi e Decreti,* II, no. 2544 (1929), 145-313. This was supplemented by the Act of December 31, 1928, respecting the Merchant Marine Code and the Commercial Code, *ibid.,* II, no. 3055, 312-313.

[26] This was the type of regulation used in putting into effect the convention on *Minimum Age* (*Sea*); it was entitled: "Royal Legislative Decree No. 744 of May 19, 1930," to issue rules for the registration of seamen; *ibid.,* III, 1930, 2639-2640.

[27] On January 1, 1936, Chile had ratified a total of 33 conventions.

[28] The convention on *Night Work* (*women*) was put in force by a single act, Legislative Decree No. 178 of May 13, 1931, to ratify the Labor Code. *Boletin de Leges y Decretos del goberno,* Libro XCX (1931), 2312-2502.

[29] The convention on *White Lead* (*poison*) was put into effect by three different types of measures: Decree of April 30, 1926, to approve the appended regulations respecting industrial hygiene and safety, *ibid.,* Libro XCV, 934-1040; Regulations of April 21, 1927, on occupational diseases, *ibid.,* XCVI (1927), 1695-1705; Legislative Decree No. 178 of May 13, 1931, *loc. cit.*

RECIPROCAL TREATMENT OF ALIENS

The treatment of aliens in respect to industrial questions has been a matter to which the Labor Organization has given considerable attention.[30] One of the purposes of the Organization is to bring about in so far as possible one universal standard of labor guarantees. An essential requisite of success in the pursuance of this end is the granting of national treatment to aliens. In some cases such treatment may be obtained through guarantees provided in broad conventions. Generally, however, conventions contain provisions for special supplementary agreements which apply reciprocally specific conditions between states.

The position of national courts in interpreting conventions has varied in many respects. Sometimes the determination of whether the application of a law based on the text of a convention shall be restrictive or non-restrictive is founded on the context. In other instances the nature of the decision hinges on the reading of the text by the court in the light of the particular circumstances. In any event, the treatment of aliens by national courts gives a definite indication of the extent of the practical benefits to be obtained from international labor guarantees.

The bearing that international labor agreements have on the equality of treatment for national and foreign workers in respect to workmen's compensation for accidents is demonstrated by two cases in French courts. The first case arose prior to French ratification of the convention on *Equality of Treatment (Accident Compensation)*, 1925.[31] The facts of the case indicated that the widow of a Russian worker killed in France did not have a residence established in French territory at the date of the accident. It was also established that there was no treaty of reciprocity between France and Russia at the time of the accident, hence there was no valid claim of compensation.[32] The court also pointed out that

[30] See "General Legislative Applications," *supra*, 165-168.

[31] See terms of the convention in *Draft Conventions and Recommendations*, 104-106. This convention was ratified by France March 30, 1928. See *Journal Officiel*, 1er Avril, 1928. The case was heard in December, 1929. See *International Survey*, 1931 (France), no. 59, 143.

[32] See decision of Cour d'Appel de Montpellier, November 2, 1928, *Veuve Nikitine V. Société Commentry-Fourchanmbault, Moniteur judiciaire du midi*, December, 1928, 298; *Gazette du Palais*, Tables du 1er semestre 1929, Responsabilité Civile No. 108.

neither France nor Russia had ratified the international convention on the subject.

Following the ratification of the draft convention on compensation by France, a case similar to the one discussed above was heard by the Court of Appeals of Riom.[33] This case related to the claim of a widow of a Spanish worker who was killed in an industrial accident. The claimant did not reside on French soil, nor had France and Spain made any special agreement concerning reciprocity.[34] In spite of these conditions the court held that the Spanish widow was entitled to compensation. For, the court stated, both France and Spain had ratified the convention on the subject of workmen's compensation, and consequently France was bound to provide compensation. Furthermore, the court held that residence on French soil was not a necessary condition of payment.[35]

The holding in the case following the ratification of the international labor convention as compared with the previous decision demonstrated the favors accruing to alien labor through the application of international agreements. The court did not attempt to hand down a decision which would be unfavorable to aliens, but resolved all doubts in favor of payment of compensation.[36]

A court ruling in France in 1932 demonstrates the liberal position of the French courts in respect to claims of alien refugees.[37]

[33] This convention was ratified March 30, 1928.

[34] See Cour d'Appel de Riom, 24 December, 1930, *Puig V. Veuve Salesquérol, Sirey,* 1931, 2, 54; also see *International Survey,* 1931 (France), 75.

[35] Article 1 of the convention provides as follows: "Each member of the International Labor Organization which ratifies this Convention undertakes to grant to the Nationals of any other Member which shall have ratified the Convention, who suffer personal injury due to industrial accidents happening in its territory, or to their dependents, the same treatment in respect of workmen's compensation as it grants its own nationals. "This equality of treatment shall be guaranteed to foreign workers and their dependents without any condition as to residence. With regard to payments which a Member or its nationals would have to make outside that Member's territory in the application of this principle, the measures to be adopted shall be regulated, if necessary by special arrangements between the Members concerned." *Draft Conventions and Recommendations,* 104.

[36] A more restrictive interpretation might have held that no payment of indemnity could be made pending the making of special arrangements between the states concerned. Compare a restrictive interpretation handed down in the German courts, *infra.*

[37] See *International Survey,* 1932, 76-77; Cour d'Appel de Grenoble, January 18, 1932, *Epoux Levine V. Société des Establissments Grammont* and *Compagnie*

This case concerned the death of an expatriated Russian refugee in France. The question to be decided was whether the pension of the deceased could be granted to refugees not resident in France. A section of the French labor code provided that "foreign representatives of a foreign worker shall receive no compensation unless at the time of the accident they were resident in French territory." [38] Owing to this clause there were some doubts as to the claim of the refugee in this case.

In the opinion of the court the Geneva arrangement concerning refugees was cited as providing a means for special protection to this group.[39] Clause 4 of this agreement, which came into force in France in 1930, gives to refugees all the rights and benefits that are accorded other foreigners. The fact that these persons were not citizens (of the U.S.S.R.) and consequently stateless was not grounds for refusing them rights and privileges. The court pointed out that the fact that reciprocity could not be obtained by this class of foreigners was cited in the Geneva arrangement as no barrier to benefits. Furthermore, in the opinion of the court, they might qualify for a pension without proving that they were legal French residents.[40] The different rulings of the French courts as handed down in 1929, 1931, and 1932 show the effect of special international agreements. At the earliest date, before an agreement was in effect, a court held that no compensation was forthcoming to a Russian alien although the contract in question stipulated benefits. In 1931, after an international convention was in effect, a claimant alien of a state which had ratified the convention was given full compensation regardless of her residence. In 1932 refugees were accorded full compensation without proving they were residents in France at the time of the accident.

The question of whether or not the mere ratification of the *Equality of Treatment (Accident Compensation) Convention*, 1925, involves mandatory reciprocity was decided February 27, 1934, by the French Supreme Court of Appeal.[41] Prior to this decision there had been some divergence between the Government's opinion and certain court decisions. However, in this opinion of the

---

d'assurances, "La Preservatrice," Gazette du Palais, 1932, I, 498; *Dalloz hebdomadaire*, 1932, 110.

[38] *Ibid.*, section 3 of Act of April 4, 1898.

[39] *Official Journal*, January 17, 1928.

[40] *International Survey*, *op. cit.*

[41] See *Summary of Annual Reports Under Article 408*, 1935, 178.

Supreme Court the Government's interpretation was accepted, and the convention was held to be applicable without the prior conclusion of special agreements.[42]

A decision in the German courts in 1930 held that the ratification of the convention on *Equality of Treatment* (*Accident Compensation*), 1925,[43] did not change the meaning of the Reich insurance code in respect to a Polish worker who had taken up permanent residence abroad.[44] This judgment, delivered by the Court of Appeal of the Reich Insurance Office, confirmed the decision of the Superior Miners Insurance Office. The alien respondent had been injured November 12, 1896, but his pension had been stopped when he left Germany permanently February 1, 1923, in accordance with the Reich insurance code.[45] The respondent relied on the clause in the convention which guaranteed "to foreign workers and their dependents without any conditions as to residence" equality of treatment.[46] The court dismissed the appeal, holding that to do so was keeping both the letter and the spirit of the convention. This point of view was based to some extent on the interpretation by the court of the report of the committee which drafted the convention.[47]

This decision appears to be less favorable to the rights of the alien workers than the decisions on the point by the French courts. Nevertheless, in this case the lapse of a long period of time between the date of the accident, the stoppage of the payment of the insurance, and the ratification of the convention probably accounted for the adverse decision.

On October 29, 1930, an arrangement was made between France and the Netherlands to the effect that students from either state should be admitted to the other for industrial employment in order that they might gain experience.[48] According to this agreement the employment of student employees in France was not conditional on production of a foreigner's identity card marked "worker." However, proof of acceptance as a student employee was required.

In a case heard on May 18, 1932, in the Tribunal Correctionnel

[42] *Ibid.* The Chilean and the Swiss courts have handed down a number of decisions confirming the right of compensation to foreigners in this regard.

[43] See *Draft Conventions and Recommendations,* 105-107.

[44] See *I. L. C., Fifteenth Session,* 1931, II, *Report of the Director,* 381.

[45] *Idem.*

[46] Article 1 of the convention. This convention was ratified by Germany, September 18, 1928.

[47] See *I. L. C., Seventh Session,* 1925, I, 212.

[48] See *Official Journal,* 1930, 13278.

de la Seine,[49] evidence was presented which showed that Lesot, a Paris publisher, employed Storm, a Dutch student, without a foreigner's identity card marked "worker," as was required by the French labor code. Under clause 6 of the arrangement between France and Holland such temporary employment had to be approved by the proper authorities.[50] If this application were accepted, the student could be employed without the worker's card. Storm accepted employment without waiting for the approval of his application. The court held that, as employment under these terms could not exceed fifty per cent of the year, it was necessary to adhere strictly to the provisions of the agreement. Accordingly, the employer had acted contrary to the provisions of the law.[51] This interpretation held to the letter of the agreement.

In 1931 a case was decided in the German courts which exhibited the manner of interpretation of the provisions of an international convention by resort to an analogy in the domain of private law. This resulted in an unrestrictive interpretation in favor of the spirit of the agreement.[52] The convention applied was on the subject of the *Repatriation of Seamen*, 1926. It appears from the facts of the case that in 1928 a seaman who was a subject of Yugoslavia was discharged by the Norwegian consul in Hamburg from a Norwegian steamer. The day after the discharge of the seaman the defendant declared that expenses incurred by the German authorities in transporting the seaman home would be guaranteed. The guarantee was made as a condition before the German police authorities would permit the seaman to land. The day following his discharge the seaman was found injured and brought to a port hospital. He was treated for a prolonged period in a public institution and subsequently transported to his home country. The public institution of Hamburg, to which the police authorities assigned the rights arising out of the undertaking

[49] See *Gazette de Palais*, 1932, 2, 380.

[50] *Official Journal*, 1930, 13278. Clause 1 of this arrangement provided that a student might be employed regardless of the condition of the labor market.

[51] The parts of the agreement which waived the possession of a worker's card and stipulated that students should be employed whatever the condition of the labor market would appear to be a valuable concession in the direction of international coöperation on labor matters.

[52] See *International Survey*, 1931, 199, for the decision of Hanseatischen Oberlandesgericht of Hamburg, May 20, 1931, in the case *Hamburg Public Welfare Authority v. Ship Owner X Hanseatische Rechts und Gerichtszeitschrift*, part B, 1931, no. 186, p. 579.

given by the ship owner, asked compensation for maintaining and transporting the seaman home.[53]

The decision of the court was that the ship owner is responsible for transportation and maintenance in case a seaman is dismissed through no fault of his own.[54] In arriving at this decision the court stated:

> "Public law does not confer upon police authorities the right to compel the shipowner to bear these expenses. However, the police authorities may demand from the shipowner an undertaking in the domain of private law to cover the expenses which have been incurred by the State as the result of sending home an alien seaman. The police authorities may make such an obligation a condition of permitting the seamen to land in Germany.[55]

The court was of the opinion that the police authorities were within their authority in granting the seaman permission to land. However, as there was no provision in the domain of public law by which the police could impose costs upon the defendant, the undertaking was considered by the court as being a private law agreement between the defendant and the police authorities. The court reasoned that, as it was impossible to deny the validity of such a private law agreement, it was of sufficient public importance to warrant legal action. Consequently, the court held the dispute was one in the domain of private law, which, according to the law concerning the constitution of courts, was within the jurisdiction of ordinary tribunals.

---

[53] See *idem.*

[54] The legal basis for this decision was sections 72 *et seq.* of the German seaman's code and Repatriation of Seamen Convention, 1926. Article 3 of this convention provides:

"Any seaman who is landed during the term of his engagement or on its expiration shall be entitled to be taken back to his own country. . . .

"Article 4. The expenses of repatriation shall not be a charge on the seaman if he has been left behind by reason of:

(a) injury sustained in the service of the vessel, or

(b) shipwreck, or

(c) illness not due to his own wilful act or default, or

(d) discharge for any cause for which he cannot be held responsible.

"Article 5. The expenses of repatriation shall include the transportation charges, the accommodation and the food of the seamen during the journey. They shall also include the maintenance of the seaman up to the time fixed for his departure." *Draft Conventions and Recommendations.*

[55] *Hanseatische Rechts and Gerichtszeitschrift,* part B, 1931, no. 186, p. 579.

The cases available would appear to indicate that national courts have generally interpreted conventions in such a manner that the rights of aliens have been respected. Most of the decisions show a non-restrictive interpretation in favor of the claims of aliens. The legal guarantees given aliens by conventions seem to have been applied by the courts without discrimination.[56]

CONVENTIONAL TREATMENT OF NATIONALS

An accurate determination of the ultimate value of international labor agreements must be based on the manner in which these agreements are applied by courts. One of the stated reasons for bringing such arrangements as international labor conventions into effect is to establish social justice. The degree to which this purpose is effected is indicated to some extent by court decisions interpreting the provisions of conventions as applied to nationals.

One of the most important and most widely ratified conventions is the draft convention concerning unemployment indemnity in case of loss or foundering of the ship, commonly designated as *Unemployment Indemnity* (*Shipwreck*) *Convention*, which was adopted in 1920.[57] The application of this convention has demonstrated its practicability, as its provisions have been the cause of a large variety of court decisions. The article of the convention which has required court interpretation and on which national legislation has been based is Article 2, which stipulates the circumstances under which seamen may receive unemployment indemnity.[58] In 1929 a

[56] It is perhaps possible that, if more recent cases than those cited were available, the results mentioned in conclusion above might be less favorable to foreigners.

[57] This convention came into force March 16, 1923. It had been ratified on January 1, 1936, by Argentina, Australia, Belgium, Bulgaria, Canada, Chile, Colombia, Cuba, Estonia, France, Germany, Great Britain, Greece, Irish Free State, Italy, Latvia, Luxemburg, Nicaragua, Poland, Rumania, Spain, Sweden, Uruguay, and Yugoslavia—a total of twenty-four states. See *Draft Conventions and Recommendations*, 45-47, for a text of the convention.

[58] The text of Article 2 is as follows: "In every case of loss or foundering of any vessel, the owner or person with whom the seaman has contracted for service on board the vessel shall pay to each seaman employed thereon an indemnity against unemployment resulting from such loss or foundering.

"This indemnity shall be paid for the days during which the seaman remains in fact unemployed at the same rate as the wages payable under the contract, but the total indemnity payable under this convention to any one seaman may be limited to two months' wages." *Ibid.*

case (The *Croxeth Hall*) arose under this clause and was appealed to the highest English court.[59]

The facts of the case were that the vessel *Croxeth Hall* was shipwrecked February 27, 1929, and the seaman involved claimed two months' wages from that date. The owners paid the seamen wages until March 11, but refused to pay more on the ground that the contract of service was due to terminate on that date in any event. The case was first tried by the Probate of Divorce and Admiralty Division of the High Court of Justice, then the Court of Appeal, and finally the House of Lords, where the claims of the seaman were upheld in each instance.[60] The case was decided on the basis of the construction of the act of Parliament which applied the terms of the international agreement on the subject.[61] The court of highest instance, the House of Lords, held that the words of the statute were clear, that the seamen were entitled to two months wages from the date of the wreck regardless of the termination of the contract of service. The opinion of the court pointed out that the only way the employer could avoid paying the wages during the specified two months period was by showing that the unemployment was due to some other cause than "loss of ship." [62] However, there was no proof in the case to show that the unemployment was not due to shipwreck.

The decision allowing the wages under the circumstances was perhaps more favorable to the rights of seamen than the text of the

[59] See *Times Law Reports,* XLVII, 147, and *International Survey,* 1930, 26.

[60] See *Times Law Reports,* XLVI, 408, for the vigorous dissenting opinion of Lord Slesser, of the High Court of Justice. His Lordship stated that according to the preamble and terms of the convention indemnity was meant to be construed in a restrictive sense. Therefore, the employers had acted legally in not paying more than loss of employment under the agreement.

[61] This was the Merchant Shipping Act of 1925, which provides: "When by reason of the wreck or loss of a ship on which a seaman is employed his services terminate before the date contemplated in the agreement, he shall notwithstanding anything in section 158 of the Merchant Shipping Act of 1894, but subject to the provisions of this section, be entitled in respect of each day on which he is in fact unemployed during a period of two months from the date of the termination of the service, to receive wages at the rate to which he was entitled at that date." 15 and 16 Geo. 5, c. 42; also *Legislative Series,* 1925, Great Britain 5.

[62] *Times Law Reports,* XLVI, *op. cit.* If, however, the court was of the opinion that the seamen had not attempted to find employment, and the employer could prove such a fact, the wages need not be paid.

international labor convention would lead one to expect. The reason for this generous interpretation is in part due to the relevant act of Parliament, for as a general rule the judges follow the terms of a legislative act with no reference to the basic convention.[63]

In 1931 a decision of the Umpire under the English Unemployment Insurance Acts was made along the same lines as that of the *Croxeth Hall.*[64] A fireman employed on a ship wrecked November 10, 1930, claimed both unemployment insurance and wages for two months under the act applying the international convention requiring the payment of indemnity. The decision was that the claimant was entitled to unemployment insurance benefit regardless of his claim under the international convention.[65]

In the same year the *Croxeth Hall* case was decided, another appeal was in the courts concerning the same convention. The circumstances of this case raised several questions not present in the former case.[66] A claim for compensation was lodged by the mother of a deceased deckhand employed on a vessel which ran aground in a storm off the coast of Iceland. The deceased, together with the rest of the crew, acting under the master's orders, remained on board exposed to wind and rain for four and one-half hours. Later they waded ashore and made their way inland through deep streams and heavy sandstorms. In crossing a stream the deceased stumbled and had to be carried by his companions until they stopped to rest for the night, where they were still exposed to intense cold. In the morning the deckhand was dead.

The county court awarded the mother compensation as a dependent, but the defendants appealed the case against the finding that death was due to accident arising out of and in pursuance of employment.[67] The appellant argued that employment ended when the wreck occurred. The Court of Appeals held that while this was

[63] This is according to the maxim of English law, *a verbis legis non recedendum est. International Survey,* 1930, 27. It is also important to note that the court decreed that the term "wages" does not include any allowance for food in addition to the money wage.

[64] See *International Survey,* 1931, no. 27, 46.

[65] The Umpire held: "A shipwrecked sailor is entitled to be regarded as unemployed and therefore entitled to benefit regardless of whether he is entitled to receive wages under the Merchant Shipping (International Labor Conventions) Act, 1925." *Ibid.*

[66] See *Maver v. Owners of Ship "Solon,"* heard in Court of Appeals, *Butterworth's Workmen's Compensation Cases,* XXII, 424.

[67] *Idem.*

a true interpretation of the legislative acts it had no bearing on the case at hand. Rather, the question was whether the deceased had suffered injury owing to the wrecking of the vessel. In the opinion of the court the evidence showed that the decision of the county court was correct. The exposure which caused the death of the deceased was begun before he had left the *Solon*. This lowered his vitality and made him less able to face the hardships of the inland journey.

This decision in favor of the claim under the convention indicates that the circumstances of the case have much to do with the decision, and that the rigidity of the law may be tempered to provide equity.[68]

An interpretation of the act applying the convention concerning the payment of wages during unemployment, which was slightly different from the other decisions of the English courts, was delivered in 1932 by the Court of Session, Scotland.[69] This case concerned an engineer who had temporarily lost his employment during repairs to his ship. His contract of service decreed that employment could be terminated at the discretion of the owner. The repairs to the vessel were made in twelve days, and the plaintiff was reemployed. He sued for wages for the twelve-day period under the terms of the parliamentary act which says two months' wages shall be paid for "wreck or loss" of ship.[70] The question the court had to decide was whether the contract was terminated under the meaning of the above act. The court decided that the ship was only a partial wreck. Furthermore, it held that, since the ship was used in fishing for the rest of the season, the contract had been terminated because of the right provided in its terms rather than because of the wreck.[71] This decision was appealed to the House of Lords, and the opinion of the lower court was upheld. In giving this reaffirmation, the court stated that the case was governed by the rule that ". . . the wreck of the ship . . . is anything happening to the ship which renders her incapable of carrying out the mari-

---

[68] Compare the decision in the case of the *Croxeth Hall, supra.*

[69] This decision was in the case of *Barras v. Aberdeen Trawling Company, Lloyds, List Law Reports* XLIII, 58, See also *International Survey,* 1932, no. 1, 7-8.

[70] See text of convention and Merchant Shipping Act, 1925, *supra.*

[71] See *International Survey,* 1932, no. 1, 8. This decision may be compared with those of the *Solon* and the *Croxeth Hall* for slightly different constructions of the same act.

time adventure in respect of which the seaman's contract was entered into...."

Since the vessel in question continued the fishing voyage and reëmployed the seaman, he could not collect indemnity.[72]

An unusual case concerning the application of the *Unemployment Indemnity* (*Shipwreck*) convention arose in the French courts in 1931.[73] This decision gives some indication of the manner of interpreting this convention in French courts.

It appears from the facts of the case that on November 4, 1929, the ship *Saida* ran aground in the White Sea in calm weather and was refloated and taken to Archangel for repairs. Owing to the closing of the Archangel harbor from January to May, the company repatriated the seamen, and they were repaid on their arrival in France. Meanwhile, as the Archangel court ordered the company to pay a large sum for salvage, the owners decided to abandon the vessel to creditors. The claimant Madec sued for the two months' wages he claimed to be due him under the terms of the act putting into force the convention concerning unemployment indemnity. The claim was allowed by the lower court, but the Tribunal Civil de Rouen, to which an appeal was taken, disallowed the claim.[74]

In the decision reversing the lower court the Rouen Tribunal Civil stated that the act bringing into force the international labor convention indicated restrictively the cases in which the indemnity for seamen thereby provided should be payable; namely, capture, foundering, or declaration of unseaworthiness. The court said that the abandonment of a vessel which had run aground did not establish a right to this indemnity.[75] In support of this decision the court observed that the vessel was not sold because of being unseaworthy, nor were the men landed for that reason; accordingly, the restrictive enumeration of the act did not cover the appellant.

An Italian judicial ruling was rendered in 1930 in regard to the application of the convention concerning unemployment indemnity in case of loss or foundering of the ship.[76] This decision by the Port Authority of Naples concerned the application of Articles 2 and 3

[72] This principle was laid down in the *Olympia* case (1913), *Summary of Annual Reports under Article 408,* 1934, 68.

[73] This case, *Société Saida v. Madec,* is reported in *Dalloz hebdomadaire,* 1931, 392. See also *International Survey,* 1931 (France), no. 46, p. 143.

[74] *Idem.*

[75] *Ibid.*

[76] See *I. L. C., Fifteenth Session,* 1931, II, *Report of the Director,* 224.

of the convention. The decision was to the effect that the provisions of the legislative decree of December 27, 1925, which brought the convention into force in Italy, was of public interest (*di ordine publico*), so a ship owner could not rely on exceptions stated in certain other laws.[77] Furthermore, the decision stated that the obligation of the ship owner was an individual obligation, and that he could not evade it by abandoning the ship to his creditors,[78] or by relying on the Royal Decree respecting compulsory insurance against unemployment.[79] Consequently, this obligation was held to be a direct charge placed on the ship owner to compensate for the dangerous and hazardous nature of a seaman's calling.

A later decision in the Supreme Court of Appeal of Italy would appear to reverse the principles laid down in the lower courts.[80] This decision was rendered as a result of an appeal by the ship owners of the S.S. *Cosmona* against a decision of the Court of Appeal of Naples. The Naples court held that it was impossible for the seamen to find employment under the existing circumstances.[81] The highest court held that this was a matter for the judge hearing the case to decide, and that in this instance the seamen could not plead involuntary unemployment.[82]

This ruling by the highest Italian tribunal reversing the liberal

---

[77] These exceptions were in section 535 of the commercial code, and the model articles of agreement of 1922, according to which, if the vessel becomes a total wreck, a seaman is not entitled to payment of his wages. *Ibid.*

[78] Under Section 491 of the Commercial Code. *Ibid.*

[79] Decree of December 30, 1923. *Ibid.*

[80] See *Summary of Annual Reports under Article 408,* 1935, 88.

[81] The Naples court held that the circumstances making the finding of employment impossible were:

(1) There was no vessel available to offer them employment;

(2) The shipwrecked seamen were entitled to be present at the enquiry on the disaster;

(3) The loss of their clothing justified the shipwrecked seamen in considering it impossible to accept immediate employment on board another ship. *Idem.*

[82] The Italian Supreme Court of Appeal answered the findings of the Naples Court as follows:

(1) That the ship owners had requested on two occasions to be allowed to supply proof that employment had been offered to all the shipwrecked seamen and that the latter had refused these offers; in regard to point

(2) That, taking into account the fact that inquiries of this nature were often prolonged, the right to attend the inquiry did not entitle the shipwrecked seamen to remain unemployed, and that it was possible for them to be present at the inquiry by proxy; and, in regard to point

(3) That this was an *a posteriori* argument. *Idem.*

decision of the lower courts would seem to place the burden of proof of involuntary unemployment on the employee.[83] Such a construction could not be regarded as favoring liberal guarantees for those protected by the international convention. The effect of this decision is to restrict narrowly the legal guarantees.

A liberal construction of the convention concerning unemployment indemnity (shipwreck) was decreed in a Spanish court.[84] This case arose in connection with a fishing vessel off the coast of Newfoundland and was heard by the Justice of Peace of St. Malo, sitting as a court of final instance. The decision was that "unemployment," for the purpose of the act, was to mean absence from employment on board ship.[85] In addition to this, the opinion stated that an advance of wages made to sea fishermen when they were engaged, but which were not fully earned, could not be reckoned against the unemployment indemnity due the fishermen.

This brief survey of a group of cases in national courts under the *Unemployment Indemnity* (*Shipwreck*) *Convention*, 1920, reveals the general methods of construction employed in the conventional treatment of nationals in the courts. It would seem, from the cases examined, that the English courts are generally very liberal in their legislation under the convention and in the application by the courts.[86] Sometimes the liberality of the decisions is due to the terms of the act of Parliament applying the international convention.[87] In another instance the court appeared to interpret the act in a manner which would fit the circumstances of the case.[88] The decision in the French Court (*Saida v. Madec*) appears to be less liberal than the English ruling.[89] While it is true that unseaworthiness was not the direct cause for the selling of the vessel or the landing of the men (rather, a number of factors contributed to

[83] The term "liberal" is used here to signify an interpretation that will accrue to the advantage of the wage earner.

[84] This case was decided November 8, 1930.

[85] This refers to Article 2 of the convention.

[86] This is demonstrated by the decisions in the case of the *Croxeth Hall*, the *Solon*, and the case concerning unemployment insurance benefit. The opinion in the *Barras v. Aberdeen Steam Trawling Company* might be cited as a slightly more restrictive interpretation.

[87] See the *Croxeth Hall* case, *supra*, 179-180.

[88] See the case of the *Solon*, *supra*. In this case the court held that, although the employment had terminated when the wreck occurred, death was partially due to exposure while employed.

[89] See *supra*.

the result), it was the beginning of a chain of events and indirectly the cause of the events that led to the result. A liberal rather than a restrictive interpretation might have decided in favor of the claims of the seamen.

The decisions in the Spanish and Italian Courts (with one exception) were inclined to be unrestrictive rather than restrictive. The circumstances were such that the authorities making the decisions could not be guided by the general terms of the convention or the legislative provisions putting it into force. Therefore, some discretion was left to them in making their decisions. In most cases the courts chose to decide in favor of the seamen.

In 1929 the Genoa Port Authority handed down a decision concerning the convention on *Seamen's Articles of Agreement*, 1926, which indicated an unrestrictive interpretation of the convention.[90] This opinion involved Article 11 of the convention, which provides that "national law shall determine the circumstances in which the owner or master may immediately discharge a seaman." [91] The decision in regard to this article was that a seaman discharged before the expiration of his agreement for non-fulfullment of his duties was entitled to the compensation provided by the Italian Commercial Code on the ground that the master of the vessel had not reported the seaman's unsatisfactory behavior to the maritime authority at the time of the discharge.[92] This decision was clearly in accordance with the spirit of the convention.

The *Childbirth Convention*, 1919, was put into effect by legislative act in Germany July 16, 1927.[93] In 1931 a case arose under the act applying this convention.[94] This case concerned the interpretation of Articles 3 and 4, concerning the period of confiement.[95]

[90] This convention had been ratified on January 1, 1936, by Australia, Belgium, Bulgaria, Chile, Colombia, Cuba, Estonia, France, Germany, Great Britain, India, Irish Free State, Italy, Luxemburg, Mexico, Nicaragua, Poland, Spain, Uruguay, and Yugoslavia. See *Draft Conventions and Recommendations*, 117. For a complete text of the convention, see 117-123.

[91] *Ibid.*

[92] *I. L. C., Fifteenth Session*, II, 1931, *Report of the Director*, 414.

[93] This convention had been ratified on January 1, 1936, by Argentina, Brazil, Bulgaria, Chile, Colombia, Cuba, Germany, Greece, Hungary, Latvia, Luxemburg, Nicaragua, Rumania, Spain, Uruguay, and Yugoslavia. *Draft Conventions and Recommendations*, 21. The text of the convention may be found on 21-24.

[94] *Reichsarbeitsgericht*, VIII, 224.

[95] Article 3 provides:

"In any public or private industrial or commercial undertaking or in any

According to the facts of the case, the plantiff was employed as a die stamper with a contract stipulating a fourteen-day period of dismissal. On March 20, 1930, the plaintiff gave birth to a child. The first day of May her employer gave notice of dismissal on the ground that there was no more work. This was the last day of the protective period under the law. The Labor Court and the District Labor Court held the dismissal took effect on May 15 instead of May 14 and that the plaintiff was due wages for that day.[96] The Federal Labor Court affirmed the decision of the lower courts.

The reasons given by the Federal Court for its holding were that by the terms of the Federal law (Motherhood Law), July 16, 1929, a notice of dismissal given by the employer six weeks before or six weeks after confinement has no legal effect if the employer knows of such confinement. In the present case the defendant had knowledge of the circumstances. The purpose of the law, the court held, went even further than that of the convention in protecting the mother before and after confinement.[97] The aim was to protect the mother from disturbance during this period. This aim would be frustrated if notice of dismissal were permissible within the protective period provided by law.[98]

---

branch thereof, other than an undertaking in which only members of the same family are employed, a woman

"(a) Shall not be permitted to work during the weeks following her confinement;

"(b) Shall have the right to leave her work if she produces a medical certificate stating that her confinement will probably take place within six weeks, etc. . . ."

Article 4 provides:

"Where a woman is absent from her work in pursuance of paragraphs (a) and (b) of Article 3 of this Convention, or remains absent from her work for a longer period as a result of illness medically certified to arise out of pregnancy or confinement and rendering her unfit for work, it shall not be lawful, until her absence shall have exceeded a maximum period to be fixed by the competent authority in each country, for her employer to give her notice of dismissal during such absence, nor to give her notice of dismissal at such a time that the notice would expire during such absence." *Draft Conventions and Recommendations,* 22.

[96] *Reichsarbeitsgericht,* VIII, 224.

[97] The court referred to Reports of the Reichstag, Third Period, 1924-1927, Document no. 3521. *Idem.*

[98] The court said, "Accordingly, notice of dismissal May 1, 1930, had no legal effect. In order to bring about the termination of the relation of work it was necessary to give notice after the termination of the period of protection, as no such notice was given before May 14, 1930, as the contracted period of notice

The judgment of the court would seem to favor the employee and to go beyond the limits laid down by the international convention. The court held strictly to the relevant national act, thus more than fulfilling the terms of the convention.

A decision favorable to the employee which gave a liberal construction to the childbirth convention was given by the Labor Court of Santiago, Chile, in 1934.[99] In this opinion the court declared that an employer must pay a worker or a salaried employee who has fallen ill during her sixth month of pregnancy her full wages both for the period of her illness and also for the twelve weeks provided for in the labor code. This application would seem to be a reasonable one.[100]

The *Hours of Work (Industry) Convention,* 1919, has been the subject of few court decisions.[101] One of the controversial sections of this convention has been the one referring to the arrangement concerning overtime.[102] On December 22, 1930, the Belgian Supreme Court of Appeal at Brussels decided that the higher rates of pay for overtime applied in regard to additional hours in undertakings of a seasonal character.[103] This decision was referred to the Court of Appeal at Liege, which delivered a judgment on March 26, 1931, declaring itself in agreement with the opinion of the Supreme Court of Appeals.[104] This holding would appear to favor the restriction of hours unless special arrangements from which benefit will accrue to the workers are in effect.

---

was a fortnightly one, the plaintiff is right in claiming payment of wages for two further weeks after her dismissal." *Idem.*

[99] *Summary of Annual Reports under Article 408,* 1935, 42.

[100] See Articles 3 and 4 of the convention, *op. cit.*

[101] This convention came into effect June 13, 1921. It had been ratified on September 1, 1934, by Argentina, Austria (conditional), Belgium, Bulgaria, Canada, Chile, Columbia, Czechoslovakia, Dominican Republic, France (conditional), Greece, India, Italy (conditional), Latvia (conditional), Lithuania, Luxemburg, Nicaragua, Portugal, Rumania, Spain, Uruguay, and Yugoslavia. See text in *Draft Conventions and Recommendations,* 9-16.

[102] Provision for overtime is made in the following manner in Article 5 of the convention: "In exceptional cases where it is recognized that the provisions of Article 2 cannot be applied, but only in such cases, agreements between workers' and employers' organizations concerning the daily limit of work over a longer period of time may be given the force of regulations, if the Government, to which the agreements shall be submitted, so decides.

"The average number of hours worked per week, over the number of weeks covered by any such agreement shall not exceed forty-eight."

[103] *I. L. C., Seventeenth Session,* 1933, *Summary of Annual Reports under Article 408,* 28.

[104] *Idem.*

A number of decisions concerning the convention on *Hours of Work (Industry)* have been given by the courts in Chile.[105] A leading case arose in the Labor Court of the Provincial Labour Inspectorate of Temuco against the General Electric Company. It was alleged that this company was working two employees a period totaling ten and one-half hours a day and sixty-eight hours a week, which was contrary to Article 5 of the convention. The company admitted the charge but stated that these employees were specialists and that it was difficult to get any one to replace them. The judge held, however, that an eight-hour day was provided for in the labor code and exceptions could be authorized only by the General Labor Inspectorate, which had not authorized such an exception. The employer must pay a fine for this breach of labor law.[106] This decision gives evidence of a strict application of the terms of the convention by the Chilean Government.[107]

A number of decisions under the *Hours of Work (Industry) Convention* were given by the Spanish Supreme Court in the years 1926-1934.[108] A judgment of July 14, 1930, was especially significant. This opinion held that a worker was entitled to payment in full for overtime, even if he had concluded a contract for a greater number of hours of work than provided for by law or for wages which were less than the legal rate.[109]

The courts in which decisions have been rendered have enforced this convention according to its letter and spirit. The fact that such enforcement is taking place in some states that do not have advanced social legislation is indicative of the significance of this interpretation.

The convention on *Workmen's Compensation (Accidents)*, 1925, came into force on April 1, 1927.[110] On January 11, 1930, a judgment was given by the Supreme Court of Justice of Luxemburg

[105] *Ibid.*, 1934, 13. [106] *Idem.*

[107] A number of Supreme Court orders putting the provisions of this convention into effect in Czechoslovakia were rendered during the years 1926, 1927, 1928, and 1930. *I. L. C., Fifteenth Session*, II, *Report of the Director*, 1931.

[108] See *Summary of Annual Reports, under Article 408*, 1935, 17.

[109] Other judgments held that overtime must be paid at a higher rate as provided by law. *Ibid.*

[110] It had been ratified on January 1, 1936, by Belgium, Bulgaria, Chile, Columbia, Cuba, Hungary, Latvia, Luxemburg, Mexico, Netherlands, Nicaragua, Portugal, Spain, Sweden, Uruguay, and Yugoslavia. *Draft Conventions and Recommendations, op. cit.* See text of the convention, 93-96.

which related to Article 2 of the convention.[111] This article relates to the responsibility of the employer in regard to the employment of individuals.[112] The court decided that "exceptional circumstances" may arise in which a third person who is not directly engaged by the employer must nevertheless be considered as his worker. But if such a consideration is held, the direct participation of the person in the execution of a piece of work must be because the work of the employer requires his assistance at that particular moment. If this were not true, the court said, the word of a third person would in effect be aiding the worker instead of the employer and no compensation could be claimed.[113]

This ruling would seem to indicate that Luxemburg is not taking advantage of the clause in Article 2 which provides that exceptions may be made in national legislation in respect to "persons whose employment is of a casual nature and who are employed otherwise than for the purpose of the employer's trade or business.[114] The effect of this interpretation of the convention would be to favor in an unrestrictive manner the protection of the worker.

In June, 1933, the Luxemburg Court of Justice laid down the rule that the right to review pensions applies only to cases where the incapacity of the victim of the accident either increases or diminishes.[115] The review cannot extend to reopening the question of the occupational character of the accident. This ruling by the Luxemburg tribunal would be a further demonstration of the liberality of judicial decisions under this convention.

[111] See *I. L. C., Fifteenth Session*, II, *Report of the Director*, 1931, 343.

[112] The text of the article in question is as follows:

"The laws and regulations as to workmen's compensation shall apply to workmen, employees and apprentices employed by any enterprise, undertaking or establishment of whatsoever nature, whether public or private.

"It shall neverthless be open to any Member to make such exceptions in its national legislation as it deems necessary in respect of:

(a) persons whose employment is of a casual nature and who are employed otherwise than for the purpose of the employer's trade or business;

(b) out-workers;

(c) members of the employer's family who work exclusively on his behalf and who live in his house;

(d) non-manual workers whose remuneration exceeds a limit to be determined by national laws or regulations." *Draft Conventions and Recommendations.*

[113] *I. L. C., Fifteenth Session*, II, *Report of the Director*, 1931, 343.

[114] Section (b) of Article 2.

[115] *Summary of Annual Reports under Article 408*, 1935, 154.

The convention on *Night Work of Young Persons* (*Industry*), 1919, came into force on June 13, 1921.[116] In Switzerland, in a case decided under this convention, the court held that the fact that certain young persons had done night work voluntarily in violation of the provisions applying the convention did not exonerate the employer from liability.[117] The court was of the opinion that it made no difference whether the work which violated the legislative act was done voluntarily or otherwise.

The *Night Work* (*Women*) *Convention*, 1919, has occasioned considerable difficulty respecting revision and ratification.[118] The Swiss courts have handed down a number of decisions for violation of the night work provisions.[119] Some of these infringements concerned the hours stipulated and others the minimum night rest period which must be observed according to the convention.[120]

Two decisions delivered in the Chilean courts on the convention on *Workmen's Compensation* (*Occupational Diseases*), 1925,[121]

---

[116] This convention has been ratified by Albania, Argentina, Austria, Belgium, Brazil, Bulgaria, Chile, Cuba, Denmark, Estonia, France, Great Britain, Greece, Hungary, India, Irish Free State, Italy, Latvia, Lithuania, Luxemburg, Netherlands, Nicaragua, Poland, Portugal, Rumania, Spain, Switzerland, Uruguay, Venezuela, and Yugoslavia. *Draft Conventions and Recommendations;* see 33-37 for a text of the agreement.

[117] *Summary of Annual Reports under Article 408,* 1934, 56.

[118] It has been in force since June 13, 1921 and has been ratified by Albania, Argentina, Austria, Belgium, Brazil, Bulgaria, Chile, Columbia, Cuba, Czechoslovakia, Estonia, France, Great Britain, Greece, Hungary, India, Irish Free State, Italy, Lithuania, Luxemburg, Netherlands, Nicaragua, Portugal, Rumania, South Africa, Spain, Switzerland, Uruguay, Venezuela, and Yugoslavia. *Draft Conventions and Recommendations,* 24-27.

[119] During the period of one year covered by the 1935 report, 52 sentences were pronounced, 17 by legal authorities and 35 by administrative authorities, *Summary of Annual Reports under Article 408,* 1935, 53.

[120] Article 2 of the convention provides that:

"For the purpose of this convention, the term 'night' signifies a period of at least eleven consecutive hours, including the interval between ten o'clock in the evening and five o'clock in the morning.

"In those countries where no Government regulation as yet applies to the employment of women in industrial undertakings during the night, the term 'night' may provisionally, and for a maximum period of three years, be declared by the Government to signify a period of only ten hours, including the interval between ten o'clock in the evening and five o'clock in the morning." *Draft Conventions and Recommendations,* 25.

[121] This convention was adopted in 1925 and had been ratified by January 1, 1936, by Austria, Belgium, Bulgaria, Chile, Colombia, Cuba, Czechoslovakia, Denmark, Finland, France, Germany, Great Britain, Hungary, India, Irish

indicate the manner in which it is being applied in Chile.[122] The first was to the effect that pulmonary tuberculosis was not compensable, as it is not directly due to the workers' employment.[123] The second was that the dependents of an agricultural worker who died as the result of anthrax infection contracted while engaged in temporary employment were entitled to a pension.[124] Both of these decisions indicate a reasonable reading of the terms of the convention in the light of existing conditions.

A number of decisions in the Spanish Supreme Court classified the diseases that were compensable and laid down the principle that in order to be compensable occupational diseases must arise directly out of the work done.[125] This ruling would appear to be in accordance with the principle set forth in the convention.[126]

This group of cases in national courts indicates to some extent the manner in which conventions are interpreted. In general the cases studied appear to record applications favorable to employees.[127] In some instances the courts construe the provisions of conventions liberally rather than restrictively so as to guarantee the rights of the persons protected.

Free State, Japan, Latvia, Luxemburg, Netherlands, Nicaragua, Norway, Portugal, Spain, Sweden, Switzerland, Uruguay, and Yugoslavia. For a full text of the convention, see *Draft Conventions and Recommendations, op. cit.,* 100-103.

[122] *Summary of Annual Reports, under Article 408,* 1935, 168.

[123] *Idem.* [124] *Idem.* [125] *Idem.*

[126] Article 1 of the convention provides "that compensation shall be payable to workmen incapacitated by occupational diseases, or, in case of death from such diseases, to their dependents, in accordance with the general principles of the national legislation relating to compensation for industrial accidents." *Draft Conventions and Recommendations,* 100.

Further provisions of the convention stipulate the diseases that should be regarded as occupational. The rulings mentioned above would seem to come within the scope of the general principles of the convention.

[127] It would appear that the existence of special types of courts (such as labor courts) possibly influence the ultimate legal action. The decisions in these bodies are arrived at by the use of more flexible principles than those applied in the ordinary law courts.

CHAPTER VIII

EFFECT ON TREATY LAW AND TECHNIQUE

GENERAL PROCEDURE STIPULATED IN THE CONSTITUTION

SOME PUBLICISTS maintain that there is nothing fundamentally new about the structural basis of the International Labor Organization, as it is in reality a type of an international union.[1] It is not the purpose of this study to examine the strength and weakness of international unions. Nevertheless, it is important to keep in mind the fact that generally the union is merely a method of co-operation between states and that it functions only to the extent that states makes use of it. Furthermore, the International Labor Organization is a special type of international union as it is created by Part XIII of the Treaty of Versailles and corresponding parts of other treaties and is a part of the larger enterprise, the League of Nations system. In addition to the special nature of its creation, the International Labor Organization is different from the usual union owing to its tripartite character.[2]

The aims and purposes of the Organization, as well as the means of attaining these objectives, are clearly stated in its Constitution. The stated objectives are found in the preamble,[3] and the Permanent Court of International Justice has held that this section determines the jurisdiction of the Organization.[4] It is instructive to note that the stipulations of the preamble might be interpreted in such a manner as to embrace all forms of labor relations. In addition to the preamble, Article 41 of the Constitution, which states the general principles to be followed, also indicates the line of action of the Organization. The methods of procedure to be followed by the Governing Body and the Conference in the making of conventions and also their consequent

[1] See A. Rapisardi-Mirabelli, "Théorie générale des unions internationales," *Recueil des cours de l' Academie de Droit International*, VII, 1925, 345-390 and F. G. Wilson, *op. cit.* 58-59.

[2] An excellent discussion of the significance of the representation of three groups in the organization is given by C. Wilfred Jenks in "The Significance for International Law of the Tripartite Character of the International Labour Organization," *Transactions of the Grotius Society*, XVII (May, 1936), 45-81.

[3] See Part XIII, Treaty of Versailles.

[4] See *P. C. I. J.*, Series B, no. 2.

application are explicitly outlined in the Constitution of the Organization.[5] The functions of these two units are defined so there will be the maximum of coöperation and the minimum of conflict in the work of the Organization. As each general step of the process of formulating conventions is legally fixed, precise action by the bodies concerned is mandatory. Thus the formation of international labor law is not left to *ad hoc* bodies or guided by opportunistic methods of procedure; rather the process is to go forward in what was designed to be an orderly and scientific manner.

The group representation of the Organization, as stipulated in the Constitution, introduces a new method in international collaboration.[6] The fact that a constitutional system of international administration embodying new methods of procedure has functioned for a number of years would tend to affect international law and technique. Utilization of this procedure with a measure of success will probably have a direct, or at least an indirect, effect on international treaty technique. A stable constitutional system, which is the means of regularly producing international agreements to meet the needs of its particular sphere, may be recognized as an example for other fields of international development. The Labor Conference and Governing Body differ decidedly from an international body which is composed of the representatives of states. With the different professional groups represented in the International Labor Organization, it can be characterized as both pre-legislative and diplomatic.[7] The administrative func-

[5] See Articles 14-37.

[6] See Articles 3-8 of the Constitution, which provide for the representation of employers, workers, and states on the Governing Body and in the Conference.

The following opinion as to the unique character of the International Labor Organization in international law is expressed by Maurice Guerreau:

"L'Organisation permanente du travail représente assurement nul ne songe à le nier . . . un élement nouveau dans la sphère du droit public qui régit les rapports des Etats; son apparition a veritablement marqué une page revolutionnaire dans les traditions jusque là reconnues et sanctionnées par la coutume internationale. Les règles posées par le Traité de Paix de Versailles ont, en effet, donne aux differents rouages de L'organisation permanente un souverainté des Etats et qui faite de cette institution un organisme exorbitant du droit commun international." *L'Organisation permanente du travail,* 42.

[7] See comment to this effect by the late Director of the Office, Albert Thomas, in *Official Bulletin,* XVI, 1931, 214.

Guerreau, *op. cit.,* 43, comments as follows: "Plus qu'une conférence, c'est une sorte de Parlement international à représentation mixte: politique et

tions of the Office in connection with the activities of the two other branches serve to broaden the nature of the Organization.[8]

METHODS OF PROCEDURE

An estimate of the effect of methods of procedure in the formulation of labor conventions on the general law and technique of treaty making will be attempted at this point. The essential methods to be considered in this evaluation are the preparatory work, which involves double-discussion procedure and the method of adoption by the Conference. In this connection it is necessary to point out that a conference composed of the representatives of three groups from many states requires a different type of procedure than that of an ordinary diplomatic conference.[9] In the past the preparation for international conferences was for the most part the task of governments.[10] Now the manner of preparation by an international body such as the Labor Organization reveals a trend toward improved methods and also relieves the governments of this burdensome task.

The discussion of the Report of the Director is possibly of significance in the work of preparing conventions.[11] This discussion usually continues for three days and is concluded by a reply from the Director to the observations made by the Conference delegates on the report. The essential characteristic of this method lies in the collective interests voiced in this discussion. Such expression is made possible by the group representation. Possibly this procedure serves to crystallize international public opinion so that conventions more expressive of a community of interests may be formed.

---

professionnelle, ce qui ne s'était pas vu jusqù'alors; et ce caractère parlementaire est établi davantage; par la faculté reconnue à la conférence d'invalider les personnes choisies pour entrer dans son sein."

[8] See Articles 6-12 of the Constitution.

An interesting comment in this connection by F. G. Wilson is as follows: "The International Labor Organization may be in fact, and probably is, a kind of international public service, but one in which by the nature of its presentation there is more genuine internationalism than in the League, in which there is frequently merely the juxtaposition of states." *Op. cit.,* 59.

[9] See the comment of F. G. Wilson, *op. cit.,* 191, to the effect that "negotiation" between these groups is one of the reasons for the complexity of the procedure.

[10] See Hudson, *International Legislation,* I, xxxix.

[11] An annual report has been submitted to each Conference since 1921 and is a summary of the work of the Organization in relation to the universal problems facing the Labor Organization.

While the influence of this action is difficult to measure, it seems possible that it may make future treaty law responsive to a broader cross section of international opinion.

The chief organs of the Labor Organization involved in the making of conventions are the Governing Body and the Office.[12] Unlike uncoördinated units of governments preparing for a conference, or the *ad hoc* procedure of special preparatory committees, these two bodies function regularly and according to rules of procedure that have developed along practical lines.[13] The leadership in the work of preparation is taken by the Governing Body. It selects the items deemed necessary for examination prior to the placing of questions on the agenda. The Office prepares the law and practice on these topics. Sometimes the study of an item will continue for several years before it is finally selected for the agenda.[14] The regular functioning of the Office and Governing Body is instrumental in creating a continuity of purpose in the work of the Organization that should make for international legal stability.

An important step in the process of placing an item on the Conference agenda is the questionnaire. This form of inquiry is not utilized to collect information on the subject proposed for international action, as that work is performed by the Office.[15] Instead, the purpose of the questionnaire is chiefly to obtain the opinions of governments as to the contemplated action.[16] In the light of these opinions, the subject is considered further.

One feature of the procedure followed by the Organization which may have some effect on treaty technique is the double-discussion requirement. This method of dealing with a subject on which the

[12] See *supra*, "Actual Making of Conventions," Chapter II, for a more complete discussion of the subject.

[13] See *Constitution and Standing Orders* (1936).

[14] The extended study of unemployment insurance following a recommendation on the subject in 1919 did not result in a draft convention until 1934. Most of the research appears to be for the purpose of improving international labor standards. Research activity is undertaken following a resolution on the subject by the Conference. A resolution sometimes originates through efforts of the members of the Office.

[15] Prior to 1921 the questionnaire was for the purpose of the collection of information. See *Official Bulletin*, III, 1921, 39-41.

[16] Prior to the adoption of the double-discussion procedure, questionnaires were sent to the governments before a new subject was adopted by the Conference. Since the adoption of the double-discussion procedure in 1926 the questionnaire has been sent out following the first discussion of the item.

Conference is taking action has been practiced successfully following its adoption by the Conference in 1926,[17] and its modification in 1929. According to this plan, the first Conference examines the law and practice reports drawn up by the Office, which contain tentative proposals for resolutions or draft decisions. If the Conference arrives at any conclusion concerning this question, the Office then frames a questionnaire on the basis of their decision,[18] which questionnaire is sent to the States Members. When the next Conference convenes, the second discussion takes places on the basis of the conclusions tentatively arrived at in the first Conference, and final decisions are made. The working out of this procedure has seemed to facilitate the task of the Conference committees. This has been true largely because of the fact that the committees have been relieved of the technical task of drafting and have been free to consider questions of policy.[19] This procedure would appear to insure careful decisions by the Conference on new questions on the agenda.[20]

The effectiveness of this method of procedure was recognized by the League of Nations in a resolution adopted in 1930 in which the "double-discussion procedure" was recommended as a method of facilitating the adoption of League conventions.[21] The action of the League would indicate that this particular procedure of the International Labor Organization is influencing the technique of treaty making.

The composition of committees of the Conference of the International Labor Organization is different from that of represen-

---

[17] See Appendix III, Report of the Committee on the "double-discussion procedure," *I. L. C., Proceedings,* 1926, I, 357-363. The examination and adoption of this method followed the failure of the first attempt to consider more carefully the making of conventions. The first unsuccessful method was called the "double-reading procedure." See *I. L. C., Proceedings,* 1925, I, 423ff.

[18] This procedure is a modification of that adopted in 1926 in regard to the unit which prepares the questionnaire and was adopted in 1929. See *I. L. C., Twelfth Session,* II, 1929, 361; also I, Third Part (appendices), 729 for note by the Legal Adviser of the Office.

[19] See comment of F. G. Wilson in this regard; he is of the opinion that this change served to preserve harmony between the various groups, as technical questions were often disruptive. *Op. cit.,* 201-202.

[20] See *I. L. C., Twelfth Session,* I, *loc. cit.*

[21] See *Official Journal,* Special Supplement No. 83 (October, 1930), 12-16. See also *The International Labor Organization: The First Decade,* 95.

tative conferences.[22] Only three committees are elected by the Conference; these are the Credentials Committee, the Committee on Resolutions, and the Committee of Selection.[23] The other committees are chosen by the Committee of Selection following nominations of prospective members by the three groups represented in the Conference. The substitution of the principle of group representation for that of the representation of states is a new feature in international conferences.[24]

The manner of voting in the Conference is distinctly different from the practice in the ordinary diplomatic conference. The Constitution provides that in the International Labor Conference "every Delegate shall be entitled to vote individually on all matters which are taken into consideration by the Conference." [25] This provision means that delegates do not vote in national blocs as is the case in the usual international conference. In the Labor Conference the government delegates sometimes act separately. They may or may not vote according to their instructions. In fact the position of a government representative is more like that of a member of a national legislature than a member of an international conference. The effect of this change in the relationship of the governmental representative to the procedure in the international conference may be far-reaching. This method of representation would seemingly detract from the importance of the sovereignty of states as represented in such a conference. The effect of such a voting procedure as that in the Labor Conference on the theory of absolute national sovereignty is especially striking when considered in the light of group action. Experience in the Conference has shown that the workers' and employers' groups generally vote as units, while the government representatives frequently divide.[26] It is

[22] See comment by Professor Norman L. Hill to the effect that the committee system of the Organization is a "departure from the current practice of representative assemblies," *The Public International Conference*, 148.

[23] See Article 7, *Constitution and Standing Orders* (Standing Orders of the Conference).

[24] Professor Hill is of the opinion that "It is most unusual for the committees of an international conference to be chosen by such a process as that which has been described, with the emphasis placed upon the representation of defined groups rather than that of sovereign states." *Op. cit.*, 149.

[25] Article 4. See comment on this article by Hugo Van Zanten, *L'Influence de la Partie XIII du Traité de Versailles sur le dévelopment de droit international public et sur le droit interne des Etats*, 58.

[26] See a study of group voting in the conference. *Annals*, CLXVI, 90-91.

conceivable that this unique method of action might bring about a modification of the concept of the sovereign authority negotiating treaties.[27]

The adoption of conventions by a vote of two-thirds as a stipulated method of procedure raises a number of serious questions in respect to its effect on treaty-making technique. Following their adoption, the conventions must be presented to the competent authorities within a specified length of time.[28] This obligation rests equally upon the States Members who voted against the convention and those who voted in favor of it. This duty of the members of the Organization has no parallel in international law. In the diplomatic conference, the state that has not signed a convention is under no such obligation; in the Labor Conference the obligation exists regardless of the votes of the delegates. Voting in the Labor Conference may be regarded as the means of registering approval or disapproval of a projected convention, just as signing it is a similar evidence in the realm of the diplomatic conference.[29] Consequently, the placing of a legal obligation concerning presentation of the convention to the competent authority on all states which are members of the Organization constitutes a new step in treaty law. It may have the effect of changing the relative importance of the public international conference. If the practice of the International Labor Organization in this regard should become a general one, the acts of conferences would possibly assume greater significance in the national affairs of the modern state.[30]

There is some basis for the position that recent developments in

---

[27] Professor F. G. Wilson is of the opinion that the group representation of the Labor Conference "involves a group theory of the state, a theory in which the governments have not a definite and controlling influence so much as a preponderant interest." *Op. cit.*, 133. This new method of representation and action would appear to project the theory of plural sovereignty within the national state into the realm of international law. Such a projection might profoundly affect international law.

[28] See Article 19, paragraph 5.

[29] See Norman L. Hill, *op. cit.*, 82.

[30] That this new procedure is not so unusual as it might appear to be, is suggested by Professor Hill, who adds that "no matter how their representatives may have voted, each government is left entirely free to take whatever final action it chooses in regard to a convention. There can be small objection to the majority rule at an international conference when it is admitted that the decisions taken are in no sense binding, but merely have the force of recommendations." *Ibid.*, 148.

international labor law have changed the relation of the powers of executive and legislative authorities of States Members in respect to ratification.[31] In the case of international labor conventions, in some instances the state has delegated no authority to its representatives to conclude such agreements; the legislature is under no moral obligation to ratify such agreements. In summary we have seen the apparent effect of the process of ratification or accession develop two divergent tendencies. The first is the compulsory submission of agreements, which adds a new state obligation. The other development is in the direction of subtracting from the obligations of the member states. This last development grows out of the lack of a moral obligation to ratify the convention on the part of the governmental representatives, who may not have given their consent to its adoption.

The unique methods of procedure of the International Labor Organization would appear to raise several questions, the most important being (1) will the new basis of representation—functional, occupational, or industrial—affect the law or technique of treaty making; (2) will the functioning of occupational groups in collaboration with state representatives eventually detract from the sovereignty of states in international law? If this new basis of representation in international agreements does indicate a more successful procedure in international affairs than has heretofore been utilized, a new epoch in the relations between states is in the making.[32] An attempt to give a definite answer to this question would be of less value, because the procedure is as yet in the evolutionary stage. Nevertheless, it appears that had there been a larger number of ratifications of conventions during the short period of the existence of the Organization the effect of this method

[31] See Van Zanten, *op. cit.*, 56.

[32] In commenting on the group representation of the Organization, Lord Burnham says: "The variety and antagonisms of classes are both the strength and weakness of the International Labor Conference. The strength because it is so drawn from the representative principle, which saves it from officialism and patronage. The weakness because it necessitates the use and sometimes the abuse of the group system of class solidarity, which is the caucus recognized openly and without pretense as the seat and source of power. The International Labor Conference differs from a diplomatic conference in that agreements come from the free play of mind and the resounding clash of interests, not as the pre-ordained and pre-arranged formula of Departments of State all engaged in 'saving face' and shirking responsibilities." *The Third International Labor Conference*, 1921, reprinted with certain additions from the *International Labour Review*, V. no. 2 (February 1922), iv.

of international action would have been of greater consequence. The lack of success of the Organization in this respect may be an evidence that the general effect of these new methods on treaty law and technique will not be great. On the other hand, the growth of international modes of procedure is necessarily slow, and the cautious beginning may mark a definite step in the direction of new techniques in forming international law.[33]

The procedure in connection with the revision of conventions has already been examined in detail. It differs from that followed in making conventions in several respects. The "double-discussion" method of action is not followed in revision. Circumstances have brought about the formulation of special procedure for placing specific questions concerning revision on the agenda of the Conference. The rôle of the Governing Body in revision is of greater importance than it is in the original act of making a convention.[34] The Governing Body must automatically review the working of conventions every ten years and consider whether total or partial revision should take place.

The method of procedure followed in revision of labor conventions is suggestive in the field of multipartite conventions of a legislative character. The working of the procedure of the International Labor Organization has demonstrated the necessity of careful adaptation of any revisory methods to the special characteristics of the subject matter of the convention being revised. This experience of the Organization will doubtless have considerable bearing on the general problem of treaty revision.[35]

CHARACTER OF THE AGREEMENTS

The international labor convention has a number of characteristics which differentiate it from the ordinary multipartite agree-

[33] Commenting on the new basis of representation found in the International Labor Organization, Mr. Ernest Mahaim says: "From the point of view of international law it was an innovation to grant delegates of industrial associations the same rights as delegates of governments, and to substitute for the traditional signature of plenipotentiaries the vote of an assembly (2/3 majority)." *Annals,* CLXVI (1933), 13.

[34] The provision in the Standing Orders of the Conference which states that in case of partial revision the question placed on the agenda by the Governing Body may not be changed by the Conference, is a concession to the workers' group. This stipulation keeps the Conference from examining the entire convention.

[35] See a comment to this effect by Jenks, "The Revision of International Labour Conventions," *British Yearbook of International Law,* XIV (1933), 64.

ment. One of the differences relates to the manner in which labor conventions are signed. The usual multipartite agreement is signed by the representatives of states which participate in the conference. International labor treaties are signed by the Director of the Office and the President of the Conference.[36] To what extent this method of signature affects the convention as an instrument in international law is a question that has already been, to some extent, examined.[37] The conclusion reached following this examination was that apparently labor conventions contain contractual obligations similar to other treaties which go into effect between states following their ratification. This would seem to be true despite the fact that these agreements are "quasi-legislative" [38] and are not signed by plenipotentiaries.[39]

The formulation by the Conference of an agreement called a recommendation appears to be an innovation in international law. This document is not binding and is presented to the States Members for the purpose of stimulating action by national legislation or other appropriate steps.[40]

In speaking of the drafting of this new type of agreement, Professor Samuel McCune Lindsay says:

---

[36] Paragraph 4 of Article 19 states: "A copy of the recommendation or draft convention shall be authenticated by the signature of the League of Nations. The Secretary-General will communicate a certified copy of the recommendation or draft convention to each of the Members."

[37] See some legal questions in revision, Chap. IV, "Contractual Nature of Conventions," *supra.*

[38] A descriptive term used by Mr. Morellet, Legal Adviser to the Office.

[39] When the first conventions were drawn up the French and Belgium authorities treated them as ordinary diplomatic instruments and the states exchanged official signatures. See *Official Bulletin,* III, no. 15 (April 1921), 448. A short time after this act the French Minister of Foreign Affairs informed the Secretary-General of the League of Nations that: "A protocol has been prepared leaving these conventions open to adhesion, one original copy of which will be deposited with the League Secretariat." This protocol was to be kept open to all members of the International Labor Organization. The Director of the Office wrote the Secretary-General that in his opinion the French adherence to the old procedure was "absolutely contrary both to the spirit and to the letter of Part XIII." This caused the French to abandon their original procedure. *Official Bulletin,* III, no. 23 (June 1921), 655-660.

[40] Article 19, paragraph 1, states: "It will rest with the Conference to determine whether these proposals should take the form (a) of recommendation to be submitted to the Members for consideration with a view to effect being given to it by national legislation or (b) of a draft international convention for ratification by the members."

> "The American Delegates would be willing to retain all of the machinery for the drafting of conventions that it is possible for the United States to accept; but alongside of it there should be introduced a new mechanism to cover a much wider field. If the only procedure were to be by way of draft treaties on labor matters, it might very well happen that the conventions would never play any serious part in the betterment of labor legislation. Professor Shotwell pointed out the field of negotiation by way of treaty is in its nature very limited and is held to rigid uniformity, while recommendations for legislation could be more readily adapted to varying conditions of national life." [41]

This early expression of faith in recommendations as a means of advancing national legislation may have been prompted by an overestimation of their value, as there is no accurate means of measuring how they have been applied.[42]

In spite of the doubt of the actual value of the labor recommendation, this instrument of expression may be a worthwhile contribution to the technique of treaty making. Action similar to recommendations may be taken in other fields to encourage states to adopt measures of universal value on matters on which they are not yet willing to establish contractual rights and duties. If the use of this method becomes widespread it might be a means of securing the approval of certain important laws which would finally result in the adoption of conventions.

The fact that the representatives of governments do not sign labor conventions and that there is no difference between the obligations of the states attending the Conference and those absent tends to make the terms "ratification" and "accession" mean the same thing. A state not present at the Conference has the same obligation as one actively in favor of the agreement. The trend away from the distinction between these two terms is not new in the

---

[41] See "The Problem of American Coöperation," *The Origins of the I. L. O.*, I, 339-340.

[42] A state ratifying a recommendation may apply only such parts of the instrument as it desires to put into effect. There is no general rule of periodic reports to the Office on the application of recommendations, although some information on the subject has been supplied by governments which have ratified them. See *International Labor Conference, Analysis of Information Supplied by Governments Concerning the Application of the Recommendations of the International Labor Conference,* 1932. In so far as the United States is concerned, no official action has been taken in regard to recommendations.

sphere of treaty law.[43] Nevertheless, this disappearance would seem to be hastened by the practice in regard to international labor conventions; for it is evident that in respect to these agreements there is no distinction between the action of the states participating in the Conference and those not taking part. The same rights and duties devolve on each group.

The clause in the constitution of the Organization which requires members to submit each convention or recommendation to the competent authority in their respective states gives these agreements a special status.[44] After they are adopted by the Conference they become something more than mere resolutions adopted by delegates representing three groups from the States Members of the Organization. The obligations placed on the members assure definite consideration in a specified period of time. According to this procedure, states, if they fulfill their obligations, cannot entirely ignore the proposals of the Conference. Thus their obligation is legal as well as moral, whereas in the ordinary diplomatic conference governments are only morally bound to submit treaties to legislative authorities.

An indication that this procedure has already affected the application of international labor law in certain states is afforded by a provision in the constitution of the Spanish Republic. This section of the constitution requires the submission of international labor conventions to the national legislative body within one year "or in case of exceptional circumstances, within eighteen months of the close of the conference at which they have been adopted." [45]

---

[43] See E. G. Fitz-Maurice, "Do Treaties Need Ratification?" *British Yearbook of International Law,* XV, 113-135.

[44] Article 19, paragraph 5, states: "Each of the Members undertakes that it will, within the period of one year at most from the closing of the session of the Conference, or if it is impossible owing to exceptional circumstances to do so within the period of one year, then at the earliest practicable moment and in no case later than eighteen months from the closing of the session of the Conference, bring the recommendation or draft convention before the authority or authorities within whose competence the matter lies, for the enactment of legislation or other action." For an excellent discussion of this point see Wilfred Jenks, "Some Characteristics of Labour Conventions," *Canadian Bar Review,* XIII (1935), 454.

[45] The complete text of the provision is as follows: "International Agreements dealing with the international organization of labor must be submitted to the Cortes within one year, or in case of exceptional circumstances, within eighteen months of the close of the Conference at which they have been adopted. Once they have been approved by the Parliament, the President must ratify them.

This makes the submission of a convention a national constitutional duty as well as an international legal one. In the recently adopted constitution of the Irish Free State, special provisions are made for the ratification of labor conventions.[46] This illustrates that as international agreements labor conventions require special treatment and that this is recognized by readjustment of the basic law of certain states to conform to the new procedure under international law.

A further stipulation concerning the peculiar character of international labor conventions is the special privilege given to federal states.[47] A government organized along federal lines may treat a convention as a recommendation if it wishes to do so. This clause was placed in the Constitution in order to accommodate the United States.[48]

The fact that federal states may treat draft conventions as recommendations would appear to produce inequalities in the obligation of states. In practice, however, this has not seemed to cause serious difficulties.[49] The federal states in recent years have attempted to solve the problem of inequality in this regard in ac-

---

This ratification must be communicated for registration to the League of Nations." *Diario de Sesiones de las cortes Constituyantes de la Republica Espanola* (Apendice 1º al numero 88) session of December 9, 1931.

[46] These provisions are as follows: "7. International Labor Conventions are approved by both Houses and the Oireachtas and ratified by means of an order of the Executive Council under their Seal." *Great Britain: Public General Acts*, 1922, 13, Geo. 5, ch. 1.

[47] Paragraph 9 of Article 405 of Part XIII states: "In the case of a federal State, the power of which to enter into conventions on labor matters is subject to limitations, it shall be in the discretion of that Government to treat a draft convention to which such limitations apply as a recommendation only, and the provisions of this article with respect to recommendations shall apply in such case."

[48] For an excellent, comprehensive discussion of the drafting of this section, see W. L. Tayler, *Federal States and Labor Treaties*, 29-68.

[49] In his study of the practice of federal states in this regard, Tayler says: "The fear expressed by certain members of the Commission on International Labor Legislation that the inequality of obligation provided in Article 19 (405) would react to the detriment of the International Labor Organization has now been dispelled. In the early years of the organization some member States took advantage of the option provided for in Article 19 (405) and treated draft conventions as recommendations. This was true of Australia and Canada. However, with the passing of time and a more detailed study of the possibilities of action as members of the International Labor Organization, new policies seem to be developing in Australia and Canada, more especially in the latter." *Ibid.*, 157.

cordance with their circumstances.[50] The action of the United States in this regard has not yet been determined, as the conventions ratified to date have been only those clearly within the scope of federal power.[51] The United States has ratified the following conventions: *Minimum Requirements of Profesisonal Capacity for Masters and Officers* (*Convention*) 1936; *Annual Holidays With Pay Seamen* (*Convention*) 1936; *Concerning the Liability of the Shipowner in Case of Sickness, Injury or Death of Seamen* (*Convention*) 1936; *Minimum Age Sea* (*Revised*) 1936. The Senate action on these conventions occurred June 13, 1938. Students of the problem differs as to whether all conventions of the International Labor Organization come within the scope of the treaty-making power of the Federal government.[52]

---

[50] The following states which are members of the International Labor Organization are federal: Argentina, Australia, Brazil, Canada, Mexico, Switzerland, Venezuela, and the United States.

[51] The United States did not become a member of the International Labor Organization until August 20, 1934. See *United States Treaty Series*, no. 874. The United States has ratified the following conventions: *Minimum Requirements of Professional Capacity for Masters and Officers* (*Convention*), 1936; *Annual Holidays With Pay Seamen* (*Convention*), 1936; *Concerning the Liability of the Shipowner in Case of Sickness, Injury or Death of Seamen* (*Convention*), 1936; *Minimum Age Sea* (*Revised*), 1936.

[52] Professor Manley O. Hudson comments on this subject as follows:

"There may be a general limitation on the treaty-making power which would prevent its exercise in such a way as to change the nature of the government, but there can be no general limitation that treaties may deal only with those matters as to which general legislative power has been delegated to the Federal Government. American participation in recent attempts to draft a treaty relating to the manufacture of arms is now clearly based on this principle, and the United States has recently become a party to the *Convention for Limiting the Manufacture and Regulating the Distribution of Narcotic Drugs* of July 13, 1931, which limits the manufacture of drugs within the States. It should be clear, therefore, that the power of the United States to enter into such labor Conventions as have been adopted by the International Labor Conference to date, is not subject to any special limitations. If this be true, paragraph 9 of Article 405 does not apply to the United States, and the mention of that provision in the preamble of the joint resolution does not establish any reservation on this point." "The Membership of the United States in the International Labor Organization," *A. J. I. L.*, XXVII (1934), 678-679. A similar point of view is taken by Tayler, *op. cit.*, as indicated in the following words: "In the United States no difficulty is expected in regard to the ratification of the international labor conventions adopted thus far as the treaty making power of the Federal Government seems to be broad enough to enable the Federal Government to ratify if it wishes," 158. After a thorough examination of the obligations of the

The standard revisory article which has evolved over a period of years and is now found in international labor conventions possesses certain characteristics not common to multipartite agreements.[53] This article explicitly defines the effect of the adoption of a revising convention.[54] The definition of the legal consequences of revision in the agreement would seem to be a step in the direction of providing a stable process of adjustment which might be valuable to multipartite instruments.

APPLICATION

There is no lack of adequate provisions for the enforcement of the standards laid down by international labor conventions. In fact, in the days immediately following the formation of the Organization it was generally believed that it could enforce these standards by the invocation of strict sanctions.[55] Nevertheless, with the resurgence of the nationalistic spirit any efforts at enforcement became impractical, so the real processes of compelling states to apply the provisions of conventions were never used. If the Organization had made use of these methods, such application, if effective, would doubtless have had a considerable effect on international practice. In the absence of attempts to force applications the effect of the existing practice is rather difficult to evaluate.

The provisions of the Constitution stipulating the means to be employed in enforcing the terms of conventions are in Articles 22-34, inclusive. The procedure to be followed by the Governing Body is explicitly outlined. Complaints received by the Governing

---

United States, Abraham C. Weinfeld, in *Labor Treaties and Labor Compacts,* reached the conclusion that conventions should be submitted to the congress and recommendations to the federal or state legislative bodies, depending on the nature of the subject matter; 52-75.

A somewhat different opinion is expressed by F. G. Wilson as follows: "On those questions upon which Congress may pass legislation Congress will be, naturally the competent authority. On those questions falling within the jurisdiction of the states, the state legislatures will be the competent authority. *Op. cit.,* 345.

There is at present no evidence of any effort to present to the states for approval conventions of this type.

[53] See Jenks, "The Revision of International Labor Conventions," *loc. cit.,* 63.

[54] See chapter III, *supra,* "The Development of Revisory Procedure."

[55] In this connection F. G. Wilson is of the opinion that those who sincerely believed sanctions could be invoked to enforce the terms of a treaty were impractical idealists. *Op. cit.,* 217-219.

Body may be legally acted upon according to the discretion of its members.[56] If the plan proposed by the Governing Body is not acceptable to the state concerned, the case may be referred to the Permanent Court of International Justice for judicial settlement.[57]

There has been no test of the practicability of the measures referred to above, as they have never been invoked. Representations have been made by workers' groups, but these have not been acted on to any great extent by the Governing Body.[58]

Thus far the action in respect to the enforcement of the application has not been effectively applied, yet the provisions set up a procedure which is unique in the field of international law.[59] One part of this procedure, which strictly speaking has to do with

[56] As the result of a legal study by the Office in 1932 on the methods of applying paragraph 4 of Article 411, the following alternatives were left to the Governing Body:

(a) it may simply reject the complaint;
(b) it may obtain additional information by the most appropriate means;
(c) it may communicate with the government in question in accordance with the procedure laid down by Article 409 for representations;
(d) it may decide at once to set up a commission of enquiry. See *Minutes of the Fifty-sixth Session of the Governing Body*, January, 1932. The use of the term "may" indicates how wide the powers of the Governing Body are until the commission of enquiry is set up.

[57] See Article 22 (408).

[58] There have been several representations under these provisions. These have been made by the Japanese, Latvian, and Indian workers respectively. In the first two cases the governments were consulted and no further action was deemed necessary. See discussion in *Minutes of the Twenty-fourth Session of the Governing Body*, 1924, and *Report of the Director, Seventh Session*, 1926, 122-124, for the Japanese representation. The Latvian complaint is recorded and the final decision given in *Official Bulletin*, XVI, 1931, 29, 265. The two most recent complaints concern the "Madras Labour Union for Textile Workers Case" and "The Labour Party of Mauritius Case." These cases were considered at the Seventh-seventh Session of the Governing Body; see *Official Bulletin*, XXII, no. 2, 61-69, and C. W. Jenks, "Some Further Representations under Article 23 of the Constitution of the International Labour Organization," *British Yearbook of International Law*, 1938, 29. In the Madras case the principle that changes in the internal constitution of a state have no effect upon the state's international obligations was reaffirmed. In the case concerning whether the Labour Party of Mauritius could be regarded as an "industrial association of employers and workers" entitled to representation under Article 23 of the Constitution, the Governing Body adopted the report of the committee which held it could be liberally interpreted but that in this case the Labour Party did not come under this meaning.

[59] See comment by F. G. Wilson, *op. cit.*, in note 20, 230-231.

the application of conventions, merits special consideration. This is Article 22 (408), which requires each state to present an annual report on the application of ratified conventions.[60] The obligations arising under Article 22 may be described as three-fold:

> "(1) An obligation on the Members to make annual reports to the International Labor Office on the measures they have taken to give effect to the provisions of conventions to which they are parties;
>
> "(2) An obligation on the Governing Body to prescribe the form of such reports and the particulars which they should contain;
>
> "(3) An obligation on the Director of the International Labor Office to lay a summary of the report before the next meeting of the Conference." [61]

The form of the report to be supplied by States Members requires certain specific information; this form has been modified from time to time by the Governing Body. In general, the information requested pertains to the effective ratification of conventions, legislative or other measures employed to put the convention into effect, with copies of the new laws, the manner in which the convention is being applied in the courts, the exceptions allowed, and any general observations that the reporting state deems advisable.[62]

The Conference Committee on Article 22 (408) examines the reports received by the Office with a view to noting any discrepancies in application or any other evidences of the failure of a state to fulfill the requirements of conventions.[63] In the process of this examination states failing to fulfill their obligations under conventions in a satisfactory manner are subject to severe criticism, especially by the workers' representatives.[64]

[60] See the Constitution.

[61] *See I. L. C., Eighteenth Session,* 1934, *Summary of Annual Reports,* 33.

[62] *Idem.* For early forms of the report, see *Report of the Director, Fifth Session,* Genoa, 1923, 375-377, and *Official Bulletin,* IV, 1920, 159-165, and VII, 285-290.

[63] This committee acts for the Conference in accordance with the section of Article 22 (408) which provides: "The Director shall lay a summary of these reports before the next meeting of the Conference." The acceptance of these reports by the Conference is a mere matter of form, but the committee devotes practical efforts to the task. In a meeting of the Governing Body in 1923 the Director explicitly stated that no effort was being made at that time to ascertain the interpretation of conventions in the various states. *Minutes of the Seventeenth Session of the Governing Body,* 1923, 21-22.

[64] These criticisms are to be found in most of the reports of the committee, which are a part of the final record of each Conference. For example, the report

Many members of the Conference felt in the early years that the considerations of the reports under Article 22 (408) were entirely too much in the nature of a summary and that more expert attention should be given to the technical meaning of the subject matter. Consequently, in 1926 the Conference approved the constitution of a body which was to be supplementary to the Committee on Article 408.[65] This new unit was to be a Committee of Experts who were especially qualified to examine the reports. Their function was to be purely technical, with no judicial prerogatives.[66] This body, it was believed, was constituted so that it could make a more comprehensive examination of the state reports and probably make suggestions that would be of value to the Organization.[67]

in 1928 criticized the failure of certain states to abide by their obligations as follows: "The conventions are international treaties. Under the general rules of international public law and the provisions of the Labour parts of the Treaties of Peace, the states which ratify are under obligation to apply without restriction and throughout their territory the provisions of Article 421 of the Treaty of Versailles and the Corresponding Articles of the Treaties of Peace. So national legislation must be brought in harmony with conventions and applied." *I. L. C. Proceedings, Eleventh Session,* I, appendix IV, 617. See also the criticism in the *Proceedings* by Mr. Kupers (Netherlands Delegate), 286-288. In 1934 the committee pointed out three unfortunate aspects of the governments' reports on conventions: (1) some states failed to make any reports; (2) others failed to report in the proper form; (3) some statements in reports revealed that ratified conventions are not strictly applied. *I. L. C., Eighteenth Session,* 1934, Appendix V, 537.

[65] See *I. L. C., Proceedings,* 1926, 239. This body was suggested by Mr. O'Rahilly (Government Delegate, Irish Free State). See *I. L. C., Proceedings,* 1925, 156-157. This new body was approved by the Conference after considerable debate. See *I. L. C., Proceedings, Ninth Session,* 1926, I, 20.

[66] When this measure was being considered some feared that the suggested committee might encroach on the soveignty of states or interfere with some of the competent bodies set up by Part XIII, e.g. the Permanent Court of International Justice or the Commission of Enquiry. Accordingly, the functions of the committee were defined as follows: (1) The committee of experts were to note the cases where the information supplied by the governments in their particular reports was incomplete, either generally or in the case of a particular country. If there is a general absence of information the committee might propose to the Governing Body the revision of the form of the questionnaire addressed to the governments. The committee might also suggest that the Office ask for further details from the governments.

(2) The committee was to draw attention to differing interpretations. (3) The committee would present a technical report to the Office to be presented to the Conference. *I. L. C., Proceedings,* 1926, 239. See also note on the composition and functions of the proposed Committee of Experts, 399-402.

[67] The first report of the Committee of Experts contained the suggestion that the forms of the reports on Article 408 should be revised so the information

The actual work of the Committee of Experts appears to be of considerable value, according to the expressions in respect to its services in the Conference records.[68] Some of the proposals of the committee have been of practical significance in furthering the co-operation among the governments and the other groups concerned.[69] In 1932 the Committee of Experts was called a "bold innovation," and its work was characterized as ". . . a procedure which represents a very noteworthy progress in international co-operation, and one which might perhaps serve as a precedent and an example for the development of effective international supervision by mutual collaboration in other spheres." [70]

Whether or not it would be possible to establish similar bodies in other international spheres would possibly depend to a large extent on a further development of international organization. Nevertheless, it seems significant to international law that a committee composed of highly trained individuals should regularly examine the fulfillment of the obligations of national states under international treaties. The development of this body might be an indication of a scientific, effective method of applying the provisions of conventions.

In the application of conventions through the interpretation by the units concerned there are possibly no innovations which would affect treaty law. The procedure followed by the Permanent Court of International Justice and national bodies in interpreting conventions is not unlike that followed in respect to other treaties.[71] Possibly the unofficial interpretations by the Office may illustrate

---

supplied by governments would be more complete. See *I. L. C., Tenth Session, Report of the Director,* 1927, II, 401, 418-419. See the list of the members of the Committee of Experts, 260.

[68] The Committee was praised highly in the Annual Report on Article 408 in 1929. The results of its work, the report emphasized, had been valuable in getting more information concerning conventions. See *I. L. C., Twelfth Session, Report of Director,* 1929, II, 294-533. See similar statement in *Eighteenth Session,* 1934, Appendix V, 538.

[69] The committee suggested in 1932 that the governments consult the workers' and employers' organizations on the subject matter of the reports and append the observations of these groups to their reports. This suggestion was modified by the Committee on Article 408 and was in no sense made obligatory. See *Minutes of the Fifty-seventh Session of the Governing Body,* April 1932, 201, 331-332.

[70] *I. L. C. Proceedings, Sixteenth Session,* 1932, 318.

[71] See *supra,* chapter V, "Interpretation by the Permanent Court of International Justice," and chapter VII, "Interpretation in National Courts."

the effect on international law of a central agency undertaking to clarify doubtful provisions of agreements.[72] However, the fact that the Office is a purely administrative body might preclude any strictly legal effect.

It appears that there is not much evidence that the application of conventions will profoundly affect international law. This is in part due to the reluctance of the Organization to put in effect the more drastic provisions concerning application. The practice of having reports regularly made by states on conventions (as provided in Article 22 (408) and of having these reports examined by experts may prove to be of sufficient value to affect the general application of treaties.

---

[72] See *supra*, Chap. V, 135-149.

CHAPTER IX

CONCLUSION

THE DEVELOPMENT of the International Labor Organization has shown the increasing importance of the legal phase of international labor legislation. The rigid Constitution of the Organization (Part XIII of the Treaty of Versailles and the labor sections of corresponding treaties) laid down the rules by which it might operate. These provisions were in some instances insufficient for the most successful functioning. The stipulations have often been regarded as limitative. The member states have been reluctant to request an interpretation from the Permanent Court. They have apparently been hesitant due to the formality of the procedure and the length of time required to get an opinion. The fact that the Constiution gives no authority to any other unit in respect to interpretation has raised a seemingly insurmountable legal barrier to official opinions other than those of the Permanent Court. The Constitution makes no provision for the revision of conventions. The bodies competent to revise derive their authority from the provisions of the constitution which concern the making of conventions. In both interpretation and revision legal difficulties have given rise to the evolution of new rules of international legal procedure.

In the formation of any practical legal system a process of change appears essential. A dynamic conception of international labor standards seems particularly indispensable in view of frequent economic, technological, and political changes.[1]

[1] Mr. Butler, a former Director of the Office, expressed the need of change, in the following words: "It may be pointed out that social legislation is not static but dynamic. There is no absolute ideal which, once achieved, represents finality. Social progress is a continuing process. What may seem the ultimate goal of one generation becomes the starting point of the next. There is certainly no reason to suppose that we are yet in sight of the millennium. Of this a glance backward over the conventions hitherto adopted furnishes ample proof. Some of them are already becoming out of date. Fifteen years ago a week of forty-eight hours seemed the maximum limit to which the reduction of hours could go. It marked the consecration of a demand that stood at the head of labor programmes for seventy years. Now a further reduction in hours is considered desirable." See *I. L. C., Nineteenth Session, Report of the Director,* 1935, 74.

Early in the history of the Organization the need of a revisory process became apparent. One of the chief causes of the effort to formulate a method of amendment was the failure of conventions to obtain wide-spread ratification. The first attempts to set up a procedure by which changes could be effected in conventions were unsuccessful. This was partially due to the lack of realization of the peculiar characteristics of labor conventions. Efforts to formulate an amendatory process which would enable the member states to make changes without a lengthy formal procedure were found to be inconsistent with the nature of labor conventions. Likewise, reservations to particular agreements were held to be incompatible with the obligations created by labor conventions. The Organization felt compelled to formulate a special revisory process.

The function of interpretation of international labor conventions looks to the application of international standards in a uniform manner. Presumably, interpretation should make the provisions of labor treaties more adaptable to specific conditions. In the field of labor this objective has been found particularly difficult to attain, as conditions concerning labor matters vary greatly. This strict adherence of the Labor Organization to the Constitution has placed the burden of interpretation on the Office and national bodies.

The development of revisory procedure by the International Labor Organization has made apparent the strength and weakness of the methods pursued. The limited provisions of the Constitution have sometimes made the formulation of flexible rules an impossibility. This situation has at times tended to delay the revision of conventions. This delay may have blocked the progress of the application of international labor standards. With the evidence available it is perhaps possible to determine whether the slow evolution of the revisory process has been an advantage or a disadvantage. The practice of revision has demonstrated that in spite of the cautious formulation of amendatory procedure, frequent modification of the procedure has been necessary. It would appear that the revision of labor conventions has not been brought about by the adherence to an untried method of procedure. This leads to the conclusion that the Organization could have justifiably acted in a more positive manner in setting up revisory procedure. It is, however, necessary to qualify this conclusion in view of the complex legal problems which have arisen in the practice of revision.

The analysis of revision has demonstrated the complexity of the problems that must be solved before modification can be successfully completed. One of these problems has concerned the need for the immediate revision of certain conventions. In order to meet this need the Governing Body has modified the existing revisory procedure. In doing so the Governing Body has given evidence of its courage and resourcefulness. The modification of set rules of procedure may be commendable in emergency situations occurring in the formative period of the Organization. Nevertheless, if such modifications of procedure were to become the rule rather than the exception, such precedents might threaten the legal guarantees set up by conventions. The constitutional limits laid down in the Constitution might be transcended with the result that the legal basis for international labor treaties would cease to support the structure. The unique character of labor conventions has made the legal problems in revision, to some extent, different from those arising from the ordinary multipartite treaty. The determination of the contractual nature of conventions has been partially solved by the Organization. The exact competence of the units concerned in revision possibly has not been permanently decided. The effect of the revising convention the original has been to some extent determined under the most recent revisory clause. The questions arising from the lack of the unanimity rule have complicated the revisory process. In spite of these difficulties the Organization has evolved a method of adjusting conventions to national needs which functions with a limited degree of success. As revisory efforts have been very recent, there is no accurate method of measuring the success of revision on the basis of the number of ratifications procured through the changes effected. In view of the results obtained from the first revisory act (*Convention for the Protection against Accidents—Dockers,* 1919) this modification would appear to have definitely facilitated ratifications.[2] The other conventions were revised at such recent dates that judgment in regard to them must be deferred.[3] It is therefore impossible to evaluate safely the

---

[2] This convention, adopted in 1929, was revised in 1932. At the date of revision four ratifications of the conventions had been deposited. In March, 1940, a total of nine ratifications had been registered.

[3] The convention on the *Employment of Women at Night* (1919) had thirty-one ratifications when it was revised in 1934. The latest figures give fifteen ratifica-

success of revision measured merely in terms of the additional number of ratifications obtained.

The interpretation of conventions has created a difficult problem for the International Labor Organization. So far no solution has been found which is entirely satisfactory. The plans to have the Governing Body or the Conference render official opinions have not been deemed valid. The unofficial interpretations of the Office have to a slight degree assisted in clarifying terms in conventions. The Office has rendered its opinion on provisions of conventions on the basis of the existing practice in other states, the preparatory work in framing the convention, and the general purpose of the document. It appears that the Office has generally interpreted conventions so states can apply their provisions. In some cases the Office may have given liberal interpretations to get more ratifications. Nevertheless, the evidence indicates that the Office has supported its opinions with valid proof. Furthermore, it has obviously tried to avoid giving interpretations which would lessen the protection of the workers.[4] The opinions of the Office have been of value to the member states. They have apparently facilitated ratifications and assisted in the application of conventions.

The one advisory opinion of the Permanent Court of International Justice demonstrated the value of its contribution to the interpretation of conventions. The Court arrived at its decision by the general canons followed in its preceding interpretations. Preparatory work was not an important factor in the Court's decision, as the tribunal believed that the text was clear. The opinion of the Court on the convention in question clarified the meaning of the doubtful clause and resulted in a satisfactory revision of the instrument. This suggests the value of using official

tions. The convention on *Workmen's Occupational Diseases* (1925) which was revised in 1934 had thirty ratifications at that time. The latest figures state that it has thirteen ratifications. The *Hours of Work Coal Mines Convention* (1931) had one ratification when it was revised in 1931. The new convention now has two ratifications. The *Minimum Age* (*Industry*) 1919, had twenty ratifications when revised in 1937; the revised convention has only one ratification. The *Minimum Age* (*Non-Industry*), 1932, had seven ratifications when it was revised in 1937. So far the new convention has received no ratifications. The *Minimum Age* (*Sea*) 1920, had thirty-two ratifications when revised in 1936; the new convention has only seven ratifications.

[4] There is a danger that unofficial interpretations might be used for the sole purpose of procuring ratifications regardless of the method of application they foster. Since the Office has been insistent on strict application in the past, it is unlikely that such a danger exists in respect to its opinions.

legal interpretations as a method of adjusting difficulties. The fact that only one advisory opinion concerning labor conventions has been rendered by the Court during the life of the Organization to date suggests the limited importance of the Court as a means of securing uniformity.

The wide variance in the legislative and administrative application of conventions by the member states has made uniform application in national courts especially difficult. To this difficulty is added the disparity in the composition of national courts and their application of different systems of municipal law. An exact comparison, therefore, appears impossible. A few limited conclusions may be drawn. By and large, national courts have interpreted conventions concerning the rights of aliens in a nonrestrictive manner favorable to the alien claimants. In some instances the decisions of national courts definitely indicate that the coming into force of conventions has materially increased the guarantees of alien workers. On the basis of the cases examined, municipal courts do not appear to have discriminated against foreign workers in their application of the provisions of conventions.

In the application of conventions concerning the rights of nationals, the decisions considered indicate that the judicial and administrative authorities have generally given interpretations favorable to the rights of those protected. The bodies rendering opinions in some states, such as Great Britain and France, appear to go further in the direction of a liberal interpretation in guaranteeing employees' rights than is the case in other states. Since the major purpose in establishing the International Labor Organization was to better the conditions of the working classes, a liberal construction of conventions by national courts is in accordance with the spirit of the Constitution.

The techniques of interpretation and revision of labor conventions are at present only in the formative stage. Interpretation is not uniform, and without an additional international body giving official interpretations there is little likelihood that any great degree of uniformity will be attained. The process of revision is not yet satisfactory from the point of view of the needs of the Organization. Procedural and legal difficulties will possibly require new adjustments in the future.

The effect of the methods examined on treaty law and technique cannot be stated with any degree of finality. A more significant evaluation can be made only after the methods in question have been in effect during a longer period of time. There are, however, several possible effects on adjective treaty law that may be safely noted. The practice of allowing functional groups within the state to participate in international action may connect legal guarantees more closely with group opinion. The formulation of conventions that are not binding until they are ratified by two-thirds concurrence of the delegates present at the Conference may weaken the unanimity rule to the extent that state sovereignty may be less jealous of international authority. The general nature of labor conventions may affect the character of future international conventions, particularly those dealing with technical subjects. The value of a workable method of revision administered by permanent agencies in a legal, scientific manner possibly will cause the application of some of the newly evolved principles in other fields of international action.

APPENDIX I

Draft Convention (No. 28) *concerning the protection against accidents of workers employed in loading or unloading ships.*[1]

Article 2

Any regular approach over a dock, wharf, quay or similar premises which workers have to use for going to or from a working place at which the processes are carried on and every such working place on shore shall be maintained with due regard to the safety of the workers using them.

In particular.

(1) every said working place on shore and any dangerous parts of any said approach thereto from the nearest highway shall be safely and efficiently lighted;

(2) wharves and quays shall be kept sufficiently clear of goods to maintain a clear passage to the means of access referred to in Article 3;

(3) where any space is left along the edge of any wharf or quay, it shall be at least 3 feet (90 cm.) wide and clear of all obstruction other than fixed structures, plant and appliances in use; and

(4) so far as is practicable having regard to the traffic and working.

(*a*) all dangerous parts of the said approaches and working places (e.g. dangerous breaks, corners and edges) shall be adequately fenced to a height of not less than 2 feet 6 inches (75 cm.);

(*b*) dangerous footways over bridges, caissons and dock gates shall be fenced to a height of not less than 2 feet 6 inches (75 cm.) on each side, and the said fencing shall be continued at both ends to a sufficient distance which shall not be required to exceed 5 yards (4 m. 50).

Article 5

(1) When the workers have to carry on the processes in a hold the depth of which from the level of the deck to the bottom of the hold exceeds 5 feet (1 m. 50), there shall be safe means of access from the deck to the hold for their use.

(2) The said means of access shall ordinarily be by ladder, which shall not be deemed to be safe unless it complies with the following conditions:

[1] *Draft Conventions and Recommendations* (1919-1934), 166ff. The excerpts in these appendices are taken from the corresponding original and revised conventions and consist of articles which have been revised by conference action.

(*a*) leaves sufficient free space behind the rungs, which in the case of ladders on bulkheads and in trunk hatchways shall not be less than 4½ inches (11½ cm.) or has throughout rungs of proper width for firm foothold and handhold;

(*b*) is not recessed under the deck more than is reasonably necessary to keep it clear of the hatchways;

(*c*) is continued by and is in line with arrangements for secure handhold and foothold in the coamings (e.g. cleats or cups);

(*d*) the said arrangements on the coamings stand out not less than 4½ inches (11½ cm.) for a width of 10 inches (25 cm.); and

(*e*) if separate ladders are provided between the lower decks, the said ladders are as far as possible in line with the ladders from the top deck.

Where, however, owing to the construction of the ship, the provision of a ladder would not be reasonably practicable, it shall be open to the competent authorities to allow other means of access, provided that they comply with the conditions laid down in this Article for ladders so far as they are applicable.

(3) Sufficient free passage to the means of access shall be left at the coamings.

(4) Shaft tunnels shall be equipped with adequate handhold and foothold on both sides.

(5) When a ladder is to be used in the hold of a vessel which is not decked it shall be the duty of the contractor undertaking the processes to provide such ladder. It shall be equipped at the top with hooks for fastening it on to the coamings or with other means for firmly securing it.

(6) The workers shall not use, or be required to use, other means of access than the means specified or allowed by this Article.

(7) Ships existing at the date of ratification of this Convention shall be exempt from compliance with the measurements in paragraph 2(*a*) and (*d*) and from the provisions of paragraph 4 of this Article for a period not exceeding four years from the date of ratification of this Convention.

Article 6

While the workers are on a ship for the purpose of the processes, no hatchway of a cargo hold which exceeds 5 feet (1 m. 50) in depth from the level of the deck to the bottom of the hold and which is accessible to the workers shall be left open and unprotected, but every such hatchway which is not protected to a clear height of 2 feet 6 inches (75 cm.) by the coamings shall either be securely fenced to a height of 3 feet

(90 cm.) if the processes at that hatchway are not impeded thereby or be securely covered.

Similar measures shall be taken when necessary to protect any other openings in a deck which might be dangerous to the workers.

Provided that the requirements of this Article shall not apply when a proper and sufficient watch is being kept.

Article 8

In order to ensure the safety of the workers when engaged in removing or replacing hatch coverings and beams used for hatch coverings.

(1) hatch coverings and beams used for hatch coverings shall be maintained in good condition;

(2) hatch coverings shall be fitted with adequate hand grips, having regard to their size and weight;

(3) beams used for hatch coverings shall have suitable gear for removing and replacing them of such a character as to render it unnecessary for workers to go upon them for the purpose of adjusting such gear;

(4) all hatch coverings and fore and aft and thwart-ship beams shall, in so far as they are not interchangeable, be kept plainly marked to indicate the deck and hatch to which they belong and their position therein;

(5) hatch coverings shall not be used in the construction of cargo stages or for any other purpose which may expose them to damage.

Article 9

Appropriate measures shall be prescribed to ensure that no hoisting machine, or gear, whether fixed or loose, used in connection therewith, is employed in the processes on shore or on board ship unless it is in a safe working condition.

In particular,

(1) before being taken into use, the said machines, fixed gear on board ship accessory thereto as defined by national laws or regulations, and chains and wire ropes used in connection therewith, shall be adequately examined and tested, and the safe working load thereof certified, in the manner prescribed and by a competent person;

(2) after being taken into use, every hoisting machine, whether used on shore or on board ship, and all fixed gear on board ship accessory thereto as defined by national laws or regulations shall be thoroughly examined or inspected as follows:

(*a*) to be thoroughly examined every four years and inspected every twelve months: derricks, goose necks, mast bands, derrick bands, eyebolts, spans and any other fixed gear the dismantling of which is specially difficult;

(*b*) to be thoroughly examined every twelve months: all hoisting machines (e.g. cranes, winches), blocks, shackles and all other accessory gear not included in (*a*).

All loose gear (e.g. chains, wire ropes, rings, hooks) shall be inspected on each occasion before use unless they have been inspected within the previous three months.

Chains shall not be shortened by tying knots in them and precautions shall be taken to prevent injury to them from sharp edges.

A thimble or loop splice made in any wire rope shall have at least three tucks with a whole strand of rope and two tucks with one-half of the wires cut out of each strand; provided that this requirement shall not operate to prevent the use of another form of splice which can be shown to be as efficient as the form hereby prescribed.

(3) Chains and such similar gear as is specified by national laws or regulations (e.g. hooks, rings, shackles, swivels) shall, unless they have been subjected to such other sufficient treatment as may be prescribed by national laws or regulations, be annealed under the supervision of a competent person as follows:

(*a*) In the case of chains and the said gear carried on board ship:

(i) half inch (12½ mm.) and smaller chains or gear in general use once at least in every six months;

(ii) all other chains or gear (including span chains but excluding bridle chains attached to derricks or masts) in general use once at least in every twelve months:

Provided that in the case of such gear used solely on cranes and other hoisting appliances worked by hand, twelve months shall be substituted for six months in sub-paragraph (i) and two years for twelve months in sub-paragraph (ii);

Provided also that, if the competent authority is of opinion that owing to the size, design, material or infrequency of use of any of the said gear other than chains the requirements of this paragraph as to annealing are not necessary for the protection of the workers, it may, by certificate in writing (which it may at its discretion revoke) exempt such gear from the said requirements subject to such conditions as may be specified in the said certificate.

(*b*) In the case of chains and the said gear not carried on board ship: Measures shall be prescribed to secure the annealing of the said chains and gear.

(c) In the case of the said chains and gear whether carried on board ship or not, which have been lengthened, altered, or repaired by welding, they shall thereupon be tested and reëxamined.

(4) Such duly authenticated records as will provide sufficient *prima facie* evidence of the safe condition of the machines and gear concerned shall be kept, on shore or on the ship as the case may be, specifying the safe working load and the dates and results of the tests and examinations referred to in paragraphs (1) and (2) of this Article and of the annealings or other treatment referred to in paragraph (3).

Such records shall, on the application of any person authorized for the purpose, be produced by the person in charge thereof.

(5) The safe working load shall be kept plainly marked on all cranes, derricks and chain slings and on any similar hoisting gear used on board ship as specified by national laws or regulations. The safe working load marked on chain slings shall either be in plain figures or letters upon the chains or upon a tablet or ring of durable material attached securely thereto.

(6) All motors, cogwheels, chain and friction gearing, shafting, live electric conductors and steam pipes shall (unless it can be shown that by their position and construction they are equally safe to every worker employed as they would be if securely fenced) be securely fenced so far as is practicable without impeding the safe working of the ship.

(7) Cranes and winches shall be provided with effective appliances to prevent the accidental descent of a load while in process of being lifted or lowered.

(8) Appropriate measures shall be taken to prevent exhaust steam from and, so far as practicable, live steam to any crane or winch obscuring any part of the working place at which a worker is employed.

Article 11

(1) No load shall be left suspended from any hoisting machine unless there is a competent person actually in charge of the machine while the load is so left.

(2) Appropriate measures shall be prescribed to provide for the employment of a signaller where this is necessary for the safety of the workers.

(3) Appropriate measures shall be prescribed with the object of preventing dangerous methods of working in the stacking, unstacking, stowing and unstowing of cargo, or handling in connection therewith.

(4) Before work is begun at a hatch the beams thereof shall be removed, unless the hatch is of sufficient size to preclude danger to the workers from a load striking against the beams; provided that when the beams are not removed, they shall be securely fastened to prevent their displacement.

(5) Precautions shall be taken to facilitate the escape of the workers when employed in a hold or on 'tween decks in dealing with coal or other bulk cargo.

(6) No stage shall be used in the processes unless it is substantially and firmly constructed, adequately supported and where necessary securely fastened.

No truck shall be used for carrying cargo between ship and shore on a stage so steep as to be unsafe.

Stages shall where necessary be treated with suitable material to prevent the workers slipping.

(7) When the working space in a hold is confined to the square of the hatch, hooks shall not be made fast in the bands of fastenings of bales of cotton, wool, cork, gunny bags or other similar goods (nor can-hooks on barrels), except for the purpose of breaking out or making up slings.

(8) No gear of any description shall be loaded beyond the safe working load, except on special occasions expressly authorized by the owner or his responsible agent of which a record shall be kept.

(9) In the case of shore cranes with varying capacity (e.g. raising and lowering jib, with load capacity varying according to the angle) an automatic indicator or a table showing the safe working loads at the corresponding inclinations of the jib shall be provided on the crane.

Article 18

The formal ratification of this Convention under the conditions set forth in Part XIII of the Treaty of Versailles and in the corresponding Parts of the other Treaties of Peace shall be communicated to the Secretary-General of the League of Nations for registration.

Draft Convention (No. 32) *concerning the protection against accidents of workers employed in loading or unloading ships (revised 1932).*[2]

Article 2

Any regular approach over a dock, wharf, quay or similar premises which workers have to use for going to or from a working place at

[2] *Draft Conventions and Recommendations* (1919-1934), 211ff.

which the processes are carried on and every such working place on shore shall be maintained with due regard to the safety of the workers using them.

In particular,

(1) every said working place on shore and any dangerous parts of any said approach thereto from the nearest highway shall be safely and efficiently lighted;

(2) wharves and quays shall be kept sufficiently clear of goods to maintain a clear passage to the means of access referred to in Article 3;

(3) where any space is left along the edge of any wharf or quay, it shall be at least 3 feet (90 cm.) wide and clear of all obstructions other than fixed structure, plant and appliances in use; and

(4) so far as is practicable having regard to the traffic and working,

(*a*) all dangerous parts of the said approaches and working places (e.g. dangerous breaks, corners and edges) shall be adequately fenced to a height of not less than 2 feet 6 inches (75 cm.);

(*b*) dangerous footways over bridges, caissons and dock gates shall be fenced to a height of not less than 2 feet 6 inches (75 cm.) on each side, and the said fencing shall be continued at both ends to a sufficient distance which shall not be required to exceed 5 yards (4 m. 50).

(5) The measurement requirements of paragraph (4) of this Article shall be deemed to be complied with, in respect of appliances in use at the date of the ratification of this Convention, if the actual measurements are not more than 10 per cent. less than the measurements specified in the said paragraph (4).

Article 5

(1) When the workers have to carry on the processes in a hold the depth of which from the level of the deck to the bottom of the hold exceeds 5 feet (1 m. 50), there shall be safe means of access from the deck to the hold for their use.

(2) The said means of access shall ordinarily be by ladder, which shall not be deemed to be safe unless it complies with the following conditions:

(*a*) provides foothold of a depth, including any space behind the ladder, of not less than 4½ inches (11½ cm.) for a width of not less than 10 inches (25 cm.) and a firm handhold;

(*b*) is not recessed under the deck more than is reasonably necessary to keep it clear of the hatchway;

(*c*) is continued by and is in line with arrangements for secure handhold and foothold on the coamings (e.g. cleats or cups);

(*d*) the said arrangements on the coamings provide foothold of a depth, including any space behind the said arrangements, of not less than 4½ inches (11½ cm.) for a width of not less than 10 inches (25 cm.);

(*e*) if separate ladders are provided between the lower decks, the said ladders are as far as practicable in line with the ladder from the top deck.

Where, however, owing to the construction of the ship, the provision of a ladder would not be reasonably practicable, it shall be open to the competent authorities to allow other means of access, provided that they comply with the conditions laid down in this Article for ladders so far as they are applicable.

In the case of ships existing at the date of the ratification of this Convention the measurement requirements of sub-paragraphs (*a*) and (*d*) of this paragraph shall be deemed to be complied with, until the ladders and arrangements are replaced, if the actual measurements are not more than 10 per cent less than the measurements specified in the said sub-paragraphs (*a*) and (*d*).

(3) Sufficient free passage to the means of access shall be left at the coamings.

(4) Shaft tunnels shall be equipped with adequate handhold and foothold on both sides.

(5) When a ladder is to be used in the hold of a vessel which is not decked it shall be the duty of the contractor undertaking the processes to provide such ladder. It shall be equipped at the top with hooks or with other means for firmly securing it.

(6) The workers shall not use, or be required to use, other means of access than the means specified or allowed by this Article.

(7) Ships existing at the date of ratification of this Convention shall be exempt from compliance with the measurements in paragraph (2)(*a*) and (*d*) and from the provisions of paragraph (4) of this Article for a period not exceeding four years from the date of ratification of this Convention.

Article 6

(1) While the workers are on a ship for the purpose of the processes, every hatchway of a cargo hold accessible to the workers which exceeds 5 feet (1 m. 50) in depth from the level of the deck to the bottom of the hold, and which is not protected to a clear height of 2 feet 6 inches (75 cm.) by the coamings, shall, when not in use for the pass-

age of goods, coal, or other material, either be securely fenced to a height of 3 feet (90 cm.) or be securely covered. National laws or regulations shall determine whether the requirements of this paragraph shall be enforced during meal times and other short interruptions of work.

(2) Similar measures shall be taken when necessary to protect all other openings in a deck which might be dangerous to the workers.

Article 8

In order to ensure the safety of the workers when engaged in removing or replacing hatch coverings and beams used for hatch coverings.

(1) hatch coverings and beams used for hatch coverings shall be maintained in good condition;

(2) hatch coverings shall be fitted with adequate hand grips, having regard to their size and weight, unless the construction of the hatch or the hatch coverings is of a character rendering the provision of hand grips unnecessary;

(3) beams used for hatch coverings shall have suitable gear for removing and replacing them of such a character as to render it unnecessary for workers to go upon them for the purpose of adjusting such gear;

(4) all hatch coverings and fore and aft and thwart-ship beams shall, in so far as they are not interchangeable, be kept plainly marked to indicate the deck and hatch to which they belong and their position therein;

(5) hatch coverings shall not be used in the construction of cargo stages or for any other purpose which may expose them to damage.

Article 9

Appropriate measures shall be prescribed to ensure that no hoisting machine, or gear, whether fixed or loose, used in connection therewith, is employed in the processes on shore or on board ship unless it is in a safe working condition.

In particular,

(1) before being taken into use, the said machines, fixed gear on board ship accessory thereto as defined by national laws or regulations, and chains and wire ropes used in connection therewith, shall be adequately examined and tested, and the safe working load thereof certified, in the manner prescribed and by a competent person acceptable to the national authorities;

(2) after being taken into use, every hoisting machine, whether used on shore or on board ship, and all fixed gear on board ship accessory thereto as defined by national laws or regulations shall be thoroughly examined or inspected as follows:

(*a*) to be thoroughly examined every four years and inspected every twelve months: derricks, goose necks, mast bands, derrick bands, eyebolts, spans and any other fixed gear the dismantling of which is specially difficult;

(*b*) to be thoroughly examined every twelve months: all hoisting machines (e.g. cranes, winches), blocks, shackles and all other accessory gear not included in (*a*).

All loose gear (e.g. chains, wire ropes, rings, hooks) shall be inspected on each occasion before use unless they have been inspected within the previous three months.

Chains shall not be shortened by tying knots in them and precautions shall be taken to prevent injury to them from sharp edges.

A thimble or loop splice made in any wire rope shall have at least three tucks with a whole strand of rope and two tucks with one-half of the wires cut out of each strand; provided that this requirement shall not operate to prevent the use of another form of splice which can be shown to be as efficient as the form hereby prescribed.

(3) Chains and such similar gear as is specified by national laws or regulations (e.g. hooks, rings, shackles, swivels) shall, unless they have been subjected to such other sufficient treatment as may be prescribed by national laws or regulations, be annealed as follows under the supervision of a competent person acceptable to the national authorities:

(*a*) In the case of chains and the said gear carried on board ship:

(i) half inch (12½ mm.) and smaller chains or gear in general use once at least in every six months;

(ii) all other chains or gear (including span chains but excluding bridle chains attached to derricks or masts) in general use once at least in every twelve months;

Provided that in the case of such gear used solely on cranes and other hoisting appliances worked by hand, twelve months shall be substituted for six months in sub-paragraph (i) and two years for twelve months in sub-paragraph (ii);

Provided also that, if the competent authority is of opinion that owing to the size, design, material or infrequency of use of any of the said gear the requirements of this paragraph as to annealing are not necessary for the protection of the workers, it may, by certificate in writing (which it may at its discretion revoke), exempt such gear from the said requirements subject to such conditions as may be specified in the said certificate.

(*b*) In the case of chains and the said gear not carried on board ship: Measures shall be prescribed to secure the annealing of the said chains and gear.

(*c*) In the case of the said chains and gear whether carried on board ship or not, which have been lengthened, altered or repaired by welding, they shall thereupon be tested and reëxamined.

(4) Such duly authenticated records as will provide sufficient *prima facie* evidence of the safe condition of the machines and gear concerned shall be kept, on shore or on the ship as the case may be, specifying the safe working load and the dates and results of the tests and examinations referred to in paragraphs (1) and (2) of this Article and of the annealings or other treatment referred to in paragraph (3).

Such records shall, on the application of any person authorised for the purpose, be produced by the person in charge thereof.

(5) The safe working load shall be kept plainly marked on all cranes, derricks and chain slings and on any similar hoisting gear used on board ship as specified by national laws or regulations. The safe working load marked on chain slings shall either be in plain figures or letters upon the chains or upon a tablet or ring of durable material attached securely thereto.

(6) All motors, cogwheels, chain and friction gearing, shafting, live electric conductors and steam pipes shall (unless it can be shown that by their position and construction they are equally safe to every worker employed as they would be if securely fenced) be securely fenced so far as is practicable without impeding the safe working of the ship.

(7) Cranes and winches shall be provided with such means as will reduce to a minimum the risk of the accidental descent of a load while in process of being lifted or lowered.

(8) Appropriate measures shall be taken to prevent exhaust steam from and, so far as practicable, live steam to any crane or winch obscuring any part of the working place at which a worker is employed.

(9) Appropriate measures shall, be taken to prevent the foot of a derrick being accidentally lifted out of its socket or support.

Article 11

(1) No load shall be left suspended from any hoisting machine unless there is a competent person actually in charge of the machine while the load is so left.

(2) Appropriate measures shall be prescribed to provide for the employment of a signaller where this is necessary for the safety of the workers.

(3) Appropriate measures shall be prescribed with the object of preventing dangerous methods of working in the stacking, unstacking, stowing and unstowing of cargo, or handling in connection therewith.

(4) Before work is begun at a hatch the beams thereof shall either be removed or be securely fastened to prevent their displacement.

(5) Precautions shall be taken to facilitate the escape of the workers when employed in a hold or on 'tween decks in dealing with coal or other bulk cargo.

(6) No stage shall be used in the processes unless it is substantially and firmly constructed, adequately supported and where necessary securely fastened.

No trunk shall be used for carrying cargo between ship and shore on a stage so steep as to be unsafe.

Stages shall where necessary be treated with suitable material to prevent the workers slipping.

(7) When the working space in a hold is confined to the square of the hatch, and except for the purpose of breaking out or making up slings,

(*a*) hooks shall not be made fast in the bands or fastenings of bales of cotton, wool, cork, gunny-bags, or other similar goods;

(*b*) can-hooks shall not be used for raising or lowering a barrel when, owing to the construction or condition of the barrel or of the hooks, their use is likely to be unsafe.

(8) No gear of any description shall be loaded beyond the safe working load save in exceptional cases and then only in so far as may be allowed by national laws or regulations.

(9) In the case of shore cranes with varying capacity (e.g. raising and lowering jib with load capacity varying according to the angle) an automatic indicator or a table showing the safe working loads at the corresponding inclinations of the jib shall be provided on the crane.

Article 18

Each Member undertakes to enter into reciprocal arrangements on the basis of this Convention with the other Members which have ratified this Convention, including more particularly the mutual recognition of the arrangements made in their respective countries for testing, examining and annealing and of certificates and records relating thereto;

Provided that, as regards the construction of ships and as regards plant used on ships and the records and other matters to be observed on board under the terms of this Convention, each Member is satisfied that the arrangements adopted by the other Member secure a general standard of safety for the workers equally effective as the standard required under its own laws and regulations;

Provided also that the Governments shall have due regard to the obligations of paragraph (11) of Article 405 of the Treaty of Versailles and of the corresponding Articles of the other Treaties of Peace.

APPENDIX II

Draft Convention (No. 4) *concerning employment of women during the night.*[1]

Article 2

For the purpose of this Convention, the term "night" signifies a period of at least eleven consecutive hours, including the interval between ten o'clock in the evening and five o'clock in the morning.

In those countries where no Government regulation as yet applies to the employment of women in industrial undertakings during the night, the term "night" may provisionally, and for a maximum period of three years, be declared by the Government to signify a period of only ten hours, including the interval between ten o'clock in the evening and five o'clock in the morning.

Article 8

The formal ratification of this Convention, under the conditions set forth in Part XIII of the Treaty of Versailles of 28 June, 1919, and of the Treaty of St. Germain of 10 September, 1919, shall be communicated to the Secretary-General of the League of Nations for registration.

Article 9

Each Member of the International Labour Organisation which ratifies this Convention engages to apply it to its colonies, protectorates and possessions which are not fully self-governing;

(*a*) Except where owing to the local conditions its provisions are inapplicable; or

(*b*) Subject to such modifications as may be necessary to adapt its provisions to local conditions.

Each Member shall notify the International Labour Office the action taken in respect of each of its colonies, protectorates and possessions which are not fully self-governing.

Article 10

As soon as the ratifications of two Members of the International Labour Organisation have been registered with the Secretariat, the Secretary-General of the League of Nations shall so notify all the Members of the International Labour Organisation.

[1] *Draft Conventions and Recommendations* (1919-1934), 24ff.

Article 11

This Convention shall come into force at the date on which such notification is issued by the Secretary-General of the League of Nations, but it shall then be binding only upon those Members which have registered their ratifications with the Secretariat. Thereafter this Convention will come into force for any other Member at the date on which its ratification is registered with the Secretariat.

Article 12

Each Member which ratifies this Convention agrees to bring its provisions into operation not later than 1 July, 1922, and to take such action as may be necessary to make these provisions effective.

Draft Convention (No. 41) *concerning employment of women during the night* (*revised 1934*).[2]

Article 2

1. For the purpose of this Convention, the term "night" signifies a period of at least eleven consecutive hours, including the interval between ten o'clock in the evening and five o'clock in the morning.

2. Provided that, where there are exceptional circumstances affecting the workers employed in a particular industry or area, the competent authority may, after consultation with the employers' and workers' organisations concerned, decide that in the case of women employed in that industry or area, the interval between eleven o'clock in the evening and six o'clock in the morning may be substituted for the interval between ten o'clock in the evening and five o'clock in the morning.

3. In those countries where no Government regulation as yet applies to the employment of women in industrial undertakings during the night, the term "night" may provisionally and for a maximum period of three years, be declared by the Government to signify a period of only ten hours, including the interval between ten o'clock in the evening and five o'clock in the morning.

Article 8

This Convention does not apply to women holding responsible positions of management who are not ordinarily engaged in manual work.

Article 9

The formal ratification of this Convention shall be communicated to the Secretary-General of the League of Nations.

[2] *Draft Conventions and Recommendations* (1919-1934), 303ff.

Article 10

1. This Convention shall be binding only upon those Members of the International Labour Organisation whose ratifications have been registered with the Secretary-General.

2. It shall come into force twelve months after the date on which the ratifications of two Members have been registered with the Secretary-General.

3. Thereafter, this Convention shall come into force for any Member twelve months after the date on which its ratification has been registered.

Article 11

As soon as the ratifications of two Members of the International Labour Organisation have been registered with the Secretariat, the Secretary-General of the League of Nations shall so notify all the Members of the International Labour Organisation. He shall likewise notify them of the registration of ratifications which may be communicated subsequently by other Members of the Organisation.

Article 12

1. A Member which has ratified this Convention may denounce it after the expiration of ten years from the date on which the Convention first comes into force, by an act communicated to the Secretary-General of the League of Nations for registration. Such denunciation shall not take effect until one year after the date on which it is registered with the Secretariat.

2. Each Member which has ratified this Convention and which does not, within the year following the expiration of the period of ten years mentioned in the preceding paragraph, exercise the right of denunciation provided for in this Article, will be bound for another period of ten years and, thereafter, may denounce this Convention at the expiration of each period of ten years under the terms provided for in this Article.

APPENDIX III

Draft Convention (No. 18) *concerning workmen's compensation for occupational diseases.*[1]

Article 2

Each Member of the International Labour Organisation which ratifies this Convention undertakes to consider as occupational diseases those diseases and poisonings produced by the substances set forth in the Schedule appended hereto, when such diseases or such poisonings affect workers engaged in the trades or industries placed opposite in the said Schedule, and result from occupation in an undertaking covered by the said national legislation.

SCHEDULE

List of diseases and toxic substances.	*List of corresponding industries and processes.*
Poisoning by lead, its alloys or compounds and their sequelae.	Handling of ore containing lead, including fine shot in zinc factories. Casting of old zinc and lead in ingots. Manufacture of articles made of cast lead or of lead alloys. Employment in the polygraphic industries. Manufacture of lead compounds. Manufacture and repair of electric accumulators. Preparation and use of enamels containing lead. Polishing by means of lead files or putty powder with a lead content. All painting operations involving the preparation and manipulation of coating substances, cements or colouring substances containing lead pigments.
Poisoning by mercury, its amalgams and compounds and their sequelae.	Handling of mercury ore. Manufacture of mercury compounds. Manufacture of measuring and laboratory apparatus.

[1] *Draft Conventions and Recommendations* (1919-1934), 100ff.

	Preparation of raw materials for the hat-making industry.
	Hot gilding.
	Use of mercury pumps in the manufacture of incandescent lamps.
	Manufacture of fulminate of mercury primers.
Anthrax infection.	Work in connection with animals infected with anthrax.
	Handling of animal carcasses or parts of such carcasses including hides, hoofs, and horns.
	Loading and unloading or transport of merchandise.

Article 3

The formal ratifications of this Convention under the conditions set forth in Part XIII of the Treaty of Versailles and in the corresponding Parts of the other Treaties of Peace shall be communicated to the Secretary-General of the League of Nations for registration.

Article 4

This Convention shall come into force at the date on which the ratifications of two Members of the International Labour Organisation have been registered by the Secretary-General.

It shall be binding only upon those Members whose ratifications have been registered with the Secretariat.

Thereafter, the Convention shall come into force for any Member at the date on which its ratification has been registered with the Secretariat.

Article 6

Subject to the provisions of Article 4, each Member which ratifies the Convention agrees to bring the provisions of Articles 1 and 2 into operation not later than 1 January 1927 and to take such action as may be necessary to make these provisions effective.

Article 7

Each Member of the International Labour Organisation which ratifies this Convention engages to apply it to its colonies, possessions and protectorates, in accordance with the provisions of Article 421 of the

Treaty of Versailles and of the corresponding Articles of the other Treaties of Peace.

Article 8

A Member which has ratified this Convention may denounce it after the expiration of five years from the date on which the Convention first comes into force, by an act communicated to the Secretary-General of the League of Nations for registration. Such denunciation shall not take effect until one year after the date on which it is registered with the Secretariat.

Article 9

At least once in ten years, the Governing Body of the International Labour Office shall present to the General Conference a report on the working of this Convention and shall consider the desirability of placing on the agenda of the Conference the question of its revision or modification.

Draft Convention (No. 42) *concerning workmen's compensation for occupational diseases (revised 1934).*[2]

Article 2

Each Member of the International Labour Organisation which ratifies this Convention undertakes to consider as occupational diseases those diseases and poisonings produced by the substances set forth in the Schedule appended hereto, when such diseases or such poisonings affect workers engaged in the trades, industries or processes placed opposite in the said Schedule, and result from occupation in an undertaking covered by the said national legislation.

SCHEDULE

List of diseases and toxic substances.	*List of corresponding trades, industries or processes.*
Poisoning by lead, its alloys or compounds and their sequelae.	Handling of ore containing lead, including fine shot in zinc factories. Casting of old zinc and lead in ingots. Manufacture of articles made of cast lead or of lead alloys. Employment in the polygraphic industries. Manufacture of lead compounds.

[2] *Draft Conventions and Recommendations* (1919-1934), 307ff.

	Manufacture and repair of electric accumulators. Preparation and use of enamels containing lead. Polishing by means of lead files or putty powder with a lead content. All painting operations involving the preparation and manipulation of coating substances, cements or colouring substances containing lead pigments.
Poisoning by mercury, its amalgams and compounds and their sequelae.	Handling of mercury ore. Manufacture of mercury compounds. Manufacture of measuring and laboratory apparatus. Preparation of raw material for the hat-making industry. Hot gilding. Use of mercury pumps in the manufacture of incandescent lamps. Manufacture of fulminate of mercury primers.
Anthrax infection.	Work in connection with animals infected with anthrax. Handling of animal carcasses or parts of such carcasses including hides, hoofs and horns. Loading and unloading or transport of merchandise.
Silicosis with or without pulmonary tuberculosis, provided that silicosis is an essential factor in causing the resultant incapacity or death.	Industries or processes recognized by national law or regulations as involving exposure to the risk of silicosis.
Phosphorus poisoning by phosphorus or its compounds, and its sequelae.	Any process involving the production, liberation or utilisation of phosphorus or its compounds.

Arsenic poisoning by arsenic or its compounds, and its sequelae.	Any process involving the production, liberation or utilisation of arsenic or its compounds.
Poisoning by benzene or its homologues, their nitro- and amido-derivatives, and its sequelae.	Any process involving the production, liberation or utilisation of benzene or its homologues, or their nitro- and amido-derivatives.
Poisoning by the halogen derivatives of hydrocarbons of the aliphatic series.	Any process involving the production, liberation or utilisation of halogen derivatives or hydrocarbons of the aliphatic series designated by national laws or regulations.
Pathologic manifestations due to: (*a*) radium and other radioactive substances; (*b*) X-rays.	Any process involving exposure to the action of radium, radioactive substances, or X-rays.
Primary epitheliomatous cancer of the skin.	Any process involving the handling or use of tar, pitch, bitumen, mineral oil, paraffin, or the compounds, products or residues of these substances.

Article 3

The formal ratifications of this Convention shall be communicated to the Secretary-General of the League of Nations for registration.

Article 4

1. This Convention shall be binding only upon those Members of the International Labour Organization whose ratifications have been registered with the Secretary-General.

2. It shall come into force twelve months after the date on which the ratifications of two Members have been registered with the Secretary-General.

3. Thereafter, this Convention shall come into force for any Member twelve months after the date on which its ratification has been registered.

Article 6

1. A Member which has ratified this Convention may denounce it after the expiration of five years from the date on which the Convention first comes into force, by an act communicated to the Secretary-General of the League of Nations for registration. Such denunciation shall not take effect until one year after the date on which it is registered with the Secretariat.

2. Each Member which has ratified this Convention and which does not, within the year following the expiration of the period of five years mentioned in the preceding paragraph, exercise the right of denunciation provided for in this Article, will be bound for another period of five years and, thereafter, may denounce this Convention at the expiration of each period of five years under the terms provided for in this Article.

Article 7

At the expiration of each period of ten years after the coming into force of this Convention, the Governing Body of the International Labour Office shall present to the General Conference a report on the working of this Convention and shall consider the desirability of placing on the Agenda of the Conference the question of its revision in whole or in part.

Article 8

1. Should the Conference adopt a new Convention revising this Convention in whole or in part, then, unless the new Convention otherwise provides,

(*a*) the ratification by a Member of the new revising Convention shall *ipso jure* involve the immediate denunciation of this Convention, notwithstanding the provisions of Article 6 above, if and when the new revising Convention shall have come into force;

(*b*) as from the date when the new revising Convention comes into force this Convention shall cease to be open to ratification by the Members.

2. This Convention shall in any case remain in force in its actual form and content for those Members which have ratified it but have not ratified the revising Convention.

APPENDIX IV

Draft Convention (No. 31) *limiting hours of work in coal mines.*[1]

Article 8

1. Regulations made by public authority may provide that the hours specified in Articles 3, 4, 5 and 7 and may be exceeded:

(*a*) In case of accident, actual or threatened, in case of *force majeure,* or in case of urgent work to be done to machinery, plant or equipment on the mine as a result of a breakdown of such machinery, plant or equipment, even if coal production is thereby incidentally involved, but only so far as may be necessary to avoid serious interference with the ordinary working of the mine;

(*b*) For workers employed on operations which by their nature must be carried on continuously or on technical work, in so far as their work is necessary for preparing or terminating work in the ordinary way or for a full resumption of work on the next shift, provided, however, that this shall not refer to the production or transport of coal. The additional time authorized by this paragraph shall not exceed half an hour on any day for any individual worker, and in the case of all mines in normal operation the number of workers concerned shall at no time exceed 5 per cent. of the total number of persons employed at the mine.

2. Overtime worked in accordance with the provisions of this Article shall be paid for at not less than one-and-a-quarter times the regular rate.

Article 22

Should the Conference adopt a new Convention revising this Convention in whole or in part, the ratification by a Member of the new revising Convention shall *ipso jure* involve denunciation of this Convention without any requirement of delay, notwithstanding the provisions of Article 20 above, if and when the new revising Convention shall have come into force.

As from the date of the coming into force of the new revising Convention, the present Convention shall cease to be open to ratification by the Members.

Nevertheless, this Convention shall remain in force in its actual form and content for those Members which have ratified it but have not ratified the revising Convention.

[1] *Draft Conventions and Recommendations* (1919-1934), 203ff.

Draft Convention (No. 46) *limiting hours of work in coal mines (revised 1935)*.[2]

Article 8

1. Regulations made by public authority may provide that the hours specified in Articles 3, 4, 5 and 7 may be exceeded in case of accident, actual or threatened, in case of *force majeure,* or in case of urgent work to be done to machinery, plant or equipment of the mine as a result of a breakdown of such machinery, plant or equipment, even if coal production is thereby incidentally involved, but only so far as may be necessary to avoid serious interference with the ordinary working of the mine.

2. Regulations made by public authority may provide that the hours specified in Articles 3, 4, 5 and 7 may be exceeded in the case of workers employed on operations which by their nature must be carried on continuously or on technical work, in so far as their work is necessary for preparing or terminating work in the ordinary way or for a full resumption of work on the next shift, provided, however, that this shall not refer to the production or transport of coal. The additional time so authorised for any individual worker shall not, except as specified in paragraphs 3 and 4 of this Article, exceed half an hour on any day.

3. Regulations made by public authority may provide that the hours specified in Articles 3, 4, 5 and 7 may be exceeded to an extent exceeding half an hour in the case of the following grades;

(*a*) workers whose presence is indispensable for the work of ventilation and pumping stations and of such compressed air stations as are necessary for ventilation;

(*b*) underground storemen; and

(*c*) winchmen and locomotive drivers and their indispensable assistants:

Provided that no worker in the above grades who is employed on operations which by their nature must be carried on continuously may be employed for more than eight hours per day exclusive of the time spent in the mine by that worker in reaching and returning from his place of work, it being understood that in each case this time will be reduced to the indispensable minimum.

Provided also that in the case of

(*a*) underground storemen;

(*b*) enginemen and men in charge of internal shafts who are engaged upon the transport of workers;

[2] An official text of this convention may be found in *Official Bulletin,* XX, no. 3 (August 1935), 62ff.

(*c*) drivers of locomotives who are engaged upon the transport of workers; and

(*d*) the indispensable assistants of the grades specified in clauses (*b*) and (*c*);

the limit of such extension shall be that fixed by the regulations of the public authority.

4. Regulations made by public authority may provide that the limit of hours specified in Articles 3, 4, 5 and 7 and in paragraphs 2 and 3 of this Article may be exceeded in the case of workers whose presence is indispensable for the work of underground ventilation, pumping and compressed air stations, but only to such extent as may be necessary to permit the periodical change-over of shifts, and time worked in virtue of this provision shall not be deemed to be overtime, so however that during any period of three weeks no worker shall work more than twenty-one shifts of the length prescribed for his grade by paragraph 2 or paragraph 3 of this Article, as the case may be.

5. In the case of mines in normal operation the number of persons coming under paragraphs 2 and 3 of this Article shall at no time exceed five per cent. of the total number of persons employed at the mine.

6. Overtime worked in virtue of the provisions of this Article shall be paid for at not less than one-and-a-quarter times the regular rate.

Article 22

1. Should the Conference adopt a new Convention revising this Convention in whole or in part, then, unless the new convention otherwise provides,

(*a*) the ratification by a Member of the new revising Convention shall *ipso jure* involve the immediate denunciation of this Convention, notwithstanding the provisions of Article 20 above, if and when the new revising Convention shall have come into force;

(*b*) as from the date when the new revising Convention comes into force this Convention shall cease to be open to ratification by the Members.

2. This Convention shall in any case remain in force in its actual form and content for those Members which have ratified it but have not ratified the revising Convention.

APPENDIX V

Draft Convention (No. 7) *fixing the minimum age for admission of children to employment at sea.*[1]

Article 2

Children under the age of fourteen years shall not be employed or work on vessels, other than vessels upon which only members of the same family are employed.

Article 5

Each Member of the International Labour Organisation which ratifies this Convention engages to apply it to its colonies, protectorates, and possessions which are not fully self-governing:

(a) Except where owing to the local conditions its provisions are inapplicable; or

(b) Subject to such modifications as may be necessary to adapt its provisions to local conditions.

Each Member shall notify to the International Labor Office the action taken in respect to each of its colonies, protectorates, and possessions which are not fully self-governing.

Article 6

The formal ratifications of this Convention under the conditions set forth in Part XIII of the Treaty of Versailles of 28 June, 1919, of the Treaty of St. Germain of 10 September, 1919, of the Treaty of Neuilly of 27 November, 1919, and of the Treaty of the Grand Trianon of 4 June, 1920, shall be communicated to the Secretary-General of the League of Nations for registration.

Article 7

As soon as the ratifications of two Members of the International Labour Organisation have been registered with the Secretariat, the Secretary-General of the League of Nations shall so notify all the International Labour Organisation Members.

Article 8

This Convention shall come into force at the date on which such notification is issued by the Secretary-General of the League of Nations, but

[1] *Draft Conventions and Recommendations* (1919-1935), 42ff.

it shall then be binding only upon those Members which have registered their ratifications with the Secretariat. Thereafter this Convention will come into force for any other Member at the date on which its ratification is registered with the Secretariat.

Article 9

Subject to the provisions of Article 8, each Member which ratifies this Convention agrees to bring its provisions into operation not later than 1 July, 1922, and to take such action as may be necessary to make these provisions effective.

Article 10

A Member which has ratified this Convention may denounce it after the expiration of ten years from the date on which the Convention first comes into force, by an act communicated to the Secretary-General of the League of Nations for registration. Such denunciation shall not take effect until one year after the date on which it is registered with the Secretariat.

Article 11

At least once in ten years, the Governing Body of the International Labour Office shall present to the General Conference a report on the working of this Convention, and shall consider the desirability of placing on the agenda of the Conference the question of its revision or modification.

Draft Convention (No. 58) *fixing the minimum age for the admission of children to employment at sea* (*revised 1936*).[2]

Article 2

1. Children under the age of fifteen years shall not be employed or work on vessels, other than vessels upon which only members of the same family are employed.

2. Provided that national laws or regulations may provide for the issue in respect of children of not less than fourteen years of age of certificates permitting them to be employed in cases in which an educational or other appropriate authority designated by such laws or regulations is satisfied, after having due regard to the health and physical condition of the child and to the prospective as well as to the imme-

[2] *International Labor Conference, Record of Proceedings, 1937, Appendix,* 408ff.

diate benefit to the child of the employment proposed, that such employment will be beneficial to the child.

Article 5

This Convention shall not come into force until after the adoption by the International Labour Conference of a Draft Convention revising the Convention fixing the minimum age for admission of children to industrial employment, 1919, and a Draft Convention revising the Convention concerning the age for admission of children to non-industrial employment, 1932.

Article 6

The formal ratifications of this Convention shall be communicated to the Secretary-General of the League of Nations for registration.

Article 7

1. This Convention shall be binding only upon those Members of the International Labour Organisation whose ratifications have been registered with the Secretary-General.

2. Subject to the provisions of Article 5 above it shall come into force twelve months after the date on which the ratifications of two Members have been registered with the Secretary-General.

3. Thereafter, this Convention shall come into force for any Member twelve months after the date on which its ratification has been registered.

Article 8

As soon as the ratifications of two Members of the International Labour Organisation have been registered, the Secretary-General of the League of Nations shall so notify all the Members of the International Labour Organisation. He shall likewise notify them of the registration of ratifications which may be communicated subsequently by other Members of the Organisation.

Article 9

1. A Member which has ratified this Convention may denounce it after the expiration of ten years from the date on which the convention first comes into force, by an act communicated to the Secretary-General of the League of Nations for registration. Such denunciation shall not take effect until one year after the date on which it is registered.

2. Each Member which has ratified this Convention and which does not, within the year following the expiration of the period of ten years

mentioned in the preceding paragraph, exercise the right of denunciation provided for in this Article, will be bound for another period of ten years and, thereafter, may denounce this Convention at the expiration of each period of ten years under the terms provided for in this Article.

Article 11

1. Should the Conference adopt a new Convention revising this Convention in whole or in part, then, unless the new Convention otherwise provides,

(*a*) the ratification by a Member of the new revising Convention shall *ipso jure* involve the immediate denunciation of this Convention, notwithstanding the provisions of Article 9 above, if and when the new revising Convention shall have come into force;

(*b*) as from the date when the new revising Convention comes into force this Convention shall cease to be open to ratification by the Members.

2. This Convention shall in any case remain in force in its actual form and content for those Members which have ratified it but have not ratified the revising Convention.

APPENDIX VI

Draft Convention (No. 5) *fixing the minimum age for admission of children to industrial employment.*[1]

Article 2

Children under the age of fourteen years shall not be employed or work in any public or private industrial undertaking, or in any branch thereof, other than an undertaking in which only members of the same family are employed.

Article 5

In connection with the application of this Convention to Japan, the following modifications of Article 2 may be made:

(*a*) Children over twelve years of age may be admitted into employment if they have finished the course in the elementary school;

(*b*) As regards children between the ages of twelve and fourteen already employed, transitional regulations may be made.

The provision in the present Japanese law admitting children under the age of twelve years to certain light and easy employments shall be repealed.

Article 6

The provisions of Article 2 shall not apply to India, but in India children under twelve years of age shall not be employed,

(*a*) In manufactories working with power and employing more than ten persons;

(*b*) In mines, quarries, and other works for the extraction of minerals from the earth;

(*c*) In the transport of passengers or goods, or mails, by rail, or in the handling of goods at docks, quays, and wharves, but excluding transport by hand.

Article 7

The formal ratifications of this Convention, under the conditions set forth in Part XIII of the Treaty of Versailles of 28 June, 1919, and of the Treaty of St. Germain of 10 September, 1919, shall be communicated to the Secretary-General of the League of Nations for registration.

[1] *Draft Conventions and Recommendations* (1919-1935), 30ff.

Article 8

Each Member of the International Labour Organisation which ratifies this Convention engages to apply it to its colonies, protectorates, and possessions which are not fully self-governing:

(*a*) Except where owing to the local conditions its provisions are inapplicable; or

(*b*) Subject to such modifications as may be necessary to adapt its provisions to local conditions.

Each Member shall notify to the International Labour Office the action taken in respect to each of its colonies, protectorates, and possessions which are not fully self-governing.

Article 9

As soon as the ratifications of two Members of the International Labour Organisations have been registered with the Secretariat, the Secretary-General of the League of Nations shall so notify all the Members of the International Labour Organisation.

Article 10

This Convention shall come into force at the date on which such notification is issued by the Secretary-General of the League of Nations, but it shall then be binding only upon those Members which have registered their ratifications with the Secretariat. Thereafter this Convention will come into force for any other Member at the date on which its ratification is registered with the Secretariat.

Article 11

Each Member which ratifies this Convention agrees to bring its provisions into operation not later than 1 July, 1922, and to take such action as may be necessary to make these provisions effective.

Article 12

A Member which has ratified this Convention may denounce it after the expiration of ten years from the date on which the Convention first comes into force, by an act communicated to the Secretary-General of the League of Nations for registration. Such denunciation shall not take effect until one year after the date on which it is registered with the Secretariat.

Article 13

At least once in ten years, the Governing Body of the International Labour Office shall present to the General Conference a report on the working of this Convention, and shall consider the desirability of placing on the agenda of the Conference the question of its revision or modification.

Draft Convention (No. 59) *fixing the minimum age for admission of children to industrial employment (Revised 1937)*.[2]

Article 2

1. Children under the age of fifteen years shall not be employed or work in any public or private industrial undertaking, or in any branch thereof.

2. Provided that, except in the case of employments which, by their nature or the circumstances in which they are carried on, are dangerous to the life, health or morals of the persons employed therein, national laws or regulations may permit such children to be employed in undertakings in which only members of the employer's family are employed.

Article 5

1. In respect of employments which, by their nature or the circumstances in which they are carried on, are dangerous to the life, health or morals of the persons employed therein, national laws shall either—

(*a*) prescribe a higher age or ages than fifteen years for the admission thereto of young persons or adolescents; or

(*b*) empower an appropriate authority to prescribe a higher age or ages than fifteen years for the admission thereto of young persons or adolescents.

2. The annual reports to be submitted under Article 22 of the Constitution of the International Labour Organisation shall include full information concerning the age or ages prescribed by national laws in pursuance of sub-paragraph (*a*) of the preceding paragraph or concerning the action taken by the appropriate authority in exercise of the powers conferred upon it in pursuance of sub-paragraph (*b*) of the preceding paragraph, as the case may be.

---

[2] *Official Bulletin,* XXII, No. 3, 89ff.

Article 6

1. The provisions of this Article shall be applicable in Japan in substitution for the provisions of Articles 2 and 5.

2. Children under the age of fourteen years shall not be employed or work in any public or private industrial undertaking, or in any branch thereof: Provided that national laws or regulations may permit such children to be employed in undertakings in which only members of the employer's family are employed.

3. Children under the age of sixteen years shall not be employed or work on dangerous or unhealthy work as defined by national laws or regulations in mines or factories.

Article 7

1. The provisions of Articles 2, 4 and 5 shall not apply to India, but in India the following provisions shall apply to all territories in respect of which the Indian Legislature has jurisdiction to apply them.

2. Children under the age of twelve years shall not be employed or work in factories working with power and employing more than ten persons.

3. Children under the age of thirteen years shall not be employed or work in the transport of passengers or goods, or mails, by rail, or in the handling of goods at docks, quays or wharves, but excluding transport by hand.

4. Children under the age of fifteen years shall not be employed or work—

(*a*) in mines, quarries, and other works for the extraction of minerals from the earth;

(*b*) in occupations to which this Article applies which are scheduled as dangerous or unhealthy by the competent authority.

5. Unless they have been medically certified as fit for such work—

(*a*) persons who have attained the age of twelve years but are under the age of seventeen years shall not be permitted to work in factories working with power and employing more than ten persons;

(*b*) persons who have attained the age of fifteen years but are under the age of seventeen years shall not be permitted to work in mines.

Article 8

1. The provisions of this Article shall be applicable in China in substitution for the provisions of Articles 2, 4 and 5.

2. Children under the age of twelve years shall not be employed or

work in any factory using machines driven by motor power and regularly employing thirty persons or more.

3. Children under the age of fifteen years shall not be employed or work—

(*a*) in mines regularly employing fifty persons or more; or

(*b*) on dangerous or unhealthy work as defined by national laws or regulations in any factory using machines driven by motor power and regularly employing thirty persons or more.

4. Every employer in an undertaking to which this Article applies shall keep a register of all persons under the age of sixteen employed by him, together with such evidence of their age as may be required by the competent authority.

Article 9

1. The International Labour Conference may, at any Session at which the matter is included in its Agenda, adopt by a two-thirds majority draft amendments to any one or more of the preceding Articles of Part II of this Convention.

2. Any such draft amendment shall state the Member or Members to which it applies, and shall, within the period of one year, or, in exceptional circumstances, of eighteen months, from the closing of the Session of the Conference, be submitted by the Member or Members to which it applies to the authority or authorities within whose competence the matter lies, for the enactment of legislation or other action.

3. Each such Member will, if it obtains the consent of the authority or authorities within whose competence the matter lies, communicate the formal ratification of the amendment to the Secretary-General of the League of Nations for registration.

4. Any such draft amendment shall take effect as an amendment to this Convention on ratification by the Member or Members to which it applies.

Part III—Final Provisions

Article 10

The formal ratifications of this Convention shall be communicated to the Secretary-General of the League of Nations for registration.

Article 11

1. This Convention shall be binding only upon those Members of the International Labour Organisation whose ratifications have been registered with the Secretary-General.

2. It shall come into force twelve months after the date on which the

ratifications of two Members have been registered with the Secretary-General.

3. Thereafter, this Convention shall come into force for any Member twelve months after the date on which its ratification has been registered.

Article 12

As soon as the ratifications of two Members of the International Labour Organisation have been registered, the Secretary-General of the League of Nations shall so notify all the Members of the International Labour Organisation. He shall likewise notify them of the registration of ratifications which may be communicated subsequently by other Members of the Organisation.

Article 13

1. A Member which has ratified this Convention may denounce it after the expiration of ten years from the date on which the Convention first comes into force, by an act communicated to the Secretary-General of the League of Nations for registration. Such denunciation shall not take effect until one year after the date on which it is registered.

2. Each Member which has ratified this Convention and which does not, within the year following the expiration of the period of ten years mentioned in the preceding paragraph, exercise the right of denunciation provided for in this Article, will be bound for another period of ten years and, thereafter, may denounce this Convention at the expiration of each period of ten years under the terms provided for in this Article.

Article 14

At the Expiration of each period of ten years after the coming into force of this Convention, the Governing Body of the International Labour Office shall present to the General Conference a report on the working of this Convention and shall consider the desirability of placing on the Agenda of the Conference the question of its revision in whole or in part.

Article 15

1. Should the Conference adopt a new Convention revising this Convention in whole or in part, then, unless the new Convention otherwise provides,

(*a*) the ratification by a Member of the new revising Convention shall *ipso jure* involve the immediate denunciation of this Convention, notwithstanding the provisions of Article 13 above, if and when the new revising Convention shall have come into force;

(*b*) as from the date when the new revising Convention comes into force this Convention shall cease to be open to ratification by the Members.

2. This Convention shall in any case remain in force in its actual form and content for those Members which have ratified it but have not ratified the revising Convention.

APPENDIX VII

Draft Convention (No. 33) *concerning the age for admission of children to non-industrial employment.*[1]

Article 2

Children under fourteen years of age, or children over fourteen years who are still required by national laws or regulations to attend primary school, shall not be employed in any employment to which this Convention applies except as hereinafter otherwise provided.

Article 3

(1) Children over twelve years of age may, outside the hours fixed for school attendance, be employed on light work:

(*a*) which is not harmful to their health or normal development;

(*b*) which is not such as to prejudice their attendance at school or their capacity to benefit from the instruction there given; and

(*c*) the duration of which does not exceed two hours per day on either school days or holidays, the total number of hours spent at school and on light work in no case to exceed seven per day.

(2) Light work shall be prohibited:

(*a*) on Sundays and legal public holidays;

(*b*) during the night, that is to say during a period of at least twelve consecutive hours comprising the interval between 8 p.m. and 8 a.m.

(3) After the principal organisations of employers and workers concerned have been consulted, national laws or regulations shall:

(*a*) specify what forms of employment may be considered to be light work for the purpose of this Article;

(*b*) prescribe the preliminary conditions to be complied with as safeguards before children may be employed in light work.

(4) Subject to the provisions of sub-paragraph (*a*) of paragraph (1) above,

(*a*) national laws or regulations may determine work to be allowed and the number of hours per day to be worked during the holiday time of children referred to in Article 2 who are over fourteen years of age;

(*b*) in countries where no provision exists relating to compulsory

[1] *Draft Conventions and Recommendations* (1919-1935), 223ff.

school attendance, the time spent on light work shall not exceed four and a half hours per day.

Article 7

In order to ensure the due enforcement of the provisions of this Convention, national laws or regulations shall:

(*a*) provide for an adequate system of public inspection and supervision;

(*b*) provide suitable means for facilitating the identification and supervision of persons under a specified age engaged in the employments and occupations covered by Article 6;

(*c*) provide penalties for breaches of the laws or regulations by which effect is given to the provisions of this Convention.

Article 9

The provisions of Articles 2, 3, 4, 5, 6 and 7 of this Convention shall not apply to India, but in India:

(1) the employment of children under ten shall be prohibited:

Provided that in the interests of art, science or education, national laws or regulations may, by permits, granted in individual cases, allow exceptions to the above provision in order to enable children to appear in any public entertainment or as actors or supernumeraries in the making of cinematographic films.

Provided also that should the age for the admission of children to factories not using power which are not subject to the Indian Factories Act be fixed by national laws or regulations at an age exceeding ten, the age so prescribed for admission to such factories shall be substituted for the age of ten for the purpose of this paragraph.

(2) Persons under fourteen years of age shall not be employed in any non-industrial employment which the competent authority, after consultation with the principal organisations of employers and workers concerned, may declare to involve danger to life, health or morals.

(3) An age above ten shall be fixed by national laws or regulations for admission of young persons and adolescents to employment for purposes of itinerant trading in the streets or in places to which the public have access, to regular employment at stalls outside shops or to employment in itinerant occupations, in cases where the conditions of such employment require that a higher age should be fixed.

(4) National laws or regulations shall provide for the due enforcement of the provisions of this Article and in particular shall provide

penalties for breaches of the laws or regulations by which effect is given to the provisions of this Article.

(5) The competent authority shall, after a period of five years from the date of passing of legislation giving effect to the provisions of this Convention, review the whole position with a view to increasing the minimum age prescribed in this Convention, such review to cover the whole of the provisions of this Article.

Should legislation be enacted in India making attendance at school compulsory until the age of fourteen this Article shall cease to apply, and Articles 2, 3, 4, 5, 6 and 7 shall thenceforth be applicable to India.

Article 10

The formal ratifications of this Convention under the conditions set forth in Part XIII of the Treaty of Versailles and in the corresponding Parts of the other Treaties of Peace shall be communicated to the Secretary-General of the League of Nations for registration.

Article 15

Should the Conference adopt a new Convention revising this Convention in whole or in part, the ratification by a Member of the new revising Convention shall *ipso jure* involve denunciation of this Convention without any requirement of delay, notwithstanding the provisions of Articles 13 above if and when the new revising Convention shall have come into force.

As from the date of the coming into force of the new revising Convention, the present Convention shall cease to be open to ratification by the Members.

Nevertheless, this Convention shall remain in force in its actual form and content for those Members which have ratified it but have not ratified the revising Convention.

Draft Convention (No. 60) *concerning the age for admission of children to non-industrial employment* (*Revised 1937*).[1]

Article 2

Children under fifteen years of age, or children over fifteen years who are still required by national laws or regulations to attend primary school, shall not be employed in any employment to which this Convention applies except as hereinafter otherwise provided.

---

[1] *Official Bulletin, XXII,* No. 3, 94ff.

Article 3

1. Children over thirteen years of age may, outside the hours fixed for school attendance, be employed on light work which—

(*a*) is not harmful to their health or normal development; and

(*b*) is not such as to prejudice their attendance at school or capacity to benefit from the instruction there given.

2. No child under fourteen years of age shall—

(*a*) be employed on light work for more than two hours per day whether that day be a school day or a holiday; or

(*b*) spend at school and on light work a total number of hours exceeding seven per day.

3. National laws or regulations shall prescribe the number of hours per day during which children over fourteen years of age may be employed on light work.

4. Light work shall be prohibited—

(*a*) on Sundays and legal public holidays; and

(*b*) during the night.

5. For the purpose of the preceding paragraph the term "night" means—

(*a*) in the case of children under fourteen years of age, a period of at least twelve consecutive hours comprising the interval between eight P.M. and eight A.M.;

(*b*) in the case of children over fourteen years of age, a period which shall be prescribed by national laws or regulations but the duration of which shall not, except in the case of tropical countries where a compensatory rest is accorded during the day, be less than twelve hours.

6. After the principal organisations of employers and workers concerned have been consulted, national laws or regulations shall:

(*a*) specify what forms of employment may be considered to be light work for the purpose of this Article; and

(*b*) prescribe the preliminary conditions to be complied with as safeguards before children may be employed on light work.

7. Subject to the provisions of sub-paragraph (*a*) of paragraph 1 above,

(*a*) national laws or regulations may determine work to be allowed and the number of hours per day to be worked during the holiday time of children referred to in Article 2 who are over fourteen years of age;

(*b*) in countries where no provision exists relating to compulsory school attendance, the time spent on light work shall not exceed four and a half hours per day.

Article 7

In order to ensure the due enforcement of the provisions of this Convention, national laws or regulations shall—

(*a*) provide for an adequate system of public inspection and supervision;

(*b*) require every employer to keep a register of the names and dates of birth of all persons under the age of eighteen years employed by him in any employment to which this Convention applies other than an employment to which Article 6 applies;

(*c*) provide suitable means for facilitating the identification and supervision of persons under a specified age engaged in the employments and occupations covered by Article 6; and

(*d*) provide penalties for breaches of the laws or regulations by which effect is given to the provisions of this Convention.

Article 9

1. The provisions of Articles 2, 3, 4, 5, 6 and 7 of this Convention shall not apply to India, but in India the following provisions shall apply to all territories in respect of which the Indian Legislature has jurisdiction to apply them.

2. Children under thirteen years of age shall not be employed—

(*a*) in shops, offices, hotels or restaurants;

(*b*) in places of public entertainment; or

(*c*) in any other non-industrial occupations to which the provisions of this paragraph may be extended by the competent authority.

3. In the interest of art, science or education, national laws or regulations may, by permits granted in individual cases, allow exceptions to the provisions of the preceding paragraph in order to enable children to appear in any public entertainment or as actors or supernumeraries in the making of cinematographic films.

4. Persons under seventeen years of age shall not be employed in any non-industrial employment which the competent authority, after consultation with the principal organisations of employers and workers concerned, may declare to involve danger to life, health or morals.

5. The International Labour Conference may, at any Session at which the matter is included in its Agenda, adopt by a two-thirds majority draft amendments to the preceding paragraphs of this Article.

6. Any such draft amendment shall, within the period of one year, or,

in exceptional circumstances, of eighteen months, from the closing of the Session of the Conference, be submitted in India to the authority or authorities within whose competence the matter lies, for the enactment of legislation or other action.

7. India will, if it obtains the consent of the authority or authorities within whose competence the matter lies, communicate the formal ratification of the amendment to the Secretary-General of the League of Nations for registration.

8. Any such draft amendment shall take effect as an amendment to this Convention on ratification by India.

Article 10

The formal ratifications of this Convention shall be communicated to the Secretary-General of the League of Nations for registration.

Article 15

1. Should the Conference adopt a new Convention revising this Convention in whole or in part, then, unless the new Convention otherwise provides,

(*a*) the ratification by a Member of the new revising Convention shall *ipso jure* involve the immediate denunciation of this Convention, notwithstanding the provisions of Article 13 above, if and when the new revising Convention shall have come into force;

(*b*) as from the date when the new revising Convention comes into force this Convention shall cease to be open to ratification by the Members.

2. This Convention shall in any case remain in force in its actual form and content for those Members which have ratified it but have not ratified the revising Convention.

BIBLIOGRAPHY

A. PRIMARY SOURCES

I. Publications of the International Labor Organization

International Labour Organisation: Constitution and Standing Orders. Years cited. Geneva: International Labour Office.

Draft Conventions and Recommendations Adopted by the International Labour Conference. Years cited. Geneva: International Labour Office.

International Labour Conference: Analysis of Information Supplied by Governments concerning the application of the Recommendations of the International Labour Conference. Geneva: International Labour Office, 1932.

International Labour Conference. Volumes, sessions, and years cited. Geneva: International Labour Office.

International Labour Conference: Provisional Record. Numbers cited. Geneva: International Labour Office, 1935.

International Labour Conference: Summary of Annual Reports under Article 408. Years cited. Geneva: International Labour Office.

Legislative Series. Years cited. Geneva: International Labour Office.

Minutes of the Governing Body. Sessions cited. Geneva: International Labour Office.

Official Bulletin of International Labour Office. Volumes and numbers cited. Geneva: International Labour Office.

Reports of the Governing Body of the International Labour Organization upon the Working of the Convention concerning Employment of Women during the Night. Conference and years cited. Geneva: International Labour Office.

Report on the Institution of a Procedure for the Amendment of Conventions submitted by the International Labour Office. Years cited. Geneva: International Labour Office.

Studies and Reports. Series and numbers cited. Geneva: International Labour Office.

International Labour Office Report Presented to the Peace Conference by the Commission on International Labour Legislation. Geneva: International Labour Office, 1920.

The International Labour Organization Year-Book. Year cited. Geneva: International Labour Office.

International Survey of Legal Decisions on Labour Law. Years cited. Geneva: International Labour Office.

League of Nations Report on the Employment of Women and Children and the Berne Convention of 1906. Report III. (*Prepared by the Organizing Committee for the International Labour Conference, Washington, 1919.*) Geneva: International Labour Office.

The Third International Labour Conference, October-November, 1921. Geneva, 1922, with a foreword by Viscount Burnham. Reprinted with certain additions from the *International Labour Review,* V, no. 2 (Feb., 1922). Geneva: International Labour Office, 1922.

II. Other Primary Sources

Boletin de la Revista general de Legislacion y Jurisprudencia (official publication of the "Illustre Colegio de Agogados de Madrid"). Volume and series cited.

British and Foreign State Papers. Volumes cited.

Butterworth's Workmen's Compensation Cases. Edited by A. H. Rugg and E. Dale. Numbers cited. London: Butterworth and Co., 1930-1932. N.V.

Chile: Boletin de Leges y Decretos del goberno. Volumes cited.

Dalloz. Numbers and series cited.

Diario de Sesiones de las Cartes Constitutyantes de la Republica Espanola (Apendice 1, al Numero 88). Session of Dec. 9, 1931.

Gazette de Palais. Numbers and dates cited. Paris: Imprimerie Nationale, current.

Great Britain: Public General Acts. George 5 and 6. Years, numbers, and chapters cited.

Hanseatische Rechts und Gerichtzeitschrift. Number cited.

Hudson, Manley O., *International Legislation. A Collection of Texts of Multipartite Instruments of General Interest Beginning with the Covenant of the League of Nations.* Volumes cited. Washington: Carnegie Endowment for International Peace, 1931.

Italia Leggi e Decreti. Volume and year cited.

Journal Officiel. Volumes cited.

The Law Times. Volume cited. London: Field Press, 1930.

League of Nations Official Journal. Volumes and years cited.

League of Nations Treaty Series. Volumes cited.

Lloyds, List Law Reports. Number cited, N.V.

Publications of the Permanent Court of International Justice. Series and numbers cited.

Records of the Assembly of the League of Nations. Numbers cited.

Receuil général des lois, décrets et arrêtes. Edited and published by Redactours du *Journal des Notaires et des Avocats.*

Reichesgesetzblatt. Volumes cited.

Reichsarbeitsgericht. Volumes and numbers cited.

Report of Proceedings of the 34th Annual Convention of the American Federation of Labor, Philadelphia, November, 1914.

Sirey. Numbers cited.

The Times Law Reports. Volume cited.

United States Treaty Series. Numbers cited.

B. SECONDARY SOURCES

I. Books

Blânqui, Jérome. *Cours d'économie industrielle: 1836-1838.* 2ème ed. receuille et annotée par Ad. Blaise. Paris: L. Mathias, 1938-39.

Brierly, J. L. "The Function of Law in International Relations," *Problems of Peace.* Third Series. London: Oxford University Press, 1929.

Chang, Yi-Ting. *The Interpretation of Treaties by Judicial Tribunals.* New York: Columbia University Press, 1933.

Follows, John W. Antecedents of the International Labor Organization. (Thesis, MS., Cornell University), 1933.

Goellner, Aladar. *L'Article 19 du Pacte de la Société des Nations.* Paris: Rousseau, 1925.

Guerreau, Maurice. *L'Organisation permanente du travail.* Paris: Librarie Arthur Rousseau et Cie, 1923.

Hill, Chesney. *The Doctrine of Rebus Sic Stantibus in International Law. University of Missouri Studies.* Colombia, Mo., 1934.

Hill, Norman L. *The Public International Conference.* Stanford University, Calif.; Stanford University Press, 1929.

House, Edward M. and Seymour, Charles. *What Really Happened at Paris: The Story of the Peace Conference, 1918-1919, by an American Delegate.* New York: Charles Scribner and Sons, 1921.

Hudson, Manley O. *The Permanent Court of International Justice.* New York: Macmillan Co., 1934.

International Labour Organization: the First Decade. London: George Allen and Unwin, Ltd., 1931. (Distributed in the U. S. A. by the World Peace Foundation.)

Kunz, Joseph L. *Die Revision der Pariser Friendenvertrage: Eine Völkerrechtlicheuntersuchung.* Wien: J. Springer, 1932.

Lauterpacht, H. *Private Law Sources and Analogies of International Law.* London, New York: Longmans, Green and Co., Ltd., 1927.

Lorwin, Lewis L. *Labor and Internationalism. The Institute of Economics of the Brookings Institute.* New York: Macmillan Co., 1929.

Lowe, B. E. *The International Protection of Labor.* New York: Macmillan Co., 1935.

Mahaim, Ernest. *Le Droit international ouvrièr.* N.V.

Mathews, J. M. *American Foreign Relations.* New York, London: The Century Co., 1928.

Miller, David Hunter. *Reservations to Treaties.* New York: The Author, 1919.

————. *My Diary at the Conference of Paris.* 20 vols. New York: Appeal Printing Co., 1924.

Périgord, Paul. *The International Labor Organization: a Study of Labor and Capital in Cooperation.* New York: D. Appleton and Co., 1926.

Phelan, Edward J. *Yes and Albert Thomas.* London: The Cresset Press, Ltd., 1936.

Riches, Cromwell A. *The Unanimity Rule and the League of Nations.* Baltimore: Johns Hopkins, 1933.

Roxburgh, R. F. *International Conventions and Third States.* London: Longmans, Green and Co., 1917.

Scelle, Georges. *L'Organization internationale du travail et le B. I. T.* Paris: M. Rivière, 1930.

Scheidtman, Ulrich. *Der Vorbehalt beim Abschluss Volkerrechtlicher Verträge.* Berlin, 1934.

Schneider, Wolfgang. *Die Völkerrechtliche Clausula rebus sic stantibus und Artikel 19 der Völkerbundsatzung.* Berlin, 1931.

Shotwell, James T., ed., *The Origins of the International Labor Organization: The Paris Peace Conference—History and Documents.* 2 vols. New York: Columbia University Press, 1934.

Tayler, W. L. *Federal States and Labor Treaties.* New York: Columbia University Press, 1935.

Thomas, Albert. *Mélanges offerts à M. Charles Andler.* Strasbourg, 1924 (N.V.).

Tobin, H. J. *The Termination of Multipartite Treaties.* New York: Columbia University Press, 1933.

Tsune, Chi Yü. *The Interpretation of Treaties.* New York: Columbia University Press, 1927.

Weinfeld, Abraham C. *Labor Treaties and Labor Compacts.* Bloomington: The Principia Press, 1937.

Weiss, Raymond. *Daniel Le Grand* (1783-1859): son oeuvre sociale et internationale. Paris: Rivière, 1926. (N.V.)

Wigniolle, Albert. *La Société des Nations et la revision des traités.* Paris: 1932.

Williams, J. Fisher. *Current International Law and the League of Nations.* New York: Longmans, Green and Company, 1929.

———. *International Change and International Peace.* London: Oxford University Press, 1932.

Wilson, Francis G. *Labor in the League System.* Stanford University, Calif.: Stanford University Press, 1934.

Zanten, Hugo van. *L'Influence de la Partie XIII du Traité de Versailles sur le dévelopment de droit international public et sur le droit interne des Etats.* Leiden: E. T. Brill, 1927. N.V.

II. Periodical Publications

Auer, Paul de. "Revisions of Treaties," *Transactions of the Grotius Society,* XVIII (Problems of Peace and War), 1933, 155-175.

Brierly, J. L. "Some Considerations on the Obsolescence of Treaties," *Transactions of the Grotius Society,* XI (1926), 11-20.

Cole, Taylor, "National Socialism and the German Labor Courts," *Journal of Politics,* III (May, 1941), 169-197.

Eagleton, Clyde. "International Legislation, and the Drafting of Treaties," *Temple Law Quarterly,* VIII (1933-34), 218-233.

Fachiri, Alexander. "Some Observations on the Interpretation of Treaties," *American Journal of International Law,* XXIII (1929), 745-752.

Fairman, Charles. "Implied Resolutive Conditions in Treaties," *American Journal of International Law,* XXIX, no. 2 (April, 1935), 219-236.

Fitz-Maurice, G. G. "Do Treaties Need Ratification?" *British Yearbook of International Law,* XV (1934), 113-137.

Garner, J. W. "Limitations on National Sovereignty in International Relations," *American Political Science Review,* XIX (1933-34), 312-329.

————. "Revision of Treaties and Doctrine of *Rebus Sic Stantibus,*" *Iowa Law Review,* XIX (1933-34), 312-329.

Gutteridge, H. C. "The Interpretation and Administration of Labour Laws in England," *International Labour Review,* X, no. 2 (Aug., 1924), 209-235.

"Law of Treaties, Draft Convention, with Comment." Prepared by the Research in International Law of the Harvard Law School. *American Journal of International Law,* Supplement, XXIX, no. 4 (Oct., 1935), 657-1225.

Hill, Norman L. "Unanimous Consent in International Organization," *American Journal of International Law,* XXII, 319-329.

Hudson, Manley O. "Advisory Opinions of National and International Courts," *Harvard Law Review,* CXXXVII (1923-24), 970-1001.

————. "The Advisory Opinions of the Permanent Court of International Justice," *International Conciliation Bulletin,* no. 214 (1925), 321-375.

————. "The Membership of the United States in the International Labor Organization," *American Journal of International Law,* XXVIII (1934), 678-699.

Hyde, C. C. "The Interpretation of Treaties by the Permanent Court of International Justice," *American Journal of International Law,* XXIV, no. 1, 1-19.

————. "Judge Anzilotti on the Interpretation of Treaties," *American Journal of International Law,* XXVIII (July, 1933), 502-506.

Jenks, C. Wilfred. "The Authority of English Courts as Decisions of the Permanent Court of International Justice," *British Yearbook of International Law,* XX (1939), 1-36.

————. "La Competence de l'Organisation Internationale du Travail examen de quatre avis consultatif rendus par La Cour Permanente de Justice Internationale," *Revue de droit internationale et de legislation comparée.* Troisième Serie, no. 1 (1937), 131-172.

————. "The Contribution of the International Labor Organization to the Development of Procedure of Peaceful Change," *"The New Commonwealth Quarterly,* IV, no. 4 (March, 1939), 43-64.

————. "The Revision of International Labour Conventions," *British Yearbook of International Law,* XIV (1933), 43-64.

————. "The Significance for International Law of the Tripartite Character of the International Labour Organization," *Transactions of the Grotius Society,* XXII (May, 1936), 45-81.

————. "Some Characteristics of Labour Conventions," *Canadian Bar Review,* XIII (1935), 448-462.

————. "Some Further Representations under Article 23 of the

Constitution of the International Labour Organization," *British Yearbook of International Law,* IX (1928), 29.

Lauterpacht, H. "The Absence of an International Legislature and the Compulsory Jurisdiction of International Tribunals," *British Yearbook of International Law,* XI (1930), 134-157.

———. "Some Observations on Preparatory Work in Treaties," *Harvard Law Review,* XLVIII (1935), 545-591.

McNair, Arnold. "The Function and Differing Legal Character of Treaties," *British Yearbook of International Law,* XI (1930), 100-118.

———. "International Legislation," *Iowa Law Review,* XIX (1933-34), 177-189.

Mahaim, Ernest. "International Labour Law," *International Labour Review,* I, 283-286.

———. "L'Organisation permanente du travail," *Recueil des cours de l'Académie de Droit International,* III (1924), 69-75.

———. "The Principles of International Labor Legislation," *The Annals of the American Academy of Political and Social Science,* CLXVI (March, 1933), 10-18.

———. "Some Legal Questions Relating to International Labour Conventions," *International Labour Review,* XX, no. 6 (1929), 765-796.

Malkin, H. W. "Reservations to Multilateral Treaties," *British Yearbook of International Law,* VII (1926), 142-162.

Pic, Paul, Garraud, P., and Lambert, Edouard, "The Sources and Interpretation of Labour Law in France," *International Labour Review,* XIV, no. 1 (July, 1926), 1-36.

Rapsidari-Mirabelli, A. "Théorie générale des unions internationales," *Recueil des cours de l'Académie de Droit International,* II (1925), 345-390.

Shotwell, James T. "The International Labor Organization as an Alternative to Violent Revolution," *The Annals of the American Academy of Political and Social Science,* CLXVI (March, 1933), 18-25.

Siefart, Hugo. "The Administration of Labour Law in Germany," *International Labour Review,* XV (May, 1927), 648-708.

Williams, J. F. "The Permanence of Treaties," *American Journal of International Law,* XXII (1928), 89-104.

Wilson, F. G. "The Enforcement of International Labor Standards," *The Annals of the American Academy of Political and Social Science,* CLXVI (March, 1933), 95-101.

Wilson, George Grafton. "Treaties and Changing Conditions," *American Journal of International Law,* XXIX, no. 2 (April, 1935), 307-308.

Wilson, R. R. "The Interpretation of Treaties," *Proceedings of the American Society of International Law,* 1930, 39-46.

———. "Revision Clauses in Treaties since the World War," *American Political Science Review,* XXVIII, no. 5 (1934), 901-909.

Winant, John G. "The International Labor Organization in Wartime and After," *Foreign Affairs,* XIX (April, 1941), 636-640.

INDEX

TABLE OF CASES

www.ingramcontent.com/pod-product-compliance
Lightning Source LLC
LaVergne TN
LVHW090314210926
848480LV00001B/245